VISIONS 2100:

Stories from *Your* Future

John O'Brien

www.visions2100.com

Published by Vivid Publishing
P.O. Box 948, Fremantle
Western Australia 6959
www.vividpublishing.com.au

National Library of Australia Cataloguing-in-Publication data:
Creator: O'Brien, John K., author.
Title: Visions 2100 : stories from your future / John K. O'Brien.
ISBN: 9781925341522 (paperback)
Subjects: Human ecology.
          Social ecology.
          Sustainability.
          Sustainable development.
          Climatic changes--Social aspects.
          Environmental protection.
Dewey Number: 304.25

Contents

Section 5 – The Benefits

Section 6 – Setting off from here

THE VISIONS

Chapter	Author		Vision
1.	Mary Robinson	Former President of Ireland & Special Envoy on Climate Change, UN	The World is Just
2.	Christiana Figueres	Executive Secretary, UN Framework Convention on Climate Change	The Climate Neutral World
3.	Dr. Renee Lertzman	Author & Psychologist	The Myth of Apathy
4.	Tessa Tennant	Director, UK Green Bank Founder, OurVoices	Peace & Plenty
	Dr Will Grant	Australian National Centre for the Public Awareness of Science, Australian National University	Is this Utopia?
	Rohan Hamden	Adaptation & Climate Risk Specialist	The Century of Awakening
	Peggy Liu	CEO, Joint US China Collaboration on Clean Energy (JUCCCE)	Living Vibrantly
5.	Bill McKibben	Chairman, 350.org	We Blew It!
	Dr Monica Oliphant	Immediate Past-President, International Solar Energy Society	Our Fragile Planet
	Professor Campbell Gemmell	Professor of Environmental Regulation, Policy & Governance, University of Glasgow	Temperatures up 4.8C
	Jan Van der Ven	Director, Asia, The Carbon Trust	Human Intelligence?
	Arlan Andrews Sr	Founder, The SIGMA Forum	Carbon Zero
	Tracy Cai	CEO, SynTao Green Finance	Once Upon a Time
	John Renesch	Founder, FutureShapers	It was close!
	Antony Funnell	Broadcaster, ABC Radio National	By the Skin of our Teeth
6.	Jack O'Brien	Student, Prince Alfred College	At Last a Happy Birthday!
	Simon Zadek	Co-Director, UNEP Inquiry into the Design of a Sustainable Financial System	Small Change

	Tony Wood	Energy Program Director, Grattan Institute	Are we Wiser?
7.	Aubrey de Grey	Chief Science Officer, SENS Research Foundation	The immutability of Aging
	Charles Landry	Founder, Creative Cities	Civic Urbanity
	Connie Hedegaard	EU Commissioner, Climate Action and Energy, 2010-14	People Knew
8.	Rachel Kyte	Group Vice President & Special Envoy for Climate Change, World Bank	Cleaner, Fairer, Smaller
	Claudia Martinez	Executive Director, E3 & Former Colombian Deputy Minister of Environment	We Live in a Better Planet
	Sam Bickersteth	CEO, Climate & Development Knowledge Network	Zero Zero Vision
	Tim Hobbs	Student, Prince Alfred College	Removing the Carbon Mask
9.	Dr Shamshad Akhtar	Executive Secretary, United Nations Economic and Social Commission for Asia and the Pacific	Windows of Opportunity
	Paul Gilding	Author	On the Other Side of the Dark Decades
	Jacqui Hoepner	Australian National University	An Australia Worth Living In
10.	John Harradine	Social Ecologist & Counsellor	Raising Consciousness
	Chandran Nair	Founder, Global Institute for Tomorrow	Austerity for All
	Yvo de Boer	Director General, Global Green Growth Institute	Green Growth
11.	Mike Duggan	Sustainability Specialist, Gladstone Ports Corporation	Pilot Vision
	Professor Barry Brook	Professor of Climate Change and Sustainability, University of Tasmania	New Resources

	Professor Peter Doherty	Nobel Laureate Professor of Immunologist, University of Melbourne	Climate Crimes
	L. Hunter Lovins	Author & President, Natural Capital	The Regenerative Economy
12.	Nina Harjula	Head of Development, Cleantech Lahti Region Development LADEC, Finland	Nordic Changes
	Carina Larsfälten	Managing Director, Global Policy Affairs, World Business Council for Sustainable Development	The Power of Collaboration
	Dr. Adam Bumpus	University of Melbourne & Co-Founder, Apidae Development Innovations	We're not afraid anymore
13.	Caleb Rice	Student, Prince Alfred College	Survival of the Species
	The Most Reverend Bernadito Auza	Titular Archbishop of Suacia & Permanent Observer of the Holy See to the United Nations	Wise Farmers
	Jonathan Woetzel	Partner, McKinsey & Company	The Rise of Home Urbanus
	Vaughan Levitzke	CEO, Green Industries South Australia	Achieving ZeroWaste
14.	George Ujvary	Managing Director, Olgas Fine Foods & www.foodologist.com	22nd Century Food
	Hyunbum (Joe) Cho	Partner, Australian CleanTech	Personal Assistant
	Dr Remo Burkhard	Managing Director, ETH Centre Future Cities Laboratory	Future Cities
	Jules Kortenhorst	CEO, Rocky Mountain Institute & Carbon War Room	Distant Memories
15.	Professor Stephen Lincoln	Research Centre for Climate Change and Sustainability, University of Adelaide	A Solar Powered Earth
	Susan Gladwin	Sustainability Strategist, Autodesk	Design Led Revolution
	Professor Ian Chubb	Australian Chief Scientist	World Saving STEM

	Kristin Alford	Founder, Bridge8 Foresight Institute	Awake!
	Ketan Joshi	Research and Communications Officer, Infigen Energy	Late Again!
16.	Anne McIvor	CEO, Cleantech Investor	USESE Results Round Up
	Andrew Affleck	CEO, Armstrong Asset Management	The Energy Silk Road
	Fred Chang	Managing Director, China Cleantech Collaboratory	Tourist Destination
	Tim Jarvis	Explorer & Environmental Scientist, Arup	Defining Growth
	Nigel Lake	CEO, Pottinger	Everything knows Everyone
17.	Tina Perfrement	Cleantech Manager, Geelong City Council	Rebuilding a Thriving City
	Omar Khan	Crescent Wealth	The Second Global Financial Crisis
	Paul Dickinson	Executive Chairman, Carbon Disclosure Project (CDP)	The Time Thieves
	Professor Peter Newman	Director, Institute for Sustainability and Technology, Murdoch University	The End of Automobile Dependence.
18.	Professor Ove Hoegh-Guldberg	Director, Global Change Institute, University of Queensland	Good News, Every Day
	Stephen Yarwood	Urban Futurist, Former Lord Mayor of Adelaide	The Information Ecology
	Christian Haeuselmann	Chair, Global Cleantech Cluster Association & Co-Founder, swisscleantech	The Great Crash of '29
	Fraser Bell	Partner, Thomson Geer Lawyers	Self-Determination
19.	Anna Skarbek	CEO, ClimateWorks Australia	Good Neighbours
	Sharan Burrow	General Secretary, International Trade Union Confederation	A Just Transition

20.	Dr Dessima Williams	Former Ambassador of Grenada to the United Nations & Advisory Committee Member of the Climate Justice Dialogue	No Island Left Behind
	Dr Martin Blake	Global Sustainability Strategist	Collaborative Culture
	Dr Sam Wells	Rhodes Scholar & Business School, University of Adelaide	Nourished
21.	Frans Nauta	Entrepreneurship, Strategy & International Cooperation, EU Climate KIC	Just a Matter of Time
	John Gibbons	Journalist, The Irish Times & Founder, www.thinkorswim.ie	The Age of Madness
	David Fogarty	Journalist	Gross Environmental Performance
22.	Claus Pram Astrup	Advisor to the CEO, The Global Environment Facility	$8 per Barrel
	Rob Day	Managing Director, Black Coral Capital	The Energy-Data Nexus
	Dr Simon Divecha	MetaIntegral Academy	Global Complexities
	Suhit Anantula	CEO, Business Models Inc	Humble Leaders
23.	Professor Chris West	CEO, Edinburgh Zoo	Those who don't know history....
	Ken Hickson	Chairman, Sustain Ability Showcase Asia – SASA	New World Order
	Simon Webb	Senior VP, Ogilvy Public Relations	For Purpose
	Mark Halle	Executive Director Europe, International Institute for Sustainable Development	Seeds of Destruction

I would give all the wealth of the world, and all the deeds of all the heroes, for one true vision.

Henry David Thoreau

INTRODUCTION

Visions can and do change the world.

Visions can mobilise communities, countries and global networks to deliver extraordinary outcomes. As we shall see, the visions that work best connect at an emotional level and are clear and concise. They do not need many words to tell of a better world. Visions do not dwell on the practicalities of getting there; they just paint a picture of the future that unites people to find a way to create that future.

This book tells stories from our possible futures through short visions. The visions come from those at the forefront of designing your future world, so it provides an insight into what they are planning for your grandchildren. It also sets out how you can be part of creating a future that you want by writing your own vision and sharing the story of your future.

The human race can do extraordinary things when it needs to. With the right motivation humans can win unwinnable wars, put men on the moon, build pyramids or create atomic bombs. We may cut off a limb in order to survive or swim the race of their lives in order to triumph.

However, the complex issue of climate change is one that our race is struggling to address. The solutions are not beyond us in any way. Technological solutions exist, scientific knowledge is plentiful, the world can afford the transition but still significant action eludes us. There are many rational arguments for clear paths forward. The complexity of climate change is now in the psychology of change.

Many very smart and powerful people have tried to build

support for taking steps towards a rational solution but have been thwarted by seemingly irrational yet infallible arguments. Now a new tack is emerging, a new way of inspiring support that has power and strength. Many of the contributors to this book are helping to drive this new approach.

This book holds stories from some of the world's leading environmental thinkers and influencers. It includes those leading the process of making global agreements on climate change and those working on leading technology solutions. These are the people who are shaping your future world. Their visions tell what they want to see in the future. They are passionate about achieving the world of their vision. This book almost certainly contains an accurate prediction of the world that your grandchildren will inhabit. Which of these versions of the future is the correct one is not so easy to say.

Enticing action to create a better world across all societies leads to a very different response to threats of global collapse. Imagine the future that you want to create and imagine what it would feel like to live there. Most people share a vision with the core themes of safety, connectedness and purpose. However, sharing these visions is not necessarily something that we feel is socially acceptable. We are afraid of ridicule and know that people may tell us to 'get in the real world' or 'to stop dreaming of utopia'. Yet, if we dare not only to dream but to share our dreams we will connect with others that have similar dreams of the future world. From this the power and passion of a group can drive extraordinary outcomes.

Incumbent powers have much to lose and may see such a thought as revolution. They warn that we should be careful of our dreams. It is however nothing more than ongoing evolution of our civilisation. It is adapting to our environmental circumstances in order to build a better world for ourselves and future generations.

The motivation that can drive the extra-ordinary comes from two sources: impending peril and reward. It works best when at least some rewards, both neuropathic and tangible, are achieved quickly or the peril immediate and intimidating. The years of training for a 100m race are spurred on by the rewards received from every race won and every personal best set along the way. Where things get more challenging is when avoiding the peril or gaining the reward takes more time. People lose their enthusiasm and the momentum for the cause can be lost.

The challenges of President Obama's first term led to much of his popular support fading away when the hope was not repaid quickly. Similarly, it is hard to maintain popular support for a war that goes on for years. The challenge only gets harder as people become less susceptible to the long-term propaganda used for the wars of the past. In addition, reducing levels of trust in government and a wealthier population with access to easier, quicker rewards makes the call to action from government less powerful. Would the challenges overcome in the twentieth century be as easy to do today? Would the populations of western countries now have the temerity to question whether it was really worth getting to the moon, building the bomb or entering the war?

The ability to organise and rise to overcome extraordinary challenges is one of mankind's most powerful characteristics. Evolution has trained us well and our success as a species has been largely delivered through being able to build passion for a cause that has a higher value than the needs of the mere individual. The cause can be fighting the 'evil' enemy, delivering the works of a 'higher being', curing cancer, reducing poverty or selling tupperware. The subjective worth of the cause may be very different but the mechanism of harnessing the passion and the power of a group is the same. This same mechanism has of course been used to deliver great ills upon the world as well as to achieve great feats.

By building a group of passionate supporters, leaders can achieve great things and far more than they would through coercion. The power of attraction to a common goal can inspire people to achieve far more than they would if they were forced into action. A leader pushing her followers into a new challenge will have less impact than the leader who convinces the followers that solving the challenge is noble or worthy.

To be aware of impending perils and rewards, the human mind is finely tuned to comb its environment for threats and opportunities: a falling child, an oncoming car, a quick buck or an empty seat. This awareness is one of the human race's finest traits. We have evolved to react with haste to imminent threats and opportunities and this has played a vital role in our survival to date.

However, any news that we do not perceive as an imminent threat is treated very differently. It is often ignored or pushed aside to be actioned only if it becomes urgent, or turns into a crisis or when your boss or partner demands that something is done. Otherwise, the natural reaction to this type of news, good or bad, is to bury your head in the sand and pretend it does not exist. There are too many other worries to justify spending time or effort on the non-urgent. We are all too stressed with the everyday challenges of paying bills, office politics, children and health to want to also chase another long term goal.

A powerful tool used to harness passion and support for a cause is the telling of stories. Hard, dry facts are useful but nothing engages an audience like telling a personal story with meaning and purpose. Think of the different levels of energy you can feel between a presenter that provides too many slides and too much data to one who shows you one picture and tells a story. The human mind engages far more easily with a story. We can visualise the setting and, if well told, can even feel the emotion. A story can engage our rational minds with facts and arguments and also our emotional minds as we take the journey with the story teller. The use of virtual senses about what we saw or heard or smelt will firmly anchor the story in our memories and enable quick recall.

There are many psychological elements at play as part of this process and many more qualified authors have addressed this subject elsewhere. Some of this thinking is referenced in this book. The solving of any complex challenge requires an effective balance of the rational and the emotional. Harnessing the power of a crowd requires a reasonable argument and lots of passion. This will win out every time over the strongest of arguments put with little emotional strength. If you can present an argument as a story with which people can identify, then the passion will be anchored to accessible memories and will be longer lasting.

President Obama's strength and following was built on passion, stories and the ability to paint a vision so strong that people believed it would come. Similarly, Indian Prime Minister Narendra Modi's rise to power has been built on his ability to harness passion and paint a vision worth fighting for.

The majority of communication on climate change and the possible responses to it have failed most of the above tests. The usual message has been about non-imminent impending peril, and the horrible consequences of not acting, presented as hard, cold rational facts that *must* not be ignored. It has rarely ignited passion in the general population. Stories are largely absent, as are compelling visions of the future. Scientists and economists are good at providing detailed and frightening data that can support an argument, but it is not their strength to convey this data in a way that builds momentum and passion.

Overall, the majority of climate communications to date have been futile and have not engaged with the emotional side of the global population. Attracting people to the idea of action requires visions of a positive future told as stories that resonate with people's world view. Once the wider population is excited about the prospects of change – how we can live better – the politics and change mechanism become merely operational challenges.

★ ★ ★

The visions in this book are told as stories from the year 2100. The writers may be looking out of their 'nano-glass' window or reminiscing on the journey that got the world to where it is 'today'. Some tell us of tourist trips to space, the 'latest' stock market results, our printed food or the traffic jams in our future cities. Others talk about the dark days when the world got to the brink of collapse and many millions suffered and died. There is much hope that, as it evolves, the human race becomes a more connected and caring race. There is shaking of heads at the time it took to act when people knew they needed to - the 'time thieves' as they are known in 2100 - and of the funny, irrational ways things were done in the olden days. The talk of retribution and climate crimes was a distraction on the journey to a more accepting world led by humble leaders and consultative governments. '*Is this Utopia?*' asks one author to which the answer is a resounding no. The world will not be perfect and there will still be many problems, but why not at least set out on the journey towards something that you really want.

That the visions are told from the year 2100 is a really important consideration. 2030 or 2050 feels more attainable and more real so why not aim for a date that is easier to contemplate? It is for this exact reason that a more distant date was chosen. If we asked people to talk about something in their lifetime, they would be constrained by the practicalities of what they think is possible, the inevitable hurdles that they can already see. They would provide practical, sensible, rational thoughts about how to step forward. No doubt these could be presented as a slideshow with lots of dot points but it would fail to provide real insight. By aiming for a date that is really hard to grasp, it removes the constraints created by today's perceptions of how the world works. It gives the authors permission to tell us what they really want and of their real hopes and fears. It removes the practicality of dismantling the politics, companies and structures of today and jumps into building a compelling story of a future world that might have sufficient attraction to make people want it. The power of the stories is that they are not constrained by practicality – they don't require a detailed account of how the vision was realised.

This presents a risk in that the pragmatists will tell us that the lack of practicality makes the content meaningless. Pragmatists have many uses and are wonderful employees but they will never achieve extraordinary outcomes. To them the unthinkable remains just that.

The contributors to this book fall into two camps and the communication style of each group is very different. As the compiler of these many visions, it appears to me that the styles derive from the motivational factors discussed above. Each of the authors is clearly passionate to create the best world possible. Some are pessimistic about our current situation. They see desperate urgency to avoid impending peril and create a world better than the one they fear. Others see the challenge of climate change as a way to improve our current societies – it is a chance to find the treasure of a better world. Whether driven by fear or by hope, there is a common goal of creating something to be proud of and of being part of a movement that achieves what at times appears impossible.

Marketing psychology uses a balance of fear and hope to sell its messages. The best marketers scare their target market and then entice them with the solution. The fear might be of missing out on a bargain or not being part of the 'in-crowd'. The hope provides the call to action – what to do or buy to provide the solution for you. So the balance of fear and hope is an important one as long as each comes with a real solution and a call to action.

As a natural optimist, I was inclined to not include the visions of fear but, on reflection, consider that they are critical to building the full story that works at all levels. Don't get despondent on reading these - just use them to build resolve that *that* is not a future you want to be responsible for.

As we will discover, behavioural psychology tells us that setting goals, even if they are never reached, has few downsides and helps people to overcome encountered obstacles more effectively. Having a vision of a better future might just result in a better world.

★ ★ ★

Having now solved the challenge of how to align global passion towards the common goal of a better world, there remains the challenge of how to start our journey and communicate progress. We know the end point but have no real idea of the best way to get there. For complex global challenges this is not an unusual situation. The 'curing' of cancer or the 'elimination' of poverty are simple goals with many options for how to proceed and much disagreement on the 'right' path to follow.

This is difficult for governments and large organisations to cope with. Their structure is built to deliver large projects in a pre-agreed way that will deliver close to expected outcomes. Such a challenge is, however, the norm in the world of innovation and entrepreneurship. Whether it be to build a business or to re-invigorate an industrial neighbourhood, the uncertainty and non-linear outcomes apparent in solving complex problems is one that many have grappled with. Research on what makes a successful entrepreneur suggests that constancy of purpose, flexibility in approach and the ability to fail cheaply many times provide the core to success.

As a global community, we are trying to solve a highly complex problem. We have a fair idea of the outcome we want but cannot yet see the 'right' way forward. The contributors to this book might be seen as the entrepreneurs of the world striving for a successful solution. Once the passion is ignited, the journey can be undertaken with innovation policy and entrepreneurship. A strategy of compelling visions, ongoing engagement, small wins and accepting some failures as inevitable should therefore be built into climate communications.

The other factor in successful innovation is that of authentic leadership. To create ongoing commitment from a group of followers requires its leaders to also have integrity and constancy of purpose. Research into effective leadership suggests that the leaders most likely to be successful in good times and bad have characteristics that include an understanding of themselves and their own motivations, being flexible in approach and focussing on the long term. These traits build trust and confidence in followers and allow ongoing progress towards a common goal.

★ ★ ★

The inspiration for this book was born out of two chapters from a book I edited in 2009 called *Opportunities Beyond Carbon*. One of the first chapters in that book was written by a friend and contributor to this book, Dr Sam Wells, who wrote about '*Envisioning what we really want*'. Sam eloquently combined the thoughts of Rachel Carson, Donella Meadows and Thomas Kuhn.

Donella Meadows wrote that '*Environmentalists have failed perhaps more than any other set of advocates to project vision. ... The best goal most of us who work toward sustainability offer is the avoidance of catastrophe. We promise survival and not much more.*'

Kuhn wrote about how paradigms become entrenched as a way of thinking and seeing the world. No matter what evidence may be produced, paradigms hold fast until an alternative world view becomes apparent. Sam writes 'When the shift finally came, it was not away from a failed paradigm, but towards a new paradigm—a new, fundamentally different, and better theoretical framework for making sense of all the evidence.'

The other chapter from *Opportunities Beyond Carbon* that inspired this book was: '*The Way We Were: Looking Back from 2100*' by Dr John Wright. In this chapter, John told the story of the century as he contemplated life 'today' on an airship journey from London to Sydney.

John's story fits well here and the goal of this book is an attempt to address the issues raised by Sam.

Opportunities Beyond Carbon sought to challenge the notions that climate change was too hard to address either because the challenge was too great or because there would be a future scientific 'silver bullet' anyway. It provided rational views of the opportunities that existed for communities, business, investors and nations from acting on the transition. What was missing from the argument were the compelling visions of where this would take us. It therefore serves as an effective prequel to this book as it remains consistent to the end point of this journey. In 2009 I wrote the following:

> *As the world community is going to make changes to its fundamental way of operating in order to reduce emissions—changes that will impact every activity and every choice—it would be foolish to ignore the opportunity to improve other outcomes as well.*
>
> *Representatives of all communities including governments, businesses, investor groups and industry networks should be asking themselves not simply, 'How do we reduce emissions?' but rather 'What changes might we make in our community to provide the greatest opportunities to improve both our physical and social environments?'*

My own vision of catastrophe came to me one evening when watching the documentary *Shake Hands with the Devil* by Canadian General Romeo Dallaire, the commander of the UN troops in Rwanda at the time of the 1994 genocide. I had recently finished a fiction book titled *The First Century After Beatrice* by Amin Maalouf.

The book that told the tale of riots and devastation in poorer countries following the discovery and widespread global use of an Egyptian bean that, when taken by a prospective mother, would ensure that her baby would be born a male. Both these sources showed that even if global devastation does not initially impact upon richer countries, genocide and mass population movements resulting from widespread, climate change induced crop failures would ultimately affect everyone.

The optimist in me dismissed this horror as an option that could not be permitted to happen. I strengthened my resolve to tell tales that could inspire visions of the opportunities that are emerging and the positive differences that can be made by mobilising global behaviour change. These stories need to be told by many people, many times over. However, the insightful writing produced by the authors in this book is, I believe, an important contribution.

Another personal story that has inspired some of my thinking is navigating the complexity of the long term health issues and chronic pain suffered by my wife, Kate. Our many interactions with a highly structured health system full of specialists who look at just one aspect of a body or want to only manage the symptoms have been incredibly frustrating. Few in the health profession seem to see the body as a single, complex, interconnected organism and few are able to step outside their own paradigms and sensibly approach patients that present as 'interesting'. There is great skill at mending holes or fixing breaks, but once we start dabbling in biochemistry, there are plenty of actions taken on the basis that it works for some, often without a full understanding of why.

Thinking of the world as a system that is enduring complex health issues, it is no wonder that the current approach taken by the various specialists is struggling to find a holistic solution that makes sense and achieves the best long term outcomes.

★ ★ ★

Compelling stories of the future provide important markers to head towards as we navigate the changes to our society that will occur during the coming century. Few of the contributors to this book see the transition as being straightforward and without pain. The change required to confront our highly evolved psychology will be hard. It may well take significant disruption and death to occur before the imminence of peril finally forces global action. The challenge is how we can accelerate the change in thinking required and thereby lessen the level of disruption that triggers the paradigm shift. Successful entrepreneurs and innovation policymakers may provide guidance on managing the options most effectively and authentic leadership will be required to hold the rudder during the storms to come. Visions provide the marker to head towards and community engagement will accelerate the call for action.

Before setting out on the journey of visions in this book, please park the pragmatist inside you to one side and instead imagine your ideal world and what you want for yourself and your descendants. Listen to the stories as they are told and take a minute to stop in each of their worlds and decide whether it is somewhere you would like to be. Which version of the future is yours? Which future story is compelling and makes you feel passionate about creating that world? Our collective future is in fact not being designed by the authors of this book, by the politicians, by the multi-national corporations or anyone else included in the term 'they'. The future will be created by each person deciding what matters and accepting nothing less.

My hope is that the power in this book allows you, dear reader, to stop feeling powerless, to stop wondering what disasters the future might bring and pushes you to get out there and create the future you want - in any way that you can. Write your own vision and tell people what it is. This will be the only way to create the world that you really want.

Remember the lesson from successful entrepreneurs that every failure should be welcomed as successfully eliminating another way that does not work - and hence inching towards the way that will. As John Harradine says in Chapter 12, '*So just get up one more time than you feel ready to and stand for what you believe in.*' If you happen to find someone standing beside you, shake their hand, give them a hug and envision the future together.

This book starts with a review of why visions are important and what they can achieve before considering how far we have got and why evolution has not catered for this circumstance. Then we dive into many of the visions that provide insight into the hopes and fears of the authors and how many of them see us touching catastrophe before finally pulling back. In Section 3, the visions tell the story from 2100, looking at how the century unfolded: why people didn't act when they knew and how the thinking and behaviours changed as we approached 2100. We also consider the fate of incumbent industries and what happened to those that innovated and those that did not.

In Section 4, you get to find out what the future will look like with some wonderful descriptions of daily life in the year 2100. Our food, cities, gadgets, holidays, investments and traffic are all profiled. More importantly, Section 5 tells how lives are lived, what is valued and how our better world has emerged.

Finally, in Section 6 we address the challenges of starting from today and how it might be possible to make all this become your reality.

The text includes 80 visions from those seeking to guide the world to this future. Enjoy their thoughts and use them to decide on what you want your own future to be.

Section 1

SETTING THE SCENE

Chapter 1

WHAT WE WANT

Never give up on what you really want to do. The person with big dreams is more powerful than the one with all the facts.

H. Jackson Brown, Jr.

Chapter 1

WHAT WE WANT

In 2100...

The World is Just

Mary Robinson, Former President of Ireland
President of the Mary Robinson Foundation - Climate Justice
Special Envoy on Climate Change, United Nations

My great-grandchildren share the world with over nine billion people; they truly share the planet. They know the reality of their interconnected dependence on their fellow human beings and therefore they respect each-other and the planet.

The decisions my generation took in 2015, to set the course for transformative change for a safe world for future generations, have been realised.

So now, poverty is eradicated. Every child goes to school regardless of sex, race, religion or place of birth. Every woman enjoys equality with every man. Every household has access to energy; energy sourced from renewables that has enabled the development of nations, communities and families while protecting our planet.

In 2100, the world is just.

People rarely talk about what they really want out of life. They fear it will be seen as self-indulgent and spoilt. Perhaps it sounds as though you are not happy with all you have which, in the Western world, is generally plenty. In the current world, being visionary and painting a picture of a perfect future seems almost taboo.

Airing grievances, talking about what we do *not* want is celebrated and heard on every bus and train every day. Western cultures relish the act of complaining. Whinging about politicians, taxes, football, immigrants and any anything else that comes to mind allows people to find an excuse for the disappointments in their daily lives. So much effort and time is devoted to explaining away why things have not changed or are getting worse. Imagine what might happen if all that energy was directed towards finding solutions to individual and societal problems.

Why do we find it so hard to imagine and discuss what we really want? To do it honestly means you have to get to the core of your values and what is important to you. This process can challenge some very deep assumptions about your life and might move you to make changes that you are not ready to make.

It may also require you to challenge the norms of society and the currently accepted version of how the world works. Looking back in history at people who advocated for a better and different world provides some clues as to the potential perils of non-conformance. Whilst ridicule or being ostracised is probably the worst fate in Western countries, you would risk death by standing up against a totalitarian regime. Ridicule and removal from a group is, however, enough of a deterrent for most people. It is not worth making too much noise if you might lose your friends, especially as an individual alone has little hope of changing the system.

Maybe your perfect world includes people living in small interconnected communities in a society that looks after all of its members with respect and care. An entirely reasonable vision and one you will see in various forms through this book. By saying it out loud, however, it might be that living in the crowded city, fighting your way into the subway each morning and doing an uninspiring office job become even more unbearable. Can you really change the world if you do not even seem to be able to change your own life? Maybe it is better just to internalise the vision and get on with living the best life possible without rocking the boat.

The taboo of openly envisioning the future might one day be seen as a quaint anachronism. When we look back at Victorian England's attitude to sex or giving the vote to woman and non-landed gentry, we consider this just about understandable given the cultural context of the time, but really quite bizarre in hindsight. There are so many cultural norms accepted at the time but seem unreal with today's view of world: the booming slave trade of the eighteenth century that made Liverpool a rich city; racial segregation in the US only fifty years ago; Australian aboriginals discounted from the census until the 1967 referendum. Who, even ten years ago, would believe that gay marriage would be largely accepted in Ireland?

So the taboo on envisioning could easily disappear and in the year 2100 maybe your descendants will focus on 'what we really want'. Maybe their leaders will get elected on competing visions for the future and the community in general will be comfortable to explore what makes it good to be human.

There is of course nothing stopping you from talking about what sort of world you want to leave behind. You might find that by starting the conversation, it gives others the courage to join in. This is about more than just election cycles, current policies and quick fixes. It is about starting a conversation about the values we cherish. In time and with enough people having this conversation, it will become the cultural norm and the world will change.

The alternative of course is to just keep your head down and decide not to bother. This is entirely understandable and is the approach taken by most of the population. But for those who have decided to opt out of influencing the discussion, there seems little justification for complaint if they do not like the outcome.

The authors in this book are all trying to make a difference. They are all happy to stand up and share their vision for the future. They want to start a conversation on what they see as important and it is wonderful to have been able to gather so many of them in one place.

Mary Robinson's vision provides a powerful picture of life in 2100 and the key steps we took to get there. In her many roles, Mary has generated admiration and respect for the integrity and intelligence she brings to difficult debates. When she became President of Ireland in 1990, it was the first time that I heard my very large Irish family all agree on anything. My family had been involved in Irish politics at the time of independence in 1922 and the sentiment of those days and the subsequent Civil War were held very deeply in some quarters. To get feisty O'Briens to come together demonstrates the gentle power that Mary holds. Her strategies of collaboration, constancy and attraction towards a common goal make her current role as a Special Envoy on Climate Change to the UN a fortunate appointment for us all.

Her vision of life in 2100 is simple and concise. It does not need many words to set out the principles of a just world in which there is equal opportunity and respect for all. The vision does not go into the detail of some others that are in this book but rather provides a guiding overview of where we want to head. How we get there is a mere detail as long as we know this is the destination.

★ ★ ★

Milton Hyland Erickson, the American psychiatrist, provides us with another piece of the jigsaw of sharing and creating an envisioned world. Erickson's 'expectant attitude' theory was demonstrated in experiments and was based on minimal non-verbal clues influencing the behaviour of other people. So, if you fully expect an outcome to happen, it is in fact more likely to occur because your behaviour will encourage others to act in the expected way. His best known experiment involved a group of twenty students who were placed in pairs in cubicles. One student was told a stranger would enter the cubicle and give them a dollar note. The other student was separately told that the stranger would give them twenty cents. The stranger was handed ten dollar notes and ten twenty cent coins and told to go into each cubicle and give a dollar note to one student and a coin to the other. This experiment was conducted many times over fifteen years with the result almost always being that in about 80% of the trials, the student received the amount they expected.

This theory may have significant limitations, but there is no doubt that a strong belief in a particular outcome will provide the believer with a greater chance of success. This is also used in sports and business psychology where envisioning success is now common at practise tracks and in executive education.

Writing in the Harvard Business Review back in 1996, James Collins and Jerry Porras wrote an article about the core aspects required to build a meaningful vision. Whilst this was written for a business audience, its key points are applicable to envisioning the future you want for the world.

They suggested that a well-conceived vision should consist of two major components: *core ideology* and an *envisioned future*. The core ideology or core values covers the non-negotiable aspects of what we stand for and why we exist. The envisioned future is what we aspire to become and create. Mary Robinson's vision includes the core values of respect and justice and details the key results produced by being true to these values.

Some of the visions in this book focus on a single issue or tell an interesting anecdote from the future world. Others however are more like this first one and tell a very honest and hopeful view of what the writer really wants. When I first read these visions, I can feel the depth of feeling that was put into the writing. On inspection, each of these visions contains both statements regarding core values and envisioned outcomes for a better world.

Similarly, research published in The Journal of Business Strategy in 2010 by Susan Kantabutra and Gayle Avery from the Institute of Sustainable Leadership suggests that visions that work have seven characteristics:

- conciseness;
- clarity;
- future orientation;
- stability;
- challenge;
- abstractness; and
- desirability or ability to inspire.

This is a useful list to reference when you are writing your own vision of the future you want. The challenge of conciseness is one that was given to the contributors for this book. Many commented that it would have been much easier to write 2,000 words on their thoughts than to bring it back to just 200 words. With a concise vision there is no room for waffle and justification. It just needs to include the nub of what is desired without worrying about the practicalities of how to achieve it.

★ ★ ★

Changing the way people think and behave through making paradigm shifts is not necessarily a straightforward task. The vision must be embedded into the core thinking of many people in such a way that it resonates as self-evident. It must become an integral part of culture at many levels.

The culture of a particular group is built up of many self-reinforcing layers. Behavioural psychology researchers consider that there are three critical steps in understanding a culture and therefore having any chance of modifying it. At the deepest level there are common assumptions across the group that are unquestioned and accepted as absolute truths and are generally unchanging with time. On top of the assumptions is built shared values across the group about the purpose of the group and its role. These can change over time as the group evolves. Finally, there is observable culture which is displayed in the '*way things are done around here*'. The observable culture can include things such as the founding story of the group, sagas of heroic tales of group members and recurring rites, rituals or activities.

Your vision of the future is so important because each social group - team, workplace, local community, tribe, or country - is built on common assumptions, shared values and observable culture, of which stories play a vital part. Telling stories is an incredibly important way to reinforce the culture and to help induct new group members. It takes a concept and brings it alive. It gives ideas meaning to the group. Telling stories is also a great place to start when seeking to change a culture. By telling and retelling a compelling story that attracts interest and support, the story will seep into the culture and become embedded as one of the shared values. In time it might even influence the assumptions that lie as the foundation of the group. Your shared vision, your story - like those of Mary Robinson and the other contributors to this book - has the potential to powerfully influence the culture and norms of all your social groups, however large or small they may be.

As is discussed in Section 3, changing these deep assumptions and the paradigms through which a group sees the world can be very difficult. Rational arguments are not enough and sometimes a shock to the system is needed to force people to change their long-held beliefs and move to a new reality.

The task of changing national and global attitudes on the way we live and interact with our planet is therefore mountainous. Changing culture will take many many stories told many times across the world to encourage people to change their values and assumptions. Increasing shocks to the current world system in the form of extreme weather events will help this transition in thinking, but it will be the quality and quantity of the stories told that will determine the timing of change.

Those convinced of a need for change will often get very frustrated with those that cannot or will not see that it is important. They will blame them for holding us back when we knew it was time to change, for wasting time, for being deliberately obstinate. The listeners to the stories are, however, just hearing something that does not fit with their world view and they have not yet been convinced that their world view is wrong. They are just behaving in accordance with their culture - it is the change agents that are breaking the unwritten rules and assumptions of their way of life. It is the story tellers that are being disruptive and trying to ruin everything.

When the stories are good enough, they will convince people to change their assumptions about how the world works. Change will then be embraced. It is therefore the quality of story telling, including that by the authors in this book, which is going to determine how far the world goes down the current road towards collapse before turning back.

No pressure there, story tellers!

Chapter 2

HOW WE ARE TRACKING

In general, anything that develops too fast will fall apart just as quickly, whereas a slow and steady development is more assured of yielding favourable results. Plants that unravel into full bloom in early morning may whither and fall by the evening, but the slow growing pine trees will not whither even in the extreme cold. Hence, a superior person does not hasten to achieve results.

The Governing Principles of Ancient China, 7th Century, Scroll 26: Wei Zhi, Vol. 2

Chapter 2

HOW WE ARE TRACKING

In 2100...
The Climate Neutral World
Christiana Figueres,
Executive Secretary, UN Framework Convention on Climate Change
Bonn, Germany

It is the start of the year 2100 and the fireworks shows held in megacities across the globe to ring in the New Year are still fresh in everyone's mind. There is much speculation as to what the next century may bring. Many of those looking forward to a new century spent weeks leading up to the new year reflecting on the last century – how we got where we are.

In almost every case progress could be traced back to the year 2015, when all governments of the world shed old divides and agreed to a long-term goal of climate-neutral growth. In that pursuit they agreed to an unprecedented level of collaboration, which stabilized a disrupted climate system that had threatened to erase prior gains and put a brake on further social and economic development around the world. In the years following 2015, global emissions peaked and deep decarbonization of the world economy was achieved as countries fulfilled commitments to move towards clean energy and sustainable development. This move to solar and wind energy was enabled by technology that drove demand – electric vehicles, energy independent buildings, intelligent micro-grids, improved electricity storage, smart agriculture and highly efficient transport systems.

Financing these advances sparked a virtuous cycle of ingenuity and innovation, resulting in global development that kept people and planet healthy and the economy prosperous even as the population surged past nine billion. Certainly, challenges arose from our many years of carbon intense growth, but the spirit of cooperation and collaboration that emerged helped countries, cities, businesses and individuals work together to overcome these challenges, adapt to our new climate and meet our global sustainable development goals.

A new century presents new opportunity and because governments enacted climate-safe development that will serve for generations, opportunity from 2100 forward is unimaginably vast and incredibly varied.

Before starting our journey and leaping into the future and all its chaos, it is important to take stock of where we are starting in the year 2015. Many of the authors have taken an historical look back to 2015 and seen important developments that occurred at that time – but this may just be their optimism talking. It may be that, in hindsight, the era of 2015 will just been seen as part of the great pause when large scale action was rational but not acceptable. However, there are some very important activities underway that have the potential to be seen as historically significant.

At the time of writing, there appears to be a growing global wave of interest in and enthusiasm for more significant steps on the road to change. There was a similar wave of interest in the mid-2000s which evaporated on the back of the global financial crisis as governments and their constituents focussed on the short term repair of damaged economies. Despite the lost ground since then, there has been good progress on the development of global institutions and the thinking on how the transition to a more resilient world might unfold.

The current wave of support is tenuous and could easily evaporate again if other more imminent crises take precedence. Whilst the winds are blowing favourably, however, there is much international progress and many of the foundations of meaningful change are being built.

With any process of change, the rate of progress is rarely smooth. There are times of rapid change followed by times spent in the doldrums with no apparent progress. The pauses in change are an important component of the process as they allow for consolidation of thinking and provide an opportunity to bring wider groups up to speed with achievements to date. In particular, where underlying assumptions are being challenged, rapid change will fail to bring along all people at the same rate. Without the pauses in progress, there will remain significant numbers of people who are still in the old way of thinking and the change will fail to be permanent.

This necessity for staged change is incredibly frustrating for the change agents, who cannot see why everyone does not just see their point of view. This is especially the case when the speed of change is critical to prevent excessive damage. There is therefore a tension between driving hard to make sure we keep moving forward and applying the brakes to make sure we bring everyone along with us. And just to complicate matters, every nation and individual needs this to be delivered in a slightly different balance to make it work for them. No wonder it is a frustrating process.

★ ★ ★

The world has come a long way towards understanding the problem of climate change and the options for technical solutions. The exact nature of the impacts on the complex ecosystems of the earth's climate and inhabitants is far from precise. However, there is overwhelming agreement on the fundamentals of the science and the overall likely consequences.

Interests that are strongly vested in denial of any meaningful need for action use their often significant financial, political and media power to fuel a debate that ended some time ago. By their very nature such interests are forged from regions that have built their wealth from industries under threat such as Texan oil and Australian coal and iron ore.

In addition, the incidence of extreme weather events is increasing. Whilst it is always difficult to directly attribute any one event to climate change impacts, there is mounting evidence that there is increasing frequency of extreme droughts, floods, heatwaves, cold snaps and cyclones.

In its Summary for Policymakers on Managing the Risks of Extreme Events and Disasters, the Intergovernmental Panel on Climate Change (IPCC) states that *'Average tropical cyclone maximum wind speed is likely to increase'* along with many other assertions about potential increased weather events. As I type this paragraph, the Category 5 Cyclone Pam has devastated a number of Pacific Islands including Kiribati, the Solomon Islands and Vanuatu and is nearing landfall in New Zealand. CNN reports that it was *'one of the most powerful storms ever to make landfall'* and it has already killed dozens of people with hundreds rendered homeless. Cyclone Pam follows on from the 2013 devastation caused by Super Typhoon Haiyan in the Philippines which killed more than 6,000 people.

The Government of Vanuatu claims that it is already suffering devastating effects from climate change with the island's coastal areas being washed away, forcing resettlement to higher ground and smaller yields on traditional crops.

According to the UN, since 2005, over 700,000 people have lost their lives, over 1.4 million have been injured and around 23 million have been made homeless as a result of disasters, including natural disasters and climate and other human–made disasters with a total economic loss of more than $1.3 trillion.

Ironically, at the same time that Cyclone Pam is wreaking havoc, the third World Conference on Disaster Risk and Reduction (WCDRR) is being held in Sendai, Japan. It no doubt helped to concentrate the minds of the attendees, some of whom are contributors to this book. The Sendai region is rebuilding after its catastrophic losses in the 2011 Great East Japan Earthquake and Tsunami.

Commenting at the opening of that conference, Helen Clark, Administrator of the United Nations Development Programme and former Prime Minister of New Zealand, said, *'This is a more important quest than it has ever been. People everywhere face increasingly deadly, destructive, and costly natural disasters; and climate change exacerbates the threat.'*

In his speech there, United Nations Secretary-General Ban Ki-moon said, *'Annually, countries across the globe suffer losses of over*

$300 billion as a result of damages caused by natural disasters, making disaster risk reduction everybody's business.'

One initiative that is being championed at the WCDRR conference is the concept of 'Building Back Better', a term first used during the Indian Ocean Tsunami recovery efforts in Aceh, Indonesia. The strategy involves restoring damaged houses, hospitals, schools and other public infrastructure to more disaster-resilient standards. The view is that post-disaster reconstruction is an ideal place to begin change as people know all too well the imminence of the peril.

Whilst the attribution of disasters to climate change is problematic and indirect, the association is starting to make the peril seem more imminent. People find it difficult to understand the practical impacts of temperature rising two degrees over 50-100 years. Increasing severity and frequency of extreme events and their consequent destruction is something far more tangible. If extreme weather-driven disasters continue to increase then the global population may well change their underlying assumptions regarding prudent short term action.

There is a plethora of technical solutions already available that could enable a transition if the political will was there. The challenge in delivering the transition to a world with a stable climate will be enormous. Industries, power systems and markets will need to be deconstructed and rebuilt and this will drive upheaval in every way. So implementing the solutions will present many challenges. However, there is no question that we already have access to proven technologies that would enable this to happen. As the century continues, we will find better technical solutions that will enable the transition to be delivered more efficiently and maybe with less disruption but it can be done today with what we have now. Some of these existing and possible future technologies are described in Section 4.

So the science is settled beyond reasonable doubt, the current technology solutions are sufficient and the impacts are becoming increasingly tangible. For rational human beings, it is now just a question of implementation. Unfortunately, we are not primarily rational so there is more work to be done before we set off on the journey. The challenge now moves to that of communications and psychology. As we will see in the next chapter, humans have not evolved to deal with climate change. We have evolved to cope with the immediate threats and are not wired to think too far into the future.

* * *

Beyond the immense challenge of greenhouse gases, the world is struggling with many other pollution issues. Driven by growing populations, industrial activity and crowded cities, the health of air, water and land is dire in many fast growing areas. Beijing and Delhi have received much publicity for their appalling air quality and I can vouch for being able to regularly taste the air pollution in Beijing. I have also experienced mixed emotions when travelling at 300 km/h on a fast train from Nanjing to Shanghai for an hour without once seeing the smog lift. I felt wonder at the technical marvel of the train and horror at the consequences of this rapid development. There are many other places not so well known that are suffering to a greater extent. In his eye-opening 2010 book titled *When a Billion Chinese Jump*, Jonathan Watts describes the appalling pollution across the country and how it is impacting the population.

Whilst those of us with the good fortune to live in the fresh air of Australia may be tempted to deride this lack of care for the environment, it was not that long ago that similar conditions were to be found in the now developed world. London recorded four thousand deaths from the Great Smog of December 1952 when '*visibility quickly dropped to five yards all over London*'.

Los Angeles also suffered from severe smog events from the 1950s through to the early 1980s. The impact of this LA smog on children's health has been reviewed in a research report published in 2015 in the New England Journal of Medicine by University of Southern California scientists. The study found that children in the Los Angeles region have substantially healthier lungs than they did just 20 years ago, following the multi-billion-dollar efforts to improve southern California's air quality.

USC's Frank Gilliland says the new findings *"show scientifically that targeting pollutants actually makes kids healthier. It's a very important message, especially for the developing world: These problems are fixable, and you can see big benefits."*

In the study, researchers followed 2,000 children aged eleven to fifteen, when lungs are growing the most. Average lung capacity increased by 10% between the period and the percentage of children in the study with abnormally poor lung function at age fifteen dropped from nearly eight per cent for the 1994–98 group to 3.6 per cent for kids between 2007 and 2011.

Manchester in the UK was known as the Chimney of the World in the nineteenth century when it was one of the most industrialised regions in the world. In 1884, the great thinker John Ruskin said Manchester was the spiritual home of pollution, calling the city's smog *"Manchester Devil's darkness"*.

A thick smog cloud descended on the city in 1931, killing 450 people. In 1950, a perfect storm of poor weather and high industrial use of coal led to smog linked to dozens of deaths from lung diseases, such as bronchitis. As late as 1995, Manchester was said to have the *"foulest air in Britain"*, with 65,000 cars entering the city centre daily.

My father worked in a hospital in Manchester in 1950 whilst playing rugby for Sale Rugby Club. As a junior doctor he was expected to have a pristine white shirt at all times. Through the times of smog this proved to be a challenge and required at least three shirts a day to ensure he was acceptably clean.

Beyond smog, the West has had many environmental challenges that it has faced and resolved. One of the most famous was the realisation that the pesticide DDT was having major impacts on ecosystems as it killed everything and not just the pests it was targeting. This was famously first publicised through Rachel Carson's 1962 book, *Silent Spring*, where she wrote about the disappearance of birds in DDT treated areas, and the implications for the health of all living things, including humans. By the time Carson died in 1967, the US had started to ban or limit the use of DDT.

The current environmental problems in the cities of the developing world are therefore nothing new and we have shown time and again that pollution is a solvable problem once there is popular support. Within 10-20 years of widespread recognition of the problems discussed above, each had been resolved, primarily through the implementation and enforcement of regulation.

Sadly, our human nature seems to require there to be a certain level of death or disaster to occur before the need for action is taken seriously. So for the already prevalent issues having severe health impacts such as poor air quality causing the 'Beijing cough' or polluted water in the West of China, it is likely that they will become just historical notes by about 2025.

In comparison, the impacts of climate change are not so direct and certainly not as widely understood. The threat is one we are not well equipped to deal with either psychologically or socially.

Another challenge is that climate change is a global rather than a local problem. Cities can regulate and change behaviours quickly and produce results within a few years. To get global agreement has proved much more problematic as governments and personalities change, and interests vary from nation to nation. Some of the authors in this book are at the centre of the current process of global negotiation and, to be successful, they will need support from wherever it can be generated.

★ ★ ★

Another important perspective in assessing where we stand as we set off on our journey is that of finance and economics. Much of the justification for not taking action on climate change has been based on preserving the underlying economic assumptions and protecting the interests of those who have created the wealth and well-being delivered to date. Many fear poverty and arguments based on maintaining economic wealth can easily find favour. However, without managing the risks of climate change impacts effectively, there will never be long term financial security. To do this we must design a world that is truly sustainable and uses its limited resources wisely.

There are, however, cracks starting to open up in this defence.

Writing in The Guardian, Professor Jeffrey Sachs, the director of The Earth Institute at Columbia University stated that, '*By separating nature from economics, we have walked blindly into tragedy. Economic policy must be combined with climate and technology if we are to stand any chance of saving ourselves.*'

Sachs details how current economic theory can be directly attributed as the cause for some environmental disasters. He states, "*We need a new way of thinking, one that tightly links the human-made world of economics and politics with the natural world of climate and biodiversity and with the designed world of twenty-first century technology.*"

One phenomenon giving powerful expression to this new way of thinking has been the surprising rise of the divestment movement that has gained traction across the globe in 2014 and 2015. It campaigns for investors, both large and small, to withdraw their investments from fossil fuel companies due to their negative impacts on climate change. The movement has been driven by 350. org which was founded by Bill McKibben, who tells of his fears for our future in Chapter 5.

The companies that have been targeted have been taken by surprise. They have claimed that they are being unfairly targeted and that fossil fuels have helped pull the world out of poverty and given many economic and societal benefits. There have been attempts to paint the divestment campaign as dangerous, radical and wanting to destroy lifestyles. Nevertheless, the movement continues to grow and is beginning to have a material impact on the market capitalisation of some fossil fuel companies.

At the same time, there is serious money has begun to be made from providing the solutions that enable the transition away from fossil fuel reliance. In January 2015, Li Hejun, founder and chairman of Beijing-based solar company Hanergy briefly became China's richest man, taking over the title from Alibaba's Jack Ma. In the US, Elon Musk's Tesla is growing quickly and currently making good money for investors.

Some of America's richest families are actively investing in the future of cleantech. Cleantech is defined as products and services that have both economic and environmental benefits. Ward McNally, a descendent of the founder of the Rand McNally map company, has joined with ten other family offices to establish the Clean Tech Syndicate. In total, the families have a net worth of some $60 billion and have so far pledged to invest $1.4 billion in cleantech.

Other groups of family offices backing the transition to a lower carbon economy include Cleantech, Renewable Energy, and Environmental Opportunities (CREO), which brings together some 50 family offices with a total of $50 billion in investable capital.

As smart investors start to see the opportunities for strong returns from companies that assist the transition to a world with a stable climate, there will be increasing interest in the sector. There will inevitably be bubbles created along the way as over enthusiasm backs companies that do not succeed, but this will just be a blip in the growth of the cleantech sector globally. Companies that deliver energy, water, waste solutions, smart cities and agriculture and those that help industry to become more efficient and sustainable will thrive. The investors in these companies will make handsome profits. At the same time, investors who have remained in support of older industries that do not evolve may well lose their money, as old industry assets get 'stranded' in the new economy.

The rich lists of the world going forward will be full of the founders of the cleantech industries, those that are more efficient and more environmentally and financially sustainable. The likes of Li Hejun and Elon Musk might then replace today's software entrepreneurs such as Bill Gates, Mark Zuckerberg and Jack Ma or the fossil fuel and iron billionaires.

★ ★ ★

Looking back from 2100, the introduction of the Sustainable Development Goals in September 2015 is likely to be seen as a vital step. This initiative has the goal to mainstream sustainable development across the United Nations and subsequently into national governments at all levels.

The Sustainable Development Goals (SDG) cover a broad range of issues from poverty reduction to nutrition, gender equality and environmental protection.

The outcome document of the Rio+20 Conference in 2012, entitled *The Future We Want*, established a process to develop the SDGs for adoption by the 193 UN member states in 2015. Member States agreed that the SDGs would serve as a driver for implementation and mainstreaming of sustainable development in the UN system as a whole.

Commenting on the SDG's, Gro Harlem Brundtland and Mary Robinson as representatives of The Elders, a group of former heads of State, said:

"Reducing vulnerability to both natural and human-made hazards is the key to building resilient communities and societies.

"There is no point, for example, in establishing a new maternal health clinic in a coastal village which risks being swept away entirely by rising sea waters. As Elders, we believe that reducing vulnerability to both natural and human-made hazards is the key to building resilient communities and societies. Only empowered and resilient communities operating in the context of global solidarity can ensure a just and equitable policy framework for tackling disaster risk and climate change.

"People around the world, from civil society to corporations, are increasingly aware that 2015 is the year when tough decisions need to be taken. As Elders, we will continue to campaign for a just and equitable solution to the world's climate challenge with human rights and solidarity at its centre."

The SDG adoption provided the perfect warm up act to the Paris UNFCCC's Conference of Parties (COP21) in December 2015. Many people were optimistic in the lead up to this event that agreements would be struck between at least the most significant nations. Many of the visions in this book hold hope that COP21 will be the start of a new level of progress.

The last time that there appeared to be this level of enthusiasm was at the COP15 event in Copenhagen in 2009 although it did not meet the expectations. The world has however moved on from

2009. The major economies of the developing world are now more supportive of global action and despite some countries, notably Australia and Canada, swimming against the tide, the politics in most countries favours taking action.

Regardless of the inevitable short term media frenzy, time will tell how COP21 turns out and what the long term impacts of its progress achieve. There is no doubt that the debate at and leading up to COP21 will make progress towards our long term future. Equally, there is no doubt that COP21 will not solve the whole problem, as that is going to take many decades and much effort. As you read this, you may know how things turned out and that the journey still has a long way to go. As you look back, hopefully you will think that 2015 was a helpful year with some good outcomes.

An overall assessment of the starting point of our journey might be that we are not doing too badly, given where we have come from. The world might be thought of as being in its 'gangly male teenager phase': grown to nearly full size, adjusting to its environment but nowhere near being mature and able to make sensible decisions. As the father of two teenage boys, my hope is that by the end of our journey to 2100, the world will have reached maturity and turned into its equivalent of a fine young man.

Christiana Figueres, who started this chapter with her vision and is driving the global agreement towards climate change, is similarly, and thankfully, optimistic. Her view from the year 2100 ends with a compelling view of what we will have created.

A new century presents new opportunity and because governments enacted climate-safe development that will serve for generations, opportunity from 2100 forward is unimaginably vast and incredibly varied.

Chapter 3

THE FAILURES OF EVOLUTION

My fear represented the failure of the human system. It is a sad truth of our creation: Something is amiss in our design, there are loose ends of our psychology that are simply not wrapped up. My fears were the dirty secrets of evolution. They were not provided for, and I was forced to construct elaborate temples to house them.

Steve Martin

Chapter 3

THE FAILURES OF EVOLUTION

In 2100...

The Myth of Apathy

Dr Renee Lertzman,
Psychologist & Author

As we look back from the world today in 2100, we wonder what could possibly have delayed action for so long at the beginning of the century. There was no shortage of good ideas about how to make the world cleaner and greener. Information about biodiversity, creatures in the deep seas and remote corners of this planet, the fragility of our home. Information about the threats.

And yet, the riddle of the time was why more people were not taking action. Actions that we knew would do us all – plants, critters, humans – a lot of good and would have avoided the many challenges we had to face.

The marketing effort to make green sexy, hot, and profitable ended up making things even more confusing. The lovely, profitable, seamless 'green dream' was confusing and ideologically incoherent. People struggled with the balance of a scary future and a wealthy today with all its 'green' gadgets.

At the time, experts berated the public for their apathy. It was assumed the community didn't care or couldn't be bothered. This was based on a way of thinking about human beings as rational, transparent, responsive to incentives and ultimately focused on self-preservation more than anything else. But this apathy was a myth. Behavioural economics as a driving framework was revealed to be limited.

When the breakthrough came it was because of the widespread acknowledgment that human psychology was more complex, and required us to innovate our understandings of how humans relate with both change and our ecological contexts. It shifted to a view of humans coping with contradiction, ambivalence, paradox and dilemmas, and in so doing, enabled us to meet people more where they are, and foster greater levels of creativity. People felt seen, heard and inspired. This view recognised that with change, there is often loss. And with loss, there is often mourning and melancholia. And with grief and loss, there can be space for creative engagement, participation, care and concern - if we can acknowledge it.

The "green dream" continues, but with it is a greater insight and understanding of how humans relate with change, what fosters our capacities for solving problems, innovating and collaborating.

As discussed further in Chapter 7, the challenges of complex health issues have many similarities to those associated with the complexities of an out-of-balance global ecosystem.

My wife, Kate, became sick in 1994 when working as lawyer in Ghana on the float of the Ashanti Gold Mine. After 21 years of mostly caring and largely incompetent medical advice, she is finally inching her way towards a reasonable quality of life. Her medical problems have been complex and have not fitted the way that the medical profession has evolved. She has suffered for years with chronic pain, to which the medical response has been largely symptom-based – either to provide enough drugs to knock yourself out or, more often, to advise you to 'just learn to cope'. Our sons have never known a well mother and I have never had a well wife – an unhealthy ecosystem has myriad impacts across all its connecting and interdependent systems.

Whilst it is sometimes hard to see, there are also benefits that come with this package of impacts. Managing through adversity brings maturity and helps to clarify priorities. Our sons probably have a greater sense of the importance of health and happiness than some of their peers at their privileged private school. I am probably a more thoughtful, patient and forgiving person through having a greater understanding that life is messy and not always easy.

Perhaps, through coping with and finding our way through the challenges of a chronically unwell global ecology, the human race will also grow in maturity and find ways to improve the quality of life for all.

Many of the contributors have this as their vision for the future.

★ ★ ★

Understanding the ecosystem in which climate change exists requires an understanding far beyond just the physical science, although of course that is critical. As discussed above, we have made good progress on the science of the problem and a range of possible technology solutions over the last 20 years. What has been largely ignored however is the behaviour and thinking of the one part of the ecosystem that must make the decision to act. It is critical to understand what is holding back the human race from acting on the overwhelmingly rational arguments for change.

In Chapter 1, we concluded that it was going to be the quality of the story telling that will determine how long it will take to precipitate change. This is a bit more complex than it may appear. Story telling done well can harness emotions and gain support for a particular way of thinking. However, to get the reaction that is sought requires an understanding of what emotional response will be useful. So, the story tellers need to listen to the psychologists to be able to frame their stories in order to be effective.

Research has been conducted into why humans are not, in general, reacting as might be expected to the threat posed by climate change. Much of this has focussed on the challenges of the temporal separation of the cause and effects and the feeling of powerlessness of an individual in the face of such a large problem.

Psychologist and researcher, Renee Lertzman, provided the vision above and has examined the issue of inaction in detail. Her book, *Environmental Melancholia*, expands on her thoughts. Her primary argument is that most people view the changes required as being too much of a threat to their way of life.

"Being green is attractive, desirable and profitable. However, it is also potentially frightening and threatens what many of us hold to be central to who we are – how we construct meaning in our lives. Until we incorporate the whole picture into our vision of being sustainable, we are going to be fighting a battle."

The strangest behaviour seems to be from those of us who understand the need for change and yet still are unable to change in any meaningful way. A bit like the overweight woman in front of me at the coffee shop this morning who ordered a 'skinny' latte and a very large custard Berliner.

Lertzman explains this dissonance between our actions and beliefs through the fact that we care an overwhelming amount about both the planet and our way of life, and this conflict appears irresolvable. The consequent apparent apathy is a bit like saying a deer stuck in the headlights does not care what happens. Rather, the deer is so worried about the consequences it is unable to move.

Daniel Gilbert, a professor of psychology at Harvard, has written about why our inability to deal with climate change is due in part to the way our mind is wired. Gilbert asserts that the human race has evolved to cope best with problems that are *Intentional, Immoral, Imminent and Instantaneous.* Climate change sets off none of these mental triggers. Climate change is not the result of malevolence so is not generally seen as intentional. It does not violate our moral sensibilities so is not seen as immoral. It is not seen as imminent, but rather a future problem, and it is proceeding very gradually so does not have an instantaneous component. Gilbert writes this is a major problem, *"because it fails to trip the brain's alarm, leaving us soundly asleep in a burning bed."*

So, whilst humans may see a rational argument, the mind is hardwired in a way that makes taking action far from a natural reaction. There may be hope that our hardwired brains may start to see more imminent threats from worsening extreme weather events. However, it will not be until this starts feeling like a real and immediate threat that humans as a whole will change their opinion.

Robert Gifford, a professor of psychology and environmental studies at the University of Victoria in Canada, has also researched the many psychological barriers to mitigating climate change. He calls them the *Dragons of Inaction*. Gifford's research continues but his initial list of seven dragons comprised:

1. *limited cognition about the problem;*
2. *ideological world views that tend to preclude pro-environmental attitudes and behavior;*
3. *comparisons with key other people;*
4. *sunk costs and behavioral momentum;*
5. *discredence toward experts and authorities;*
6. *perceived risks of change; and*
7. *positive but inadequate behavior change.*

Gifford also now includes the lack of perceived behavioral control in his list of key barriers. People feel that they are such a small part of the problem and the solution that they cannot have an impact.

As an example of this last point, a Climate Change Council colleague overheard a conversation in the supermarket of an Australian country town in 2009. Two locals were in the next aisle discussing climate change. At the time, there was much media debate over the proposed introduction of a carbon price into Australia. One lady was asking the other what she thought of this new 'tax' and what she thought of all this climate change talk. The reply was simple and telling. Her friend said, "*Well, if climate change was really that much of a problem, then the Government would already be doing something about it. If they're arguing about it, then it is just some political rubbish.*"

How can an individual, whether in a country town or elsewhere, possibly feel as though they have any influence or control over something that requires global governments to cooperate? The challenge for democratically elected governments of course is therefore that they must advocate for changes with no immediate apparent benefits to an electorate that may not yet be fully convinced of the need for the changes. This neatly brings us back to the need for good story telling to help communities to see the need and benefits in change and provide the mandate to governments to deliver those changes.

★ ★ ★

There are also are many other psychological angles at work in the reluctance of humans to recognise and act upon the problem. These can be loosely grouped under the term behavioural economics which attempts to understand why humans often make irrational decisions.

There has been much research into conspiracy theories and why they often fit with prevalent mental models of the world, despite both apparent irrationality and statistical improbability. The success and support of conspiracy theories often stems from a perceived lack of control of destiny and a preference for a belief in control being exerted by unknown forces. This might involve divine beings, aliens or secret government agencies.

Robert Brotherton at the University of London says that believing in conspiracy theories fits with the way our brains make sense of the world.

"One of our psychological biases is that, whenever anything ambiguous happens, we connect the dots," Brotherton says.

Brotherton also suggests that 'proportionality bias' can lead to false conclusions. Proportionality bias is when people believe that a serious consequence must have a serious and intentional cause. This fits with Gilbert's suggestion above that in order to take action, something must be seen as intentionally bad. *"When JFK got shot, people wanted to think that something big caused that, not just that some guy you'd never heard of could have killed the president."*

A commonly recounted conspiracy is that governments support MMR vaccine programs to appease pharmaceutical companies and deliberately risk increasing autism as a consequence. This stems from an entirely discredited article that was published in the Lancet in 1998. The author was struck off the medical register and no other research has ever found a link. The myth continues however and, as a consequence, the instance of childhood whooping cough and measles is increasing. There is no evidence and no rational argument for avoiding the vaccine and yet many people persist in believing that the government is out to deliberately harm them.

The comfort of having someone to blame for something bad

is very cathartic. It is a natural reaction for humans. Whether it is tripping over a pavement, failing an exam, having a car crash or getting sick, if there is an external reason to be found, then that allows the sufferer to take out their anger on someone else. It is so much easier than confronting the possibility that both our good fortune and our bad luck are the result of random events and that we have little real control over where our lives take us.

The conspiracy theories surrounding climate change rage on each side. Either the science community is making it all up to win research grants or that governments are looking after their donors in the oil companies and deliberately not taking action. Sadly, the reality is far more complex and there is no easy 'baddie' to blame that would make the issue one of intentional bad consequences.

As Gilbert says in his entertaining Harvard Thinks Big 2010 talk, '*Global warming isn't trying to kill us and that's a damn shame. If climate change were some kind of nefarious plot visited upon us by bad men with worse moustaches, right now we would be fighting a war on warming*'. He goes on to say, when addressing the fact that global warming does not strike humans as immoral, that '*if global warming was caused by gay sex or caused by the act of eating puppies, Americans would right now be massing in the street calling for its end*.'

On a similar theme, Law Professor Alberto Alemanno at HEC Paris spoke in his 2014 TEDx talk about the concept of free choice and why humans rarely make the best rational choice. His argument is that every decision is heavily influenced by the context in which the decision is made. A compelling example is the disparity between rates of organ donation in different countries. In countries where you are required to opt out of organ donation, the rates of donation are significantly higher than those where you have to opt in. Alemanno describes this as the 'power of inertia'. It is much easier and requires much less conscious thought for people to do nothing and continue with the status quo than to make a proactive decision. We are '*cognitively lazy*' and the '*default matters*'.

He also argues that social pressure is extremely important in decision making and people generally want to be seen as part of the group, complying with its unwritten rules and cultural norms.

He summarises, '*We think much less than we think we think*'. This, he argues, leads humans to fall into 'cognitive traps', such as those used by marketers to trick us into buying stuff we do not want. These same marketing strategies and cognitive traps are also effectively used to sell us policies and beliefs that critical thinking would lead us to dismiss.

However, he suggests that we can use the same marketing strategies to deliver benefits to the world. He cites the example of the collection of UK taxes which has been enhanced by around 5% by means of a letter to tax payers informing them that 95% of their fellow citizens pay on time and that currently the letter recipient was in the minority.

Others term this technique as gamification. Gabe Zichermann CEO of Gamification Co in New York tells the story of how gamifying speeding fines in Sweden made a step change in driver behaviour. The concept was simple: everyone who was caught speeding had to pay a fine whilst those who passed the same camera driving below the speed limit were entered into a lottery to win the proceeds from the fines. By changing a negative reinforcement loop into a positive reinforcement loop, the behaviour of a 'game's' participants can be radically changed.

The discipline of behavioural economics tries to pull together all the reasons for decision making and its impact on the economy. The field was pioneered by Richard Thaler at the University of Chicago. Thaler investigated the implications of relaxing the standard economic assumption that everyone in the economy is rational and selfish, instead entertaining the possibility that some of the agents in the economy are sometimes fallibly human. Thaler is the co-author of the global best seller *Nudge* in which the concepts of behavioural economics are used to tackle many of society's major problems.

Examples of seemingly irrational but consistent human decision making include selling more black cars on cloudy days, the guy who refused to pay $10 to have someone mow his lawn but would not accept $20 to mow his neighbour's and the woman who drove ten minutes to save $10 on a $45 clock radio but would not drive the same ten minutes to save \$10 on a \$495 television.

Marketers also use the Fear of Missing Out (FoMO) extensively in their tactics to entice people to make seemingly irrational decisions. When cornered by the threat of losing out on a soon to end price on a much desired product, used perhaps by those we wish to emulate in some way, many of us succumb to the risk of a quick, ill thought out buying decision.

As an aside, the rise of social media has prompted a number of psychological studies, including that by Andrew Przybylski from the University of Oxford who suggests that people with below average self-esteem are attracted to social media more than others to help build relationships. The same people have the tendency to find social media very addictive because they do not want to miss anything and this can result in high anxiety levels. This is of course a huge simplification of the processes at work, but intuitively has some merit.

Behavioural economics also suggests some ways that the same tricks can be used to create benefits. These can include reducing eating by using a small plate or forcing yourself to go to the gym by committing to a friend to go together.

So it appears that, by exploiting the weaknesses in our entrenched mental models, there are psychological ploys we can use to change behaviour. Are these tricks and frame changing strategies really sufficient to make the scale of changes we need? The conclusion of most of the contributing authors seems to be that societies' mental models are too entrenched to be altered until the world faces impending catastrophe. Only then will responses at the scale required finally be provoked. This can lead to some depressing views of the future as we shall see.

★ ★ ★

Now for the good news! Maybe our brains are not as inflexible as once thought. Neuroplasticity is a relatively new field of research that is exploring the brain's capacity to rebuild its connections to create new ways of thinking and behaving. The focus of this work has been on overcoming strokes, chronic pain and ageing. My wife's chronic pain has led us to this emerging field in the hope of a different solution to the many failed physical and chemical interventions.

Baroness Susan Greenfield of the University of Oxford sees the downside of this with children that spend lots of time using electronic devices. In her book, *Mind Change: How Digital Technologies Are Leaving Their Mark on Our Brains*, she cites findings from different researchers who claim that playing video games and spending long hours in front of the screen online can significantly change how we perceive things.

She argues that computer games over-stimulate the player through rewards perceived in the thrill centres of the brain and simultaneously remove any consequences of failure - just play again! I have seen her lecture on this subject and compare the reduced prefrontal cortex of a teenage gamer to that of addicts and gamblers who are unable to effectively assess risk and reward.

Mind Change sets out the case for our long-term screen-centric behaviour having an impact on our evolutionary path. Greenfield's view is mostly pessimistic on how these changes will impact our ability to cope with and react to complex problems and big challenges. She fears that the generation nearing adulthood will be severely disadvantaged in their ability to empathise, will be desensitised to bad consequences and unable to assess long term risks.

In contrast, Gabe Zichermann spoke compellingly at TEDx Brussels on his view that games are making kids better problem-solvers and better at everything from driving to multi-tasking. He speaks of 'fluid intelligence' and how the process of gaming builds the interconnectedness of the brain increasing problem solving capabilities.

Both of these examples focus on the plasticity of children's brains as they grow and mature. Whilst both sides are arguable, neither is probably that far removed from historical thinking on how maturing brains start to build new connections that allow adults to behave as adults.

The most promising and innovative area of work, however, is in the retraining of adult brains.

In his book *The Brain that Changes Itself*, Norman Doidge of Columbia University's Center for Psychoanalytic Training and Research in New York reviews global progress in this concept, providing fascinating case studies of successful transformations. Neuroplasticity breaks the concept that the brain is hard-wired and that brain cells just die off as we get older and do not regenerate.

Doidge writes about Michael Moskowitz who has established a chronic pain management unit in California where he works with people who have suffered '*intractable pain*' for many years. The patients had undergone every conventional treatment using drugs and other physical interventions.

> '*Moskowitz spends most of his time immersed in the chronic pain of others. Their agony is unknown to most people, in part because they are often so drained by their pain that they stop wasting what little energy they have to express distress to those who can't help them. Chronic pain may be invisible on a patient's face, or it can give its victim a drawn, ghostly presence, because it sucks the life out of a person.*'

The idea that chronic pain was caused by a neuroplastic event of the brain had been proposed by the German physiologist Manfred Zimmermann in 1978, but was largely ignored. Moskowitz suffered from chronic pain for many years following a boating accident in 1994. After retraining his brain to not be over-stimulated by the pain signals, he almost entirely cured his own pain. He now helps others to do the same.

The process involved what he calls *competitive plasticity* where one region of the brain steals resources from another area if needed. Chronic pain will cause the pain centres to expand resulting in the sufferer being unable to concentrate, move gracefully or effectively manage emotional responses. The areas that regulate these activities have been hijacked to process the pain signal.

Moskowitz used this same process to fight back. Every time the pain increased, he focussed on other things that would use the areas of the brain that might otherwise be subsumed. In this way over time, he appeared to teach his brain to ignore the pain signals coming in by rewiring the circuits that had been previously over-reacting.

The most exciting bit of this theory is that once the rewiring has been completed it does not seem to unravel - it has been changed for good. Moskowitz has patients who have kept their gains for five years. I hope to report a personal anecdote to this effect in the years to come!

So perhaps the fixed mental models that lead us to conclude that we will not be able to change human behaviour before getting perilously close to catastrophe may not actually be hardwired. The opportunities presented by adult neuroplasticity are therefore exciting. It is however yet to be seen whether Doidge's examples can be replicated on a global scale.

Through the telling and retelling of visions of a desirable future world, some of the apparent hardwired assumptions of the way the world is can be weakened and space created for change to occur.

The solution is by no means certain, but it feels as though the science might just be suggesting it is possible and that is certainly good news. Now all we have to do is work out how we do it.

★ ★ ★

Many of the visions told in this book foresee the human race heading towards the brink of disaster before pulling back and being forced into a new way of thinking and behaving. This is consistent with the majority of current views of psychological barriers to change. Doidge's neuroplasticity may allow us to avoid this circumstance if we manage to collectively rewire our systems, but there is clearly the potential to cause much suffering along the way.

Paul Gilding, whose vision is in Chapter 10, wrote in his book *The Great Disruption* that the human race was '*slow but not stupid*'. By this he meant that generally, when perils are apparent, humans are poor at taking preventative action to stop the peril worsening but that eventually they react with great force and ingenuity to prevent complete catastrophe.

A well known story of survival in which there was an immediate and significant sacrifice was that of Aran Ralston in 2003. Aran was an experienced adventurer and went to Utah's Bluejohn Canyon for a planned eight hour, thirteen mile day-hike. On his hike, Aran dislodged a large boulder that pinned his hand and forearm. He had limited supplies and had not told anyone where he was going.

After five days of being a prisoner to his immobile limb and with no hope of rescue, Aran decided to take drastic action in order to survive. He resolved to amputate his own arm using his pocket knife. He broke his radius and ulna then cut through the remaining skin and tendons, freeing himself. He managed to walk out and get medical assistance in time to save his life.

Whilst it seems incredible to be able to cut off your own arm with a pocket knife and no anaesthetic, it was merely a choice between the lesser of two very bad outcomes. Aran created a future for himself by sacrificing something that he valued very highly: his arm! In order to make this extreme decision, he needed to reach the point where he had exhausted all other options and was faced with death or sacrifice.

This fits with the views of many of the contributors of this book who see that the world will get to the edge of collapse or disaster before pulling back. The longer we go on, the greater the sacrifice will need to be. The question then will be 'what is the world's equivalent of cutting off your arm?' What sacrifices will be required to give the human race an acceptable – or perhaps even better – future? Much of the psychology discussed in this chapter indicates that we will take a long time before deciding to make the big changes.

I hope to change this by encouraging individuals to think about what they really want for the future world and then share that vision with others. With this we will encourage discussions about our future and what is important. It is time to pull our collective heads from the sand – it is time to stop the ostrich act! The risks we face need to be confronted.

★ ★ ★

So the context for our journey is now clear. The powerful role of story telling and visions in changing the way people think and our cultural norms is incredibly important. The world has mostly realised it has a serious problem and that it already has the technical capability to overcome this problem and yet it is not taking concerted rational action. The psychology of climate change presents many barriers that at times seem insurmountable if they are hardwired. What is unclear is whether the entrenched thinking is driven by our cultural context or our evolutionary needs – or a combination of the two. Neuroplasticity suggests that, even if evolution has designed our brains such that we struggle with this issue, we have the power to retrain our thinking.

The world is not yet at Ralston's day five but we are certainly trapped in a difficult position with some tough decisions to make. Collapse is not yet sufficiently imminent to force drastic action. The challenge for our story tellers is to rewire human perceptions of the way the world works and move the boulder before we need to amputate.

Section 2

DREAMS, FEARS & HOPES

Chapter 4

DREAMS...

I have a dream that one day every valley shall be exalted, and every hill and mountain shall be made low, the rough places will be made plain, and the crooked places will be made straight.

Martin Luther King, Jr.
28 August 1963, at the Lincoln Memorial, Washington D.C.

I'll let you be in my dreams if I can be in yours

Bob Dylan
Talkin' World War III Blues, 1963

Chapter 4

DREAMS...

Peace & Plenty

Tessa Tennant, Non-Executive Director, UK Green Investment Bank
Founding Chair of The Association for Sustainable
& Responsible Investment in Asia (ASrIA)
Trustee, Carbon Disclosure Project
Innerleithen, Scotland

In 2100 my grandson will be 90 years and still an active, happy man comfortable about his imminent, self-chosen exit from this life. In his early years he will have witnessed the world go through great convulsions as the new world order took shape. There was much needless pain and suffering but in the end justice prevailed and a clean economy proliferated the world over. Everyone was now a student, had healthcare, good food and a home. Time had taken new meaning - no more 9-5 working days, commutes or manic, show-off holidays. Instead people enjoyed truly holy-days, contemplating and rejoicing in the peace and plenty won. 'Plenty' had the new definition in the diversity of possibility in learning, sharing and play. It was safe and a joy to travel walk-about, anywhere in the world.

This is my dream... my fear is we won't seize the chance we have now to make this world. We have to switch fast to clean, close-looped, intelligent production systems because there aren't enough resources otherwise. This switch is happening. It just needs to be faster, as does the shutdown of destructive industries. Ecological communication is the advertising industry's new task, replacing its deluge of consumer soma.

In 1963, Martin Luther King Junior spoke with passion about this now famous dream and changed the world. It cemented the vision of a better future firmly in the minds of many and, for this reason, has gone down in history as a critical moment in the path towards building a better America.

The removal of racial segregation and provision of equal opportunities for all was, and remains, eminently rational. However, the change was slow in coming because the powerful people of the Southern United States were entrenched in a way of thinking that could not countenance the change. Delivering a powerful vision helped to change this thinking.

As discussed by leadership expert Simon Sinek in his 2009 TEDx talk, had King shaped his speech around '*I have a plan*' rather than '*I have a dream*', it would have ended up too grounded in the thinking of the day. It would not have provided inspiration. It would not have been remembered. By sharing a dream, the thought gained power and connected with the emotional side of many Americans, whether black or white.

Had Martin Luther King Jr lived, it seems highly likely that his dream, expressed on that 1963 summer's day in Washington, would have been lived out in all his actions. He set out his vision of a better future and would then have exerted his energy into finding ways to bring it to reality. Life for black Americans in 2015 is far from perfect but it is a long way along the road towards King's dream.

In Selma, Alabama on the sixtieth anniversary of one of the bloodiest episodes in the civil rights struggle, Barrack Obama said, "*Fifty years from Bloody Sunday, our march is not yet finished, but we're getting closer*". He was speaking near the Edmund Pettus Bridge in Selma where police and state troopers beat and used tear gas against peaceful marchers who were advocating against racial discrimination at the voting booth. The event became known as "Bloody Sunday" and prompted a follow-up march led by King that spurred the passing of the 1965 Voting Rights Act.

The dreams in this book provide a way to attract people towards a better future and will help to overcome all the psychological barriers considered in Chapter 3. They also provide an insight into the thinking of those leading our collective journey to the future. The people at the forefront of global negotiations are telling us where they want to take us. They are sharing their dreams with you. Take heed of where we are being led and decide if that is where you want to go.

★ ★ ★

The motivational author Jerry Gillies is best known for his books on how to get rich and on transcendental sex – a powerful mix! His blog, MoneyLove, claims to show '*you how you can become prosperous beyond your wildest dreams.*' His original MoneyLove book has sold more than two million copies. Whilst Jerry does not have his dream included in this book, there are clearly some things to learn from how he has attracted people towards his vision, even if that vision is short term.

Gillies uses two phrases when looking to inspire people to make changes:

Make sure you visualize what you really want, not what someone else wants for you.

You will recognize your own path when you come upon it, because you will suddenly have all the energy and imagination you will ever need.

Both of these are very relevant when discussing dreams. Whilst there are dreams here that you might relate to, none of them can be *your* dream. I encourage you to challenge yourself by writing your own 200 word dream for the future and include what is important to you – what you want to work towards. Maybe even write one version now and then write another one when you finish this book. See what, if anything, has changed in your thinking after visiting the dreams of others.

Gillies' second quote above is useful when deciding when you have hit on the answer that meets the needs of your subconscious. When writing our dreams and our fears it is very easy to be led by the words of others or to stick with fairly shallow ideas that do not expose real feelings. This is an understandable cultural defence mechanism as opening up entirely may present areas of weakness that others might exploit. This has become so entwined with how we behave, that it can often be hard to express our own true feelings, even to ourselves.

So, when you write your vision for how you want the world to be, challenge yourself to go past the obvious and the constraints of practicality and find out what excites you. Once you feel excited and energised by the vision you have conjured up, it will be the one that you will then strive towards.

Tessa Tenant's dream at the start of this chapter is a very real one. Her grandson is set to live through the full journey of this book as I hope my sons will too. Every generation wishes to provide a better life for their progeny. Historically, this has largely been around wealth creation. There are, however, many studies showing that, once people are able to have food, shelter and security, wealth accumulation does not correlate in any way with happier, more fulfilled lives. Yet countless people in rich countries strive tirelessly to earn more money, buy a bigger house, have more expensive holidays and manage to feel as though they are outdoing their peers. This sort of drive is what allows authors such as Jerry Gillies to outsell authors who provide more sage, less selfish and longer-term advice.

Tessa has built her dream on the tenets of respect for life, justice, education, health and security for all. She hopes for peace and safety and sees the world valuing *plenty* in a way that includes the things that make it a joy to be human. It is difficult to see how that can be argued against. Who would not want to create such a world for their grandchildren?

Tessa is used to being ahead of her time. In 1988, when I was busy downing yards of ale as a pesky first year student at Oxford, Tessa set up the UK's first sustainable investment fund, Jupiter Asset Management. In the nearly thirty years since, the sustainable investment sector has become a multi-billion dollar global industry. So maybe her foresight is better than most and her vision might be more accurate than many.

Of course, this right-brain influenced dream does not come with a practical guide to securing the perfect world that the left-brain requires. As we drift back to reality, it is easy to say that, even in this 'perfect world', the weaknesses of human nature will mean that some people will not behave by the rules. Pragmatists might say that aiming for the perfect world can only lead to disappointment.

In a 2010 paper published in the American Sociological Review, John Reynolds from Florida State University examined whether setting high expectations and failing had any long term detrimental impacts. Entitled *'Is There a Downside to Shooting for the Stars?'* its research was based on two national longitudinal studies of school-children hoping to get accepted into college. It tested whether unrealized educational expectations were associated with the onset of depression in adulthood.

The results indicated that there were almost no long-term emotional costs of *'shooting for the stars'* rather than planning for the probable outcome. There appears to be no harm in having a dream and failing to achieve it. The dream might of getting the best marks, scoring the winning goal or riding an elephant into the sunset with a princess! When we do not achieve our lofty goals, humans usually successfully cope with the disappointment through compensatory strategies that protect our *'motivational resources and self-esteem'*.

Of course that is not to say that failure to achieve goals does not create frustration. This seems to be particularly the case when an individual feels that they are not in control of the situation and that failure is seen to be caused by others. This can often be the case in larger organisations where employees who want to make step changes are thwarted by the cultural inertia of the system. The dying days of my corporate career included a good dose of this frustration!

There is also much research that suggests that ambitious goals promote high levels of attainment, well-being and physical health via perseverance through difficulties. This *'optimism bias'* gives people the resilience to see hurdles as mere temporary setbacks rather than impassable roadblocks.

In the Clinical Psychology Review in 2010, Charles Carter looked at the performance of optimists in numerous areas of life. In all cases, the optimistic bias led to greater perseverance through difficult times in order to strive towards desired goals.

> 'The energetic, task-focused approach that optimists take to goals also relates to benefits in the socioeconomic world. Some evidence suggests that optimism relates to more persistence in educational efforts and to higher later income. Optimists also appear to fare better than pessimists in relationships.'

He concluded that 'In sum, the behavioral patterns of optimists appear to provide models of living for others to learn from.'

So having a vision and being optimistic about achieving it has few, if any, downsides and many advantages.

Having a vision of a better world is therefore likely to result in the world being better.

★ ★ ★

Is this Utopia?

Dr Will Grant, Centre for the Public Awareness of Science, Australian National University Canberra, Australia

How do you tell if you live in a dystopia? How do you tell if you live in a utopia?

I share the planet here at the start of the twenty-second century with just over ten billion people. I share the solar system with about ten million more. I don't know if that's too many or just right. Some people worry about that.

Like most people, my family and I grow lots of our own food. (Ok, Robogardeners do most of the work. But we tell them what we'd like). We eat real meat occasionally, and Newmeat more regularly. The kids like Newmeat better but they don't really have adult palettes yet.

We travel by bike. We all have Copenhagen Wheels for the hills and I love our LaserBubbles that protect us in the rain. We live just a few kilometres from work and school. Parceldrones carry the big things for us when we go shopping. I guess I work but to be honest I wouldn't call what I do work.

We use a bunch of energy - but to be honest we generate more than we could ever use. We don't really think about it.

So is this utopia? It seems pretty good to me. Not everyone is so lucky, but more and more are every year. But mainly, I think as a species we're not crushing the rest of the world to live happy lives. And that's utopia for me.

Will Grant's vision steps a little bit back from the perfect world envisioned by Tessa Tennant. He sees a world vastly improved on today but knows that it can be even better going forward. He has not reached the end point of development by 2100. But he has much to celebrate and appreciates the world that has been created. He paints a vision of a more connected and functional community that grows some of its own food, provides local and purposeful jobs and in which energy is no-longer an issue. There are concerns over the ten billion population and '*not everyone is so lucky*' but these seem to be minor concerns. The world is now sustainable and he is living a happy life and that is *his* utopia.

Visions of the far future free us from the constraints of practicality and allow a discussion on what is important. Living a happy and fulfilled life in a sustainable, connected community meets most of our human needs. This provides so much more than the formal forecasts of the future world painstakingly assembled by statisticians.

As an example, every five years the Australian Government publishes a detailed Intergenerational Report in an attempt to briefly focus the policy debate on long-term needs rather than the daily short-term political fighting. The legislated scope of the report is to assess '*the long-term sustainability of current Government policies and how changes to Australia's population size and age profile may impact on economic growth, workforce and public finances over the next 40 years.*' Bizarrely the 2015 version of the report manages to do all this without considering the impacts of climate change!

Whilst a useful document to some extent, it contains little that inspires people to see a better life but rather narrowly focuses on 'economic growth'. Its remit is not to address how to help people to have happier and more fulfilled lives. Maybe this should be a goal for the 2020 report. Perhaps a non-governmental organisation might take on the challenge of simultaneously publishing '*The Real Intergenerational Report*' on how to build a better community.

Arlan Andrews Senior, who writes a pessimistic view of the future in the next chapter, has formed a career from providing forecasts that are not conducted by statisticians. He founded an organisation called SIGMA Forum, which is a group of science fiction writers who offer futurism consulting to the United States government and NGOs. Andrews states that he '*formed SIGMA because I had heard more original and appropriate futurism on panels at any given science fiction convention than in all the forecasting meetings I ever attended while in D.C.*'.

Whilst not substantiated with research, this is a fascinating concept. That there is more truth in fiction than in forecasts is something that goes against the structures that prop up our supposedly rational world. Facts and science can provide the starting point for assessment but forecasts are constrained by the requirement that decisions are seemingly rational and, often, concerned with only increasing wealth and material possessions. As we have seen, actual decisions are mostly driven by right brain emotional responses and are not necessarily rational. The science fiction writers are grounded in reality of what is possible but then allow their creative brain to envisage where this might take us. Maybe this process is closer to the reality of how the world evolves. If so, such a rational and creative process may result in more accurate predictions of the future than are currently allowed. Of course, many science fiction 'predictions' are a long way from coming true whereas statistical forecasts just end up being inaccurate. However, by including creativity in predictions of the future we open up our minds to what is possible, allowing for more choice of a preferred future.

★ ★ ★

The Century of Awakening
Rohan Hamden, Adaptation and Climate Risk Specialist
Adelaide, Australia

What astonished people the most was just how solvable those seemingly intractable problems were. Poverty, equity, energy, hunger, resource consumption – all were overcome so swiftly, some wondered if they were even problems at all. Climate change has bitten deep, but we continue to overcome through ingenuity and cooperation.

It was the internet that ultimately saved us. Or more correctly, it was the information system that instantly connected every human on the planet. With eleven billion minds to think about our problems, there was always someone somewhere who was able to generate a wise solution. That solution was quickly propagated and built upon by the next connected mind.

It turned out that 99% of people just wanted to live happy and purposeful lives. Values they realised they shared with almost every-one on the planet. Democracies suddenly found they could not be elected on fear based polices. Even autocracies found little support for hatred and protectionism.

It became known as the Century of Awakening. The time when we finally shook off our fear of the natural world, and our fear of each other, and became the real stewards of the planet. Instead of cursing us for the world we left them, those born in the twenty-second century looked back and praised us for the peace and sustainability we created.

Rohan Hamden's vision sees global collaboration solving intractable problems. He sees that by increasing connections, people all over the world will realise that they have the same values and desires and that difficult problems can be solved. We will cast off our fears and create a more inclusive world, and future generations will thank us.

Ideas like this can create movements that change the world.

An example of an idea that is now changing the world is the

one that Bill McKibben, a contributor to the next chapter, was conceived after seeing a talk from James Hansen in December 2007. McKibben said in his chapter in Opportunities Beyond Carbon:

I almost never write about writing—in my aesthetic the writing should disappear, the thought linger. But the longer I've spent working on global warming—the greatest challenge humans have ever faced—the more I've come to see it as essentially a literary problem. A technological and scientific challenge, yes; an economic quandary, yes; a political dilemma, surely. But centrally? A crisis in metaphor, in analogy, in understanding. We haven't come up with words big enough to communicate the magnitude of what we're doing.

How do you say: the world you know today, the world you were born into, the world that has remained essentially the same for all of human civilisation, that has birthed every play and poem and novel and essay, every painting and photograph, every invention and economy, every spiritual system (and every turn of phrase) is about to be something so different? Somehow 'global warming' barely hints at it. The same goes for any of the other locutions. And if we do come up with adequate words in one culture, they won't necessarily translate into all the other languages whose speakers must collaborate to somehow solve this problem.

Hansen's talk was about the climate challenge and how we had to keep greenhouse gas concentrations to below 350 parts per million to avoid catastrophic changes. This was the answer to Bill's conundrum: forget the words and just focus on the number as it will have the same meaning worldwide.

As a result, Bill and some colleagues formed 350.org. From humble beginnings in 2008, 350.org now operates worldwide and has started to change the global conversation. It delivers high profile public events to communicate the scale of the problem and initiate community actions that achieve results. In recent times, campaigns have included fighting coal power plants in India, stopping the Keystone XL pipeline in the U.S. and divesting public institutions everywhere from fossil fuels.

The vision of harnessing global interest in good environmental outcomes has transformed into an active global movement in just a few years. This is a wonderful example of how an idea can take hold. In 2009, Bill summarised the start of the movement as follows:

> *It makes sense that we need a number, not a word. All our words come from the old world. They descend from the time before. Their associations have congealed. But the need to communicate has never been greater. We need to draw a line in the sand. Say it out loud: 350. Do everything you can.*

The positive visions presented here may, I hope, similarly inspire the global community to not only avoid the 350.org's stark scenarios but also to create a better world.

★ ★ ★

Change cannot happen without risks being taken. By sharing their visions, the authors face a risk in exposing what they *really want*. Encouraging people to change behaviours necessarily accepts that some changes will fail to be effective - and failure is always a risk.

However, risk-taking, within reason, is liberating. Suddenly the frustrating constraints of the world today are not quite so tight and people start to feel empowered to create a better way of doing things. Of course, excessive risk-taking without an eye on the possible consequences is not what is under consideration here. It is educated risk-taking that steps into the unknown to see if there is a better way to move forward.

I admire my teenage sons for their willingness to take risks. They sometimes fail, but mostly do not, and failure is never the catastrophe that might have feared. At their age and for many years after, I was very cautious in my risk taking and always made sure I was almost certain of success before taking the plunge. With the wisdom, or recklessness, of age I am now finally starting to take more, albeit calculated, risks.

The biggest regret of many people is that they didn't take a risk because they were not quite brave enough to do so. The hurt of what might have been is often much harder than of having tried and failed.

In her book, *The Top Five Regrets of the Dying*, Bronnie Ware, an Australian nurse who worked in palliative care, describes the regrets she heard from those preparing for their deaths. As reported in 'The Guardian', *'Ware writes of the phenomenal clarity of vision that people gain at the end of their lives, and how we might learn from their wisdom.'* Ware recorded these top five regrets of the dying:

1. *I wish I'd had the courage to live a life true to myself, not the life others expected of me.*
2. *I wish I hadn't worked so hard.*
3. *I wish I'd had the courage to express my feelings.*
4. *I wish I had stayed in touch with my friends.*
5. *I wish that I had let myself be happier.*

None of these are regrets about giving something a go and failing to succeed: that is rarely the case in hindsight. It is a similar thought to the classic phrase from Alfred Lord Tennyson in his 1850 poem *In Memoriam: 27*:

Hold it true, whate'er befall; I feel it, when I sorrow most;
'Tis better to have loved and lost
Than never to have loved at all.

Or, in the words of the famous Irish Playwright Samuel Beckett: *'Ever tried. Ever failed. No matter. Try again. Fail again. Fail better.'*.

Tessa Tennant and others also see a huge risk in not taking action. In her vision, Tessa looks back to a time of *'much needless pain and suffering'*. Many of the authors here, especially those in the next chapter, are motivated by a fear of what the world might become. To those who can see this future it is very powerful and really very scary. The challenge is that most humans are unable to envisage this future and so are not motivated by it. To most, the consequences of short-term change weigh more heavily than the perception of the long-term consequences of continuing on our present path.

The visions of a better world provided here offer people an

option for their future. Imagine the all too common situation of being too scared to ask the person you really fancy out on a date because of the fear that they might say no. Yet the long-term benefits of success far outweigh the temporary pain of failure. The future is a beautiful, if challenging, partner. Your choice is to take a risk in having a 'first date' with this attractive future or, instead, to accept a life of regret.

Our final vision for this chapter is from Peggy Liu, the inspirational founder of the Joint US-China Collaboration on Clean Energy (JUCCCE). She envisages an over-populated world where most live in crowded cities. Despite this, the quality of life is good and we have developed in a way that enables us to use and re-use our resources efficiently. Living '*vibrantly without being overwhelmed*' provides a vision of fulfilled lives living within their means. A simple vision with great power.

Living Vibrantly
Peggy Liu, Chairperson, Joint US-China Collaboration on Clean Energy (JUCCCE)
Shanghai, China

In 2100, the world is divided in two. The Earthscaped world and the paved world. In the first, the sky is blue. The rivers run clear. I drink from the tap. Children eat grapes off the vine. Neighbours walk to green sanctuaries from their homes and walk in soil that looks like rich coffee grounds.

But most of the world's population lives in the paved world of dense skyscrapered cities. Omnipresent subways and rail dominate over shared driverless cars.

We eat in a way that is good for us, and good for the planet. Our factories manufacture food – from 3D printed Wagyu for the rich to tasty pellets of fuel for the poor. College students major in 'Big data analysis', 'Large-scale aquaculture' and 'Precision agriculture'.

Every resource - even human waste - is used to its highest capacity via 'Need and Want' sharing apps. All of our stuff is designed to neatly turn into other stuff - or fuel. We dress in virtual, chameleon-like clothing for our virtual adventures to make holographic videos to show our virtual friends. We are free to live vibrantly without being overwhelmed.

Chapter 5

FEARS...

You take people, you put them on a journey, you give them peril, you find out who they really are.

Joss Whedon

Chapter 5

FEARS...

We Blew It!
Bill McKibben, 350.org
Vermont, USA

Looking back on the century, the only real thought is: why didn't we do this sooner? The technology we're using - solar panels, windmills, and the like - were available in functional form a hundred years ago. But we treated them as novelties for a few decades - and it was in those decades that climate change gathered its final ferocity. Now we live in a low carbon world and it works just fine - except that there's no way to refreeze the poles, or lower the sea level, or turn the temperature back down to a place where we can grow food with the ease of our ancestors. Timing is everything, and it hurts to think we blew it.

The risk of not changing creates fear in many. They can see what the consequences might be. They can see the statistics of scientists wreaking havoc on civilisation as they know it. Those that do not choose to put their head in the warming sand feel a growing sense of desperation as the world twiddles its collective thumbs.

Bill McKibben is one such person. Whilst Tessa Tennant was establishing her investment fund in London, a 28 year old Bill published his first book, *The End of Nature*. So he too is no newcomer to this story. Having spent a lifetime successfully raising awareness of the impact that the growing human race inflicts upon its fragile environment, he also is not an optimist.

His vision is of regret and lost opportunity. It fits with the fears Tessa expressed in the previous chapter but here it sits on its own. Almost all we know about the psychology of climate change would indicate that this dystopia is a highly likely outcome – the result of our evolved human nature. Maybe this is the version of the future in this book that is correct.

As a student, I spent a summer driving tractors on a pear farm in Lake County, California with some very generous friends of friends. Mo and Jim Carpenter took me in and treated me as family. When I was not out on the farm carting pear-laden 'caja', I played chess with Mo and learnt to water ski with Jim. I remember them laughing at how incredibly stubborn I was, both in defending a losing position in chess and in managing to stay upright for a few more seconds when wipe-out was imminent. I will not be persuaded that stubbornness is anything but a virtue!

It is for this reason that I have found this the hardest chapter to write. I can see the downsides and I know that action is critical. I just cannot accept that the fears of some can be allowed to become reality. Whilst accepting the possibility, there often seems little value in talking up all the downsides: surely it is better to inspire and attract people to something they want rather than to scare them into submission.

These fears are however very real and can provide the context to move forward.

Fear is one of the most powerful of emotions. In his 2004 book, *Psychology of Fear,* Paul Gower describes how fear is *'a built-in survival mechanism'* that *'serves a protective purpose -- signalling us of danger and preparing us to deal with it'*.

Behaviour that results from fear is driven by the 'fight or flight' mechanism, an idea originally developed by Dr. Walter B Cannon in 1915 and then expanded to also include 'freeze' or 'fright'.

The emotion of fear induces the release of adrenaline and, the hard to pronounce, norepinephrine causing the immediate physical reactions of increased heart rate and breathing, constricted blood vessels and tightened muscles. This is a short-term reaction that prepares the body for immediate action. Long-term fears may produce a short burst of this reaction but the body is unable to maintain this level of readiness without detrimental health impacts.

Longer-term worries are more likely to surface as anxieties, although may still produce physiological arousal such as nervousness and apprehension. To differentiate between the two, Swedish psychologist Arne Öhman suggests that '*anxiety is foreboding and puts you on alert to a future threat, fear immediately leads to an urge to defend yourself with escape from an impending disaster.*'

Research also suggests that it is possible at times to turn off anxiety in order to get on with daily life. When the anxiety arises from a phobia of spiders, the ability to turn it off is extremely useful, but far less so when the source of anxiety is a real approaching threat such as climate change.

Many of the contributors to this book see climate change as a current threat and many of them feel *fear* at this prospect. Where engaged at all, the general public however, perceive climate change as a future threat and so merely suffer from a mild *anxiety*.

In her article *The Psychology of Irrational Fear* in the *The Atlantic* published in 2014, Olga Khazan discusses how irrational fear can take hold in individuals and societies. The article was spurred by public reactions to Ebola contagion worries. Khazan quoted a survey from Chapman University that found Americans were '*most afraid of: walking alone at night, identity theft, safety on the Internet, becoming the victim of a mass shooting, and having to speak in public.*' These fears are rarely rational once probabilities are examined. '*Despite the fact that crime rates have decreased over the past 20 years, most Americans, the survey found, think all types of crime have become more prevalent.*'

In general, humans' ability to rationally assess non-imminent risk is one of our greatest weaknesses.

Fears seem to be more prevalent when they involve things that are unfamiliar, unexpected, learnt as being 'scary' or in close proximity. This is consistent with Dan Gilbert's characteristics of what causes humans to react most strongly that were discussed in Chapter 3. Examples of each of these could include immigrants, noises at night, spiders and crime in your neighbourhood respectively. We also tend to be susceptible to fear when we start from a baseline of vulnerability such as poor health or, more generally, when we feel a lack of control. This explains why people are more scared of flying than driving despite the overwhelming statistics showing road deaths are more common.

Climate change can be presented as 'unfamiliar', 'unexpected' by many and something over which people feel they have little control. However, it is not a learned fear, its proximity is not widely believed to be imminent and, in the western world, we do not feel particularly vulnerable. People living on low-lying Pacific Islands such as Kiribati or Vanuatu do feel imminently vulnerable to climate change and the community's view there is very different to that of those living in the relative safety of London or New York.

The telling of fears may well complete the argument for action on climate change. If the story tellers of climate fear can convince their audience that they really should be scared, that the problems are indeed imminent and that, even in big western cities, we are vulnerable to serious impacts, then perhaps they can spur people into action.

This is a very different psychological mechanism to that provided by hope and attraction towards a better future, where the mechanism is *positive psychology,* a term coined by renowned psychologist Martin Seligman.

Seligman argues that positive psychology can lead to permanent changes in the brains' connections. It re-wires how we think and is connected with the neuroplasticity discussed in Chapter 3. The fear reaction is chemical and temporary whereas the 'dream reaction' delivers long-term outcomes. Combining the two could provide the perfect balance needed to alter community attitudes.

★ ★ ★

Our Fragile Planet

Dr Monica Oliphant, Immediate Past President of the International Solar Energy Society
Adelaide, Australia

Most countries use their own local renewable resources for major energy needs and dependence on imported non-renewable resources has largely ended.

Unencumbered by massive expenditure on fossil fuels the wealth disparity between the "haves and have nots" has reduced and with equity in energy, poorer nations have developed faster than previously. Toxic air pollution in large cities is virtually nonexistent and amongst all nations conflict over energy resource ownership, that was rife in the last 100 years, is rarely seen.

The long path to a renewable energy future started about 130 years ago, influenced by the Middle East oil crisis of the 1970s. Then solar was mainly for water heating, PV for satellites and wind for farmers. The next five decades saw the establishment of the renewable energy revolution - predominantly community driven. A paradigm shift occurred in the way utilities delivered power from centralised to distributed systems. Later, the discovery of new cheap superconducting materials reduced long transmission line losses, enabling interconnections within and between nations to make strategic use of excess dispatchable renewable power. This plus the discoveries of more efficient renewable technologies, innovative storage options, non fossil transport fuels and renewable industrial process heat, made change possible.

Countries that tried to ignore the low carbon transition had sanctions imposed on them.

With renewable energy leading the way 2100 could see a safer, more equitable, and sustainable world.

My fear however, is that the lack of political will, global co-operation and an accepted viable transition plan will prevent realisation of the Vision – with disastrous consequences for our fragile planet.

Dr Monica Oliphant has worked in renewable energy technologies for decades and was a prior president of the International Solar Energy Society. She, like many of the authors, sees that it is eminently possible to create a better world and deploy technology solutions that resolve the climate change challenge. Whilst her vision could easily fit elsewhere in this book, the strongest statement in her vision concerns her fear that we will not act in time. Like Bill McKibben, she sees that we will miss our opportunity to change destructive behaviour patterns and look back with dismay at what we have done to our *'fragile planet'*.

The telling of fears and specific dire consequences may also have another role to play in this war of the mind. In addition to potentially spurring action through inducing a fear reaction, they can provide a rational context for an emotional decision made for other reasons.

Because behaviour changes that are driven by long-term benefits are permanent, my view is that the final support for transition will be driven by positive visions and the desire for a better world. However, humans always then look for a rational explanation for making decisions based on gut-feeling. When instinctively being inspired towards creating a better world, we can fall back on the rational reassurance that we are avoiding all this bad stuff too and that is the real substance of the decision.

Our fear-carrying story tellers therefore provide an incredibly important piece of the solution. I also think that those who tell of their fears are braver than those that just reassure us that everything will be wonderful. I cannot let my fears come too close to the surface as it might be too much to bear. Life as a stubborn optimist is a much easier existence than that of a pessimist bearing the weight of knowledge of catastrophe.

So be gentle with our fear-mongers. They are the holders of our collective fears and allow the rest of us to move forward.

★ ★ ★

Temperatures up 4.8°C

Professor Campbell Gemmell,
Consulting Partner, Canopus
Professor of Environmental Regulation and Policy, University
of Glasgow
Previously CEO of Scottish EPA
Glasgow, Scotland

Thirty years of the second dash for gas ....that crazy big backward step in managing our carbon before the YuanDollar union that helped get trading working sensibly, funded big scale carbon capture and storage, hydrogen and other renewable-electric charging networks everywhere for the, now already gone, FamCars and FreightCars.

We then transcended into a full blown socialized investment model for real new technologies, like the AI/brainlinks for data and creative transfers, 3DNanofabrication built on the commercial and domestic upscaling and cost drops of the old 3D Printing.

Anyway, we now have global temperatures 4.8°C up, 50°C a six week standard in Australia, storminess greatly increased and sea levels up just over one metre on average from the 2000 benchmark. With storm damage and insurance not just through the roof but removing the houses of 1.85 billion of our eleven billion people, mass migrations and disputes over who has water all costing tens of trillions of Ch$ annually...we had finally to "get it"!

But it took too much time. Don't politicians hate leading for good transformations!

Elder lifecare re-integrated into AllAge areas is massive now. Add all the required cooling, catering, shared resource-cycling has changed so much of our lifestyle, architecture and spatial planning. Then the on and offshore arcology, plans advanced for Moon and Mars and already on Antarctica.

So, we see it works when it makes sense for economy, society and ecology. Sound familiar? Not sustainability anymore, just constant creativity and adaptation.

The current global consensus is that we are striving towards keeping the average global temperature rise to two degrees Celsius or below. 350.org advocates that to achieve this we must drop the existing level of greenhouse gases from 400 parts per million (ppm) back to 350 ppm.

The Intergovernmental Panel on Climate Change (IPCC) in its Fifth Assessment Report describes the impacts of a two degree rise as follows:

> *It is very likely that heat waves will occur more often and last longer, and that extreme precipitation events will become more intense and frequent in many regions. The ocean will continue to warm and acidify, and global mean sea level to rise.*
>
> *Key risks that span sectors and regions include the following:*
>
> 1. *Risk of severe ill-health and disrupted livelihoods resulting from storm surges, sea level rise and coastal flooding; inland flooding in some urban regions; and periods of extreme heat.*
> 2. *Systemic risks due to extreme weather events leading to breakdown of infrastructure networks and critical services.*
> 3. *Risk of food and water insecurity and loss of rural livelihoods and income, particularly for poorer populations.*
> 4. *Risk of loss of ecosystems, biodiversity and ecosystem goods, functions and services.*

To achieve this level of climate stability requires rapid changes to be made. The fears in this chapter and elsewhere in this book mostly result from the feeling that we are not moving fast enough and will end up with a world much worse than it might have been.

Worryingly, the Report warns us that just stopping temperature rise will not prevent further changes:

> *Stabilization of global average surface temperature does not imply stabilization for all aspects of the climate system. Shifting biomes, re-equilibrating soil carbon, ice sheets, ocean temperatures and asso-ciated sea level rise all have their own intrinsic long timescales that will result in ongoing changes for hundreds to thousands of years after global surface temperature has been stabilized.*

Professor Campbell Gemmell from the University of Glasgow sees this outcome in his vision of a world with average temperature increases of 4.8 degrees Celsius. He sees that we are coping with this change but that things are very very different.

According to the IPCC, the impacts of the sea level rise envisaged by Campbell will have significant impacts for coastal communities:

> *The height of a 50-year flood event has already increased in many coastal locations. A 10- to more than 100-fold increase in the frequency of floods in many places would result from a half metre rise in sea level in the absence of adaptation. Local adaptation capacity (and, in particular, protection) reaches its limits for ecosystems and human systems in many places under a one metre sea level rise.*

The increased storm damage that Campbell sees making nearly two billion people homeless would ravage coastal areas across the world.

Life goes on in Campbell's world but it is a different world to that painted by Tessa Tennant in the last chapter. There is no Century of Awakening and no 'Living Vibrantly' in this world.

It is a scary picture!

★ ★ ★

Human Intelligence?
**Jan Van der Ven, Director, Asia, The Carbon Trust,
Founder, greencred.me
Beijing, China**

*It was long thought that the seeds of mankind's collision with
nature were sown by the invention of agriculture 10,000 years ago,
because material possessions no longer had to be carried from one
encampment to the next, and instead could be accumulated by
newly sedentarized communities.*

*By 2015 however, there was increasing evidence that as far back
as 200,000 BC, when early humans began their exodus from
Africa, megafauna on every continent they set foot became extinct
– merely a prelude to the destruction humans would wage next,
cutting down 80% of the Earth's primeval forests, turning 40% of its
land surface into farmland, cities and roads, leading to an extinction
of species on a scale not seen since the meteor impact that caused
the demise of the dinosaurs.*

*This suggested that not a stable food supply, but the ability
to analyse, communicate and organize constituted the most
formidable threat to life on Earth.*

*Yet also in 2015, anyone with an internet connection could read
about climate change, and simulate various scenarios to stay below
the safe limit of 2C warming recommended by the IPCC with the
Global Calculator, financed by the UK government's International
Climate Fund. These scenarios ranged from changes in energy
mix to simple changes in diet. All of them required effort, none
were impossible to achieve, and all lead to a better outcome than
dangerous climate change, for which there was no reset button.*

*The question was therefore: could human intelligence save itself?
The odds weren't good.*

When I grew up in the UK, the country stopped for the Grand National horse race. In Australia, the first Tuesday in November is the country's own 'Super Tuesday' when every workplace puts on the TV at 3.10pm for the Melbourne Cup. People who would never otherwise place a bet on a horse race rush to the 'bookies' to lose their money. The human lack of ability to accurately assess risk is on show in abundance on such days. The final betting decision is usually made based on gut-feel or identification with the horse's name. The pretence of studying the form guide merely justifies this emotional decision.

We ignore the statistics on road crashes because we think that we are in control and will be able brake quickly if needed. We think that air travel is dangerous because we are stuck down the back with no control. We think wind turbines are killing us and that coal plants have always been there and so they must be benign.

At a recent event in Adelaide I had a conversation with a seemingly sensible, intelligent, well-educated woman who told me with conviction of the damage that wind turbines were causing. When I suggested that living next to a wind farm might be preferable to living next to a coal mine, she told me that she grew up in the La Trobe valley next to some of the world's dirtiest coal and that was just fine.

The imperfections of the familiar are often far less scary than the uncertainties of change. Emotional responses are more powerful than rational evidence of likely outcomes. 'Better the devil you know' is more than a mere cliché.

Jan Van der Ven lives in Beijing amidst the frequent smogs caused by rapid industrialisation. He sees the challenge as one of humans being able to adapt their way of thinking and applying human intelligence in a different way. The way of thinking that has enabled humans to dominate the world will not be sufficient to stop living beyond its means. Jan thinks the probability of making this change is low and fears what that might mean for the world.

Looking at historical human behaviour, this is an entirely reasonable fear. However, we also know that optimism, combined with a healthy dose of stubbornness, can create a better future than pragmatism because it allows us to negotiate barriers with more vigour and not accept failure as an option.

Arlan Andrews Sr provides a very different view of the future. Andrews is not convinced that anthropogenic climate change exists but sees increased volcanic activity causing catastrophe.

Interestingly, in February 2015 the *New Scientist* reported on a research project, conducted by the University of Arizona, which examined the link between melting glaciers and increased volcanic activity as the weight of the ice reduces. So maybe Andrews' vision is less fantastic than it might seem at first glance.

Carbon Zero

Arlan Andrews, Sr., SIGMA Forum
Former ASME White House Fellow in the White House Science
Office, 1992-93
Corpus Christi, Texas, USA

I don't know why I am writing this, or to whom. There are only a few dozen survivors left in our subterranean redoubt in the Peruvian Andes, and we give thanks to Mad Mike Manx, eccentric billionaire and our unlikely savior.

Manx, always rebellious, made his first fortune by playing odds against that early twenty-first century pseudoscientific version of the Medieval "dancing sickness" (whereby for unknown reasons, normal people take up destructive fads and practices, without rational thought). They called it "global warming."

Manx bought thousands of abandoned wind turbines -- obsoleted in the 2030s after new petroleum engines became 99.5% efficient, and compact nuclear reactors appeared on every corner--for pennies on the dollar, converting his "aerial Cuisinarts" into the coolest high-rise housing for the uber-rich.

Then, of course, the Sun had a severe Minimum; simultaneously the world's volcanoes began spewing out gigatons of the Earth's toxic inner gases, sun-blocking the thickened atmosphere, and all the glaciers returned with a vengeance.

Manx knew the Andes would be the safest place, but instruments now show all exits are blocked, under a kilometer of ice.

It's ironic, but our "carbon footprint" is now zero.

It appears unlikely that global warming will just disappear and not cause all the fears we have seen here. Even if it does then it would seem crazy not to have some insurance in place just in case the vast majority of scientists happen to be correct.

As part of this insurance policy of lower greenhouse gas emissions, if we also happen to build a better, more functional, happier world then there really seems little to lose - unless of course Andrew's vision of the volcanoes occurs!

In our final vision for this chapter, we go to the extreme. Tracy Cai is another Beijing resident and is doing ground-breaking work on green finance for the Chinese market. SynTao is one of China's first and most proficient advisers to industry on the cross-over between finance and the environment.

Tracy sees that all her good work and that of others in this book fails. The world is finished but luckily we have managed to save the race by colonising other planets. Hopefully, the humans in her vision treat their new homes with more respect.

Once a upon a time...
Tracy Cai 蔡英萃
Co-Founder & CEO, SynTao Green Finance
商道融绿,
Beijing, China

In 2100, the ambassador from the United Planets (UP) of the universe knocks on the door of the last man on earth to deliver the decisions of the UP: As the heavy pollution from earth is seriously threatening the survival of other planets, we have decided to blow up the earth within 24 hours. The man is too weak to fight for the cruel news or even to say "No". All he could do is cry.

Look at what the earth once was! All beautiful islands such as Maldives, Hawaii and Tahiti that disappeared as the ozone layer made the planet almost naked and all the Antarctic and Arctic glacier and icebergs melted. All fossil fuels have been depleted. The people began to burn out all the forests. The habitat for wild animals disappeared, making them homeless. One of the dangerous insects survived and killed millions of people. The mountainous trash made by the human beings was everywhere. The sand storms visited every day. Most people died because of lack of safe food, clean water, solutions for various illnesses or even sufficient oxygen. The whole earth looked not green or blue. It is now a black and yellow dirty ball.

Thousands of years later, when a little girl is gazing at the stars from a liveable planet, she finds that there are some twinkling stars like floating objects. Her grandma tells her "that should be the debris of the earth". "What is the Earth?" "Once upon a time, it was a very beautiful blue planet..."

Chapter 6

HOPES!

I am prepared for the worst, but hope for the best.

Benjamin Disraeli, 19th Century British Prime Minister
The Wondrous Tale of Alroy, pt. 10, Chapter 3.

If one advances confidently in the direction of his dreams, and endeavors to live the life which he has imagined, he will meet with success unexpected in common hours.

Henry David Thoreau

Chapter 6

HOPES!

It Was Close!
John Renesch, Founder, FutureShapers,
San Francisco, US

What a journey! Given where we were at the turn of the last century, it is amazing that we are where we are as we begin the twenty-second century. It got really scary for several decades but we finally got our heads on straight and found new ways to live together, new ways to transform all the life support systems upon which we relied for survival. But it was close. Some actually collapsed. More functional systems replaced the collapsed ones. People started getting hopeful.

We now have a world where every human being has his or her basic needs met. Everyone has clean drinking water, access to nutritious food, basic education and health care, shelter from the elements and the opportunity for fulfilling work. We have achieved environmental sustainability worldwide and widespread social justice. With few exceptions, the world is free of conflict, violence and wrong-doing. The global culture no longer tolerates anti-social behavior, organizational dysfunction and organizational domination of anyone. It is widely agreed that the well-being of everyone takes precedence over the desires or wants of any one person or group.

Our ancestors had a vision that this kind of world was possible but global crises threatened the survival of the human race so many doubted it was possible. But they made it happen and we are grateful for the world we have inherited.

John Renesch has worked as a futurist and influencer for 25 years. As his website says, he '*believes that commerce holds the key to bringing about a global shift of human consciousness thus creating a future of tremendous possibility for humankind — the possibility that will allow humanity to transcend the inevitable future that can be projected from current trends.*'

John's latest book, *The Great Growing Up*, discusses the need for humanity as a whole to stop behaving like a spoilt teenager and start taking some responsibility for themselves and others. He presents this as a conscious choice that we can make and that will drive the first '*conscious evolution of our species*'.

His vision sees us achieving this by 2100, but, like many of his co-authors, he sees it taking a long time for the world to reach this maturity. He also suggests that many people '*doubted it was possible*' to get to this outcome because we took so long and caused so much damage on the way.

The theme of this chapter is one of timing. The consensus is that we will finally achieve a positive outcome for the world but what is uncertain is how long we will take to change our ways and how much suffering and damage we will chose to inflict along the way.

We have looked at the largely binary outcomes of the optimists and the pessimists and at the psychology of what is holding us back from making rational decisions. Most of our authors assume that resistance to change will dissolve as we continue to edge towards catastrophe. Just when global outlook changes will then determine the extent of damage we have caused along the way.

It is therefore vitally important to understand why people resist change so strongly. One common theory revolves around the concept of 'psychological capital'. If one has invested in a particular way of thinking it is hard to admit that this is wrong. Psychological capital goes beyond human capital ('what you know') and social capital ('who you know') and is focussed on 'who you are' and 'who you are becoming'. Change that is perceived as adverse to who you are, or want to be, will be resisted as a threat with negative consequences.

In a 2011 paper, Professor Joan Freeman of Middlesex University in London compared the 1960s psychological capital of tobacco company executives with those of fossil fuel managers today.

When news of the ill-effects of tobacco began to be made public in the 1960s, there was a famous quote by an American tobacco executive. He said that "doubt is our product", meaning that they were no longer only selling tobacco, but also uncertainty, promoting the thought that maybe tobacco was not really poisonous, in spite of the scientific evidence. In the same way today, some still refer to climate change as though it were merely a possibility.

Freeman goes on to talk about aspects of anti-smoking campaigns that might be effectively applied to climate change communications. The key to much of this is making the discussion local and personal rather than big and global.

Challenge to beliefs can open the possibility of change. As with smoking, concern about climate change raises three challenging questions which need resolving before many would be prepared to change their assumptions and habits.
  i.   What is true and what is not true?
  ii. What are the immediate benefits to the individual as well as to the wider world?
  iii. What can each individual do about it?

The science of climate change is not a matter of much debate within the scientific community although remains so in some portions of the media. To help create wider community acceptance it is critical to provide consistent and conclusive evidence of 'what is true'.

Freeman's second question about immediate benefits to the individual is much easier to answer for tobacco consumption than it is for climate change. This presents one of the biggest hurdles to challenging the community's psychological capital of what a good life should be.

The most confronting aspects of climate change are unlikely to be fully recognised for many years in the western world. As for those in poorer countries who are more vulnerable, we only have to look at news coverage to see that catastrophes affecting people of nations and cultures other than our own are fairly easy to shrug off. Action on climate change is generally perceived as providing no immediate benefit to the individual and so fails Freeman's second test. This is where it is important to expand the conversation to also consider building more liveable cities and creating more fulfilling lives – this is where the immediate benefits will be felt.

Finally, there is the challenge of convincing individuals that they can have an impact on such a large problem. The first step here is for individuals to have a vision of what they want the world to be and to then communicate this vision as widely and as often as they can. Tell your friends, post it on websites, maybe even make a YouTube video about your future world.

Dr Niamh Murtagh of University College, London has explored similar themes when looking at resistance to change with respect to environmental issues. She found that one of the key drivers for resistance is 'self-identity' and that threatened identities motivate both change and resistance to change to a greater extent than past behaviour or habit. So, if self-identity is strongly correlated with a particular action, a particular way of living or past success, then there will be significant resistance to any change which threatens that.

A detailed research study was published in 2014 by Mbongeni Andile Mdletye from the University of Johannesburg on resistance to change by prison officers in South Africa. At the time prison philosophy was undergoing transformational change from '*punishment-oriented philosophy to the rehabilitation-driven philosophy in terms of the treatment of sentenced offenders*'.

The key causes for the resistance to change were found to be the officers' previous experiences of change and their perceptions of whether the change was fair. These perceptions were influenced by:

'Loss of control, status, routines, traditions, relationships, security, competence, as well as fear of the unknown, failure, lack of support, confidence and trust, inappropriate or poor management styles, low tolerance for change, distorted perceptions of change'.

Clearly action on climate change is seen by many in the developed world as a threat to their way of life. They are easily convinced by those interested in maintaining the status quo that such action will lead to financial insecurity, unknown results and a loss of control to 'radical greenies'. The result being that they are uncertain of veracity of the science, see little immediate benefit and think they are powerless to do anything anyway.

Conversely, many in the developing world can already see the impacts occurring, know that action will be provide significant local benefits and are lobbying hard to get the world to see the peril that they are in. The lack of action is the greatest threat for them.

By the Skin of our Teeth

Antony Funnell, Author
Presenter & Producer, Future Tense, ABC Radio National
Brisbane, Australia

How did we get to a low carbon world? Barely; with enormous difficulty; by the skin of our teeth; with absolutely no time to spare; with a constant eye for any other option.

We got there through fair and foul - through market economics as much as enlightenment; through dirty politics and national self-interest, not just fine words and good intentions.

But we got there - just in time.

Now we have to live with the consequences of taking so long to make the journey.

How did we create a low carbon world? Through high-tech luck more than dogged persistence; through scientific game-changers like nuclear fusion and artificial photo-synthesis.

But we created it - just in time.

So, what did we discover along the way?

We prided ourselves that human beings are ultimately self-correcting – perhaps, maybe. But we were also forced to acknowledge that we like to avoid taking difficult decisions until the very last moment – until the hour is about to strike. Until we absolutely have to.

We learned that – grudgingly.

Still, we got there – with not a moment to spare.

And now we have to deal with the consequences of taking so long to make the journey.

Antony Funnell published a book in 2012 titled 'The Future and Related Nonsense' that took a fairly light-hearted look at how our future world might evolve. In a chapter on environmental issues, he portrays a fairly pessimistic view of the human race's ability to act in good time to achieve sensible outcomes. In support of his argument he considers finishing assignments at university and Europe's reaction to the rise of Nazism. He concludes that:

> 'The greater the size and complexity of the task, the greater the chance that no one will get around to doing anything about it until the eleventh hour.'

Antony explores why writing about efficiency and sustainability is very hard to make interesting. Efficiency, in particular, is a passionless argument involving no right brain thinking – it will never excite or inspire despite, or maybe because of, its rationality.

I am not however so convinced on the Jevons Paradox concerns that Antony also raises. The Jevons Paradox suggests that increased efficiency means that it is cheaper to produce the product in question so more of the product is produced and consumed. As a result, efficiency gains are usually negated. There are clear sets of data that show that both increased efficiency and increased consumption can happen simultaneously but there is little evidence to tie these together in a straight forward cause and effect relationship. No doubt there are some elements of truth in the theory of the Jevons Paradox but I am not convinced it is the fatal flaw that some suggest.

Both Antony's view that we will get to a low carbon world 'just in time' and Paul Gilding's view that the human race is 'slow but not stupid' indicate that, worryingly, we will not be taking decisive action any time soon.

As we have already seen, the resistance to change for this particular problem is strong. We have looked at the psychological reasons for this and it seems likely that attracting people to a positive future would be a good way to start re-wiring our underlying assumptions and overcome the psychological capital so many of us have invested in our current way of living. Some of the practicalities involved in this are further explored in Chapter 11. There has been significant research into effective change management techniques and in particular where this is concerned with environmental issues.

Professor Dexter Dunphy of the University of Technology in Sydney has explored the role of change agents in successfully changing attitudes towards environmental issues. In his book with the very left-brain orientated title of *Organizational Change for Corporate Sustainability*, Dunphy describes the competencies required for successful change agents as including *'clarity of vision, knowledge of what we wish to change and the skills to implement the changes'*.

In my corporate energy career, I unsuccessfully set about trying to be an environmental change agent with the naiveté of someone who thought that rational thought would always prevail. However, as Dunphy warns, *'Changing entrenched power structures can be a career-threatening move!'* With the status of a failed 'intrapreneur', I set upon a path of wanting to understand the psychology of change and leadership along with a better understanding of the innovation process and how to successfully deliver disruptive projects.

Dunphy stresses the point that change agents can never control the process they are trying to change but rather are *'co-creators; midwives aiding the birth of a new order'*. He continues:

> *'Managing corporate change is rather like white-water rafting or surfing. The first lesson is not to try and control the environment but to move with it.'*

We have some challenges in this respect when it comes to climate change. The longer the delay, the more people will suffer and the greater the damage will be to clear up. Yet we cannot force the pace of action; we will not be able to coerce the world to move. Dunphy stresses the importance of vision, clarity of purpose and resilience in staying on the course for the long-term. There will be inevitable failures when change is being prescribed and especially when *'entrenched power structures'* are being threatened.

So it seems likely that it will be a long haul before the necessary change is accepted and becomes the 'new normal'. We can however influence when this happens and whether we can actually make the leap and survive by more than just the '*skin of our teeth*'. The more we can do to accelerate the '*birth of the new order*', the less suffering we will have chosen to inflict on the world and its inhabitants.

At Last a Happy Birthday!
Jack O'Brien, Year 12 IB Student, Prince Alfred College Adelaide, Australia

Energy has been of particular concern over the last few decades as natural resources have become scarce. Hybrids have entirely replaced all previously petrol powered machines. While the world mainframe is entirely powered from hundreds of thousands of square miles of solar panels as well as the millions of wind and nuclear power stations that now litter Africa, allowing them to boost their economy into the fastest developing region in the world.

People seemed unable to, both mentally and economically, convert to an entirely renewable energy system. As such, fossil fuels were, until recently, still in high demand across the world stage. This forced radical actions. Big Oil Co went under 20 years ago when their extensive extraction of fossil fuels led to a massive landslide taking out the island of Hong Kong and leading to the deaths of millions.

Now, finally, with the rising prices of fuels to the point where they are no longer practical for everyday use, countries across the world have begun dedicating huge sums of their budget into an as yet elusive solution. The World Space Program has explored thousands of planets for more efficient forms of energy, and with synthetic meats now being easily produced farming animals and global hunger have become completely obsolete.

So I'm going to have Happy 102nd Birthday this year because the future finally seems bright.

Jack O'Brien is a smart, generally optimistic and annoyingly tall young man who happens to be my son. His view of the future ends on a positive note but he is not hopeful of the human race's ability to change its systems in the near future. Jack's view that fossil fuel use will survive to nearly 2100 would push the world towards catastrophic climate change and create much chaos and suffering.

There has been some good progress with renewable energy, nuclear power, space exploration and global hunger but there are '*as yet elusive*' solutions to the complete replacement of fossil fuels. Towards the end of his years, he looks forward to the world having a bright future as it finally understands how it needs to adapt.

Jack is therefore on the less optimistic end of when the change might happen. Maybe this is the most likely outcome if we just let things progress in the same way that they have to date. Maybe by changing the conversation and focussing on the positives, we can bring this date forward to create a level of damage that is less than catastrophic.

We will need some luck to come along in this process and to be ready to recognise and capitalise on the opportunity when it does arrive. Maybe we will get some really severe weather events that shut down rich cities and change the perception of the imminence of the threat. That might help people leap to the optimistic visions of the future as a form of comfort and security when they feel that the world as they know it is collapsing.

★ ★ ★

Humans often turn to religion in hard times as it gives them hope for the future and comfort when they have to endure suffering. The decline in religion in the developed world could be correlated with the decline in hardship and suffering.

Gregory Paul, a Baltimore-based palaeontologist published research in 2009 that compared twenty-five socioeconomic indicators against statistics on religious belief and practice in seventeen developed nations. He concluded that "*religion is most able to thrive in seriously dysfunctional societies.*"

People do not feel they need so much spiritual support when

life is mostly easy. Maybe, if people start to feel threatened by increasingly severe weather events then there may be a reverse in this trend and a more arduous search for a positive future to hold on to. Whether this is a return to passively asking for help from the gods or proactively building a more functional society is something that we will find out.

The rational response to this would of course to be proactive! However, there is a risk that we will waste more years of delayed action declaring '*the end of the world is nigh*' and fervently praying for a solution. I am not intending here to disenfranchise any reader who is of a religious persuasion but rather to suggest that there are clear, tangible actions that humans can take immediately that will reduce future suffering, and it is incumbent on us to get on with it and not delay further.

So whatever the reason for the final change of our collective heart, we will turn back from the brink and the challenge is just when this will happen. The conscious decision we are making as we dither is how many millions of lives and species will be lost and how much damage is wrought.

Simon Zadek is another author who has been active in the environmental sector for a long time and lives in the smog of Beijing. His first published paper, in 1993, was on '*The Practice of Buddhist Economics*'. It considered how Buddhist principles might enable the creation and appreciation of greater value than just financial wealth.

In that paper, Simon references the original coining of the term by E.F. Schumacher in his 1966 essay. Schumacher's vision was that Buddhist Economics is a system where '*the economy should exist to serve people, not vice versa, and that it should be in harmony with, rather than exploiting of, nature.*' To achieve this outcome, he envisages '*a multitude of vibrant, self-sufficient villages which, from their secure sense of community and place, work together in peace and cooperation*'. This vision is not dissimilar to the Greenvilles of Christian Haeuselmann's vision in Chapter 19.

Simon's poetic vision below is generally optimistic and sees us ending up in a world built upon Anarres, the fictional inhabitable moon in Ursula Le Guin's novel, *The Dispossessed*. Anarres is supposed to be a society without government or coercive authoritarian institutions where its inhabitants put the needs of society ahead of their own personal desires: a form of anarchic utopia.

The utopia in the novel is far from perfect. Simon has envisioned a more caring world that has suffered through its '*march of folly*' but has emerged with a new structure that is greatly improved. That is his hope for the future.

Small Change

Simon Zadek, Co-Director, UNEP Inquiry into the Design of a Sustainable Financial System
Senior Fellow, Global Green Growth Institute and the International Institute of Sustainable Development
Visiting Scholar, Tsinghua School of Economics and Management
Advisory Board Member, Generation Investment Management
Beijing, China

Arrival.
Quiet, save for the ever-sounds of children at play.

Smart people doubted it, cynics dismissed its relevance
Passion and neglect, inevitable bedfellows, forged the march of folly.

History forgetfully claims every moment.
Thirteen billion born, twenty billion loved and were loved.
Six billion did not arrive.

Joules as the gold standard, finance is energy.
Ten billion real time energy merchants,
Generated from the wind in their wired hair to their light tread on receptive pavements.

Production is consumption, here and now, no there.
Disembodied immediacy, encircled loop.
Balanced confinement.

Climate is us.
Solitary technological species, adopting universes
Integrating them to our way, modifying to their absolutes.

Gods, abandoned longevity for the select, conscious departure.
Rebuilt from soulless bricks and mortar, reimaging ourselves,
Whilst the unselect ground prematurely into dust.

Governed by the commune, the We,
Reinforced by lost memories.
Anarres.

Chapter 7

COMPLEXITY

It is good to have an end to journey toward; but it is the journey that matters, in the end.

Ernest Hemingway

Chapter 7

COMPLEXITY

Are We Wiser?

Tony Wood, Energy Program Director, Grattan Institute Melbourne, Australia

The twenty-first century's achievement of reliable, affordable and sustainable energy for today's six billion people was not without pain. The dislocation and decimation of many populations in the second quarter of the century did finally galvanise global leaders to real action. And we did turn the climate change juggernaut. Yet, are we wiser?

First, we learned that policies driven by hope, such as moving quickly to 100 per cent renewable energy, never work and that well-designed, market-based policies can address major environmental issues associated with energy and water. But, galvanising agreement to such policies against individual self-interest depended on enough disruption for the common interest to emerge.

Second, we learned that there is no destination for this journey. The days of burning fossil fuels have long passed, even though we have a legacy of billions of tonnes of CO2, captured and stored decades ago. Transforming all of our stationary energy and then land transport to low-emissions electricity happened quickly once emissions were fully priced. But even now we are not entirely comfortable with roughly equal shares of solar and nuclear energy in the supply mix.

Finally we are learning a new definition of economic growth beyond consumption of physical resources – perhaps the greatest learning of all.

Another theme that emerged through a number of the visions included in this book was that there is huge complexity in the challenge we are facing. There is no simple solution and there will be no end point to our journey to create a better world. We will not reach utopia where everyone can just relax and enjoy the perfect world.

Tony Wood is one of Australia's leading independent commentators on energy policy. He provides insightful opinions on options to transition the energy sector in a way that will create the least disruption. He advocates that the most sensible approach to transition is through '*well-designed, market-based policies*' but, in his vision, sees that we will need the '*dislocation and decimation of many populations*' before we are able to overcome '*individual self-interest*'.

As we have seen, the need for threat and decimation is one that fits well with almost everything we know about human psychology. Countries that feel the least threat are often those that are least willing to take action. The irony of this is of course that these are also the countries that are most able to take action. Any short-term cost increases would not substantially impact anyone but yet there is the most vigorous resistance from those who have most. Perversely, as people get richer they generally appear to become more selfish. The greatest generosity of spirit and action is often found in the poorest of communities as they appreciate the value of looking after each other.

As I sit here writing on a sunny fall day in the comforts of Adelaide, Australia, it is not hard to understand this disconnection. Adelaide is a beautiful, gentle city with clear air, few traffic jams and a largely wealthy and healthy community. People from here often travel and move elsewhere for good jobs but then come back to bring up their kids and live an easy, unchallenging life. As in every community, people here will always find something to complain about but it is hard to take many of these complaints too seriously.

Adelaide, and Australia in general, is a very conservative parochial society and many in positions of power do not see global issues as any of their concern. Whether poverty, war or climate change, then a common attitude is that the concern belongs to those not lucky enough to be Australian and is theirs alone to sort out. The country is rich and stable and Australians are rightly proud of this fact. Australians just need to look after themselves!

This is a very different attitude to the pioneering spirit that built the country. The pioneers were adventurers who worked hard and took risks in a bid to create a fairer, better world than the one they had left. At the same time they built their fortunes. The descendants of these pioneers have become lazy and self-satisfied. They no longer want to see change or to push the boundaries of what is possible. They would prefer instead to have a barbeque with a nice bottle of red! The country's founding fathers would be appalled: that is not what they set out to create.

The lifecycle of a nation can be compared to that of many a family dynasty. The founders come from nothing and build a fortune and the descendants progressively get lazier and more risk-adverse and end up losing the fortune. This has led to the well known phrase: one [generation] to make, one to consolidate and one to lose.

Sadly, it seems that the rich nations, such as Australia, are stuck in the third phase of this cycle. They are too egocentric and in-ward-looking to see that the world, and their place in it, is changing rapidly. Without adjustment, their privileged place may not survive. Without collaboration with other countries on world issues such countries will, like spoilt brats, find themselves ostracized and side-lined. We are now very much a global society and no nation can afford to face the future alone.

Despite the risks, politicians play on human's susceptibility to selfishness and short-termism. In rich countries with frequent elections, rhetoric, grab lines and policies aimed at this work well in winning votes. Such is our ability to self-justify that the politicians that espouse the virtues of short-term, selfish policies may even sincerely believe that they are doing the best thing for their country. Looking back from the year 2100, history may tell a different story. Our descendants will shake their heads at the foolishness of their forebears.

Australian investors are also inhibited by this same shot-term attitude. Investment in environmental technologies is low at the best of times. Rich Australians have made their fortunes from digging up dirt, running casinos or peddling celebrity gossip in the media. There are no cleantech billionaires in this part of the world - yet! Australian entrepreneurs with world beating technologies move to the US West Coast or to Asia to get funded and build the industries of the future. Even if they maintain a token office here and plan to return in retirement, Australia will have lost the technology and its jobs forever. This no longer is a country that supports innovation or venture investing. Australia faces a future in which it resembles an aging and scruffy British aristocrat standing in front of a now ramshackle manor house. The money has gone elsewhere.

Tony Wood asks his world in 2100 'Are we wiser?' He knows that we will have got through the climate crisis once there is a sufficient level of devastation. Will the world in 2100 still be stumbling along in the same manner, averting crises only after we have decimated communities and reduced the global population back to six billion? Will we have managed to mature sufficiently to avoid repeating these mistakes? Evolution is an unpredictable process so there is hope that we, as a race, might have become less egocentric and have come to value growth beyond the 'consumption of physical resources'.

Of course, 2100 does not represent journey's end. It does however give us a focal point and achieving improvements will give purpose to many people along the way. In the words of Ernest Hemingway, 'It is good to have an end to journey toward; but it is the journey that matters, in the end.'

In 2100, there will still be plenty of things to improve. The hope is that we will indeed be wiser and thus willing to strive towards increasing wealth in the widest meaning of the word. Maybe even the politicians and other leaders will be respected for their far-sightedness and determination to deliver meaningful change in all the areas that make it wonderful to be human. Wouldn't that be wonderful?

The Immutability of Aging

Dr Aubrey de Grey, Chief Science Officer,
SENS Research Foundation www.sens.org
Mountain View, California, USA

Can we truly relate to the way we thought about humanity's worst problems in 2020? Arguably, our mindset then was even more different from today's than it was from 1800, before the Industrial Revolution and the germ theory. During those 220 years, as we automated away the nastiest jobs and healed away the most prevalent infections, we remained fatalist concerning the oldest enemy of all - the inexorable decline that was the punishment for daring to survive. And our coping strategy of putting the immutability of aging out of our minds, by classing it as not really a medical problem, contaminated our thinking more broadly - we were similarly nonchalant about everything else that seemed infeasible, above all the environmental impact of fossil fuel use.

But as the 2020s unfolded, with ever more dramatic rejuvenation of already-old laboratory animals, our psyche changed forever. We all remember the headlong rush to translate laboratory breakthroughs to the clinic, with decisive success emerging in the 2030s and soon becoming universal. But by then we had already taken climate change seriously too, and capitalisation on the breakthroughs of the 2010s in nuclear fusion and solar energy was no longer left to market forces but was expanded to dominate energy production within a decade. Global temperature remains too high despite rapid carbon sequestration, but we alleviate its effects with hurricane pre-emption and graphene-based desalination on a scale not imagined in 2020. Looking back, there can be no doubt that the defeat of aging empowered us to overcome all the other challenges that nature offers us. Earthquakes: you're next...

Aubrey de Grey is tackling another highly complex problem that challenges the human race: that of aging. He has researched and characterised all of the key elements that comprise the aging process. This has involved looking at the damage to our complex systems from the '*accumulating and eventually pathogenic molecular and cellular side-effects of metabolism*'. Furthermore, he has gone on to design interventions to repair and/or obviate that damage. His Strategies for Engineered Negligible Senescence (SENS) considers the seven major classes of damage and identifies detailed approaches to address each one. This work could lead to an ability to extend '*healthy lifespan without limit*'.

The approach to human aging and how to identify and repair damage is no different to the global approach needed to ensure that our planet too has a '*healthy lifespan without limit*'. Aubrey sees the two as interlinked and as we understand and treat human aging, we will start having more respect for our planet and how to treat it. The challenge of what happens with population levels as aging is 'solved' is another matter. SENS has funded research on this topic at both the University of Chicago and the University of Denver. The final results of this work are not yet published but will consider the balance of impacts that '*extended years of healthy and productive life*' against the planetary impacts of more humans.

My sunny fall afternoon writing was interrupted by a visit to Kate's pain specialist, which quickly removed the facade of all Adelaide life being easy. The doctor is fairly new to us and is the first time we have had a female pain specialist. The meeting went well. The doctor has a skill for looking beyond the immediate to providing an environment that allows for space to cope with the daily ups and downs of chronic illness. She understands that the system is complex and the symptoms and treatments react in non-linear and often unpredictable ways. It feels as though this is a powerful ability in a medical world that is mostly full of male egos wanting to find the cure: the single right answer.

Aging treatment and medicine in general too often go for 'end-of-the-pipe' solutions. Treatment of symptoms does not provide resolution of the problem; it merely delays or prolongs the decline. The medical world is full of specialists who partly understand their own little sub-systems. These discipline experts are often far too focused on their own area of specialisation to see the best solution for the full system.

The issues of chronic pain or aging are too complex to be solved by a single 'silver bullet'. With chronic pain we have worked with many doctors who thought they were able to provide Kate's own silver bullet, only to become disheartened, disinterested or even angry when they failed. This is just the result of the weakness of being human but can be devastating for the patient.

To enable a system to recover needs many consistent actions that provide an environment to encourage the recovery. We cannot control the outcome but rather must act like Dunphy's midwife in helping to provide the best chance of a successful delivery.

Backing a single solution to provide all the right outcomes will be destined to failure. A complex problem, whether it is for pain, aging or climate change, is rarely a static one, so one single solution will never be able to address the continually evolving problem

The best chances of success in complex challenging situations such as climate change come from pursuing multiple partial solutions and enabling the system to heal itself in the best way possible. The best solution at any one time will be selected by the system depending on the needs of the most pressing problem of that moment.

For chronic pain, this can be a mixture of physical or chemical interventions combined with lifestyle changes and providing a nurturing, caring environment. For aging, it may be Aubrey's seven areas of damaging. For climate change it will need to be a mixture of technological solutions, policy initiatives and behavioural change that will jointly provide the planet's system the space and options it needs to recover.

★ ★ ★

Another complex and evolving problem is that of cities and how to make them functional and productive. Many large growing cities are beset with problems ranging from smog to gridlocked traffic to the development of dysfunctional neighbourhoods.

Charles Landry has worked on the challenge of building better cities since the 1980s. He has published numerous books and advised many of the world's leading cities on how to improve functionality and create a thriving, healthy ecosystem. His vision below includes a ten step guide that helped cities at the turn of the twenty-second century to become more connected, inclusive, creative and sustainable. His starting points are to think in an integrated way, share knowledge, be sustainable, break silos of expertise and increase the understanding of others. This is the perfect recipe for negotiating any complex challenge.

Charles' '*civic urbanity*' has delivered a world that has '*realigned individual desires and self-interest within a collective consciousness focus instead on 'us' or 'our joint world or city'.*'

In his vision, Tony Wood notes that '*galvanising agreement to such policies against individual self-interest depended on enough disruption for the common interest to emerge.*' The extent of malfunction that is required to deliver support for these changes is not clear. However, many global cities are on the brink of significant dysfunction and, through their unfettered growth, are inefficient and unhealthy places to live. So once the population is ready to accept action, this provides the framework to deliver effective results.

Complex problems present challenges to the way the world has worked to date. We have succeeded as a race through building armies of soldiers or workers to conquer specific tasks. We have created task forces to knock over mighty challenges. Overcoming complex, non-linear global challenges requires a different way of thinking. They can be addressed but require a different approach. Bureaucratic institutions and professions such as governments and medicine have not been constructed to deliver the flexibility and entrepreneurial attitude required when there is a moving target. We will explore later how innovation and entrepreneurial systems might be able to overcome this barrier.

Whether we are able to address this complexity will determine the state of the world in 2100 and how close we come to the fears expressed in Chapter 5. Understanding the systems we are trying to influence, both physical and psychological, is a critical step in building a world in which we will be proud to live.

Civic Urbanity
Charles Landry
The Creative City
Oxford, UK

*The **ten themes** of civic urbanity shaped the dilemmas, challenges and opportunities of the twenty-first century city. It realigned individual desires and self-interest within a collective consciousness focus instead on 'us' or 'our joint world or city'.*

1. *The starting point was to think in an **integrated and connected** way. Only then could we discern the linkages and dependencies that shaped life.*

2. *A reinvigorated public and **shared commons** was an ethos adopted against the increasingly self-centred public culture in the early part of the century.*

3. *Cities started to not only talk of **sustainability** but also to 'walk the talk'.*

4. ***Unhealthy urban planning** was what we used to do. Rigidly separating functions, we now plan to make us healthy.*

5. *We learnt about **cultural literacy**, an understanding of others so we could negotiate difference.*

6. *Cities were once becoming increasingly unequal, but clever cities now demand greater **equality and inclusiveness.***

7. *The **demographic time bomb** hung over everything that cities did, but now we do not isolate the aged and instead take an inter-generational perspective.*

8. *The **aesthetic imperative** was also crucial and old fashioned words like beauty and ugliness have re-entered the planning debate.*

9. *The escalating intractable urban problems that cities were facing were only solved through harnessing the **imagination and creativity** of its citizens.*

10. *Finally we had to reinvent how we administered, managed and governed through a **creative bureaucracy**.*

Section 3

THE JOURNEY

Chapter 8

PEOPLE KNEW

The secret of success is constancy to purpose.

Benjamin Disraeli
24 June 1872, Crystal Palace, London

Chapter 8

PEOPLE KNEW

People Knew
Connie Hedegaard
EU Commissioner, Climate Action and Energy, 2010-14
Copenhagen, Denmark

Today it is hard to understand. But at the beginning of the twenty-first century people labelled "growth" so differently to what we do today. In those days, if something was produced it was valued as "growth" without factoring in the impact on the environment, depletion of natural resources or pollution. They did not even think to talk about the consequences for future generations. And the strangest thing was that it was not because back in the 2010s people did not understand the implications of climate change or the challenge in providing for the billions more people due to inhabit Planet Earth. People knew. Governments said they knew. Business knew. But oddly enough many thought they could make profound change through continuing business as usual.

Only when in 2015 the international community started to embrace a new way of measuring growth, GDP+, and started to change investments away from fossil fuels and to phase out subsidies to fossil fuels, things came back on track. And maybe most interestingly: this shift also meant a new focus on the more qualitative aspects of life, on communities and how to create meaningful jobs in a world of automation. Actually it was around 2015 that the circular economy, that today we take for granted, got started.

The journey from our current addiction to fossil fuels and high carbon consumption to a world where we live within the means of the planet is not going to be plain sailing. There are many people that will be motivated by the drive to protect existing business models and others greedily eying new profits streams. Democratically elected politicians need to sell complex messages on why we need to act now for a non-Imminent problem.

Looking back from 2100, Connie Hedegaard sees it hard to understand how the world behaved back then when 'people knew'. Future generations will marvel at our inaction. History has blamed Emperor Nero for taking the same action during the six day Great Fire of Rome in the year 64 CE. Will we be known as the great Neroan generation for fiddling whilst the world started to burn?

Ms Hedegaard could not be accused of 'fiddling' whilst in office. Her four years as the European Union Commissioner for Climate Action and Energy culminated in October 2014 with ambitious and binding targets across the European Union. The agreed targets include a cut in greenhouse gas emissions by at least 40% by 2030 compared to 1990 levels, an EU-wide binding target for renewable energy of at least 27% and an indicative energy efficiency target of at least 27%. These targets have set the benchmark of what can be done and the Commissioner had a significant role in bringing these commitments to fruition. Yet these targets on their own are not enough to avoid catastrophic climate change so there is much more work to do.

People knew that cigarettes caused lung cancer for a long time before action was taken. Even the ravages of Mesothelioma from inhaling asbestos fibres were known by those involved whilst they continued to sell the product. How can people continue to act in the face of compelling evidence that everything they do is harmful? It might be easy to surmise that these company executives are all psychotic or evil. This is not the case however.

There are often instances where beliefs and action are inconsistent. Cognitive dissonance, first described by Festinger in 1957, describes how people cope with this inconsistency by finding a satisfactory explanation that justifies their behaviour. A cigarette executive might talk about how they have reduced advertising or added warning labels to justify why they are actually doing a good job in lessening the harm caused from cigarettes. Anyway if they resigned, another manager would just do their job, so it is better that they stay and do the best job possible.

Those in the fossil fuel industry similarly justify the benefits of their work to the human race. A few years ago, I met an old university friend in London for a reunion Christmas lunch. He is now a senior manager in a big oil company and became remarkably defensive when talk turned to cleantech and climate change. '*So you got here from Australia without using any fossil fuels, did you?*' is the phrase I remember most clearly.

Politicians come under pressure to support old industries especially when the economic outlook is bleak. In the same month that the European Commissioner announced her ambitious binding targets, the Australian Prime Minister said '*Coal is good for humanity, coal is good for prosperity, coal is an essential part of our economic future, here in Australia, and right around the world.*'

There is no question that fossil fuels have played an enormous part in creating the wealth enjoyed by much of the world today. They have enabled transport, materials and a multitude of other elements that are essential to our daily lives. Fossil fuels have also created the wealth that has enabled the research into delivering the same quality of life in more sustainable ways.

Fossil fuels have been essential to date but that does not mean that they are essential going forward. A transition is necessary and there is now no *rational* reason for this not to proceed as quickly as possible.

DDT, Thalidomide and asbestos all had their benefits but in the end the mostly unintended consequences proved to be too costly. Fossil fuels will have the same fate regardless of the dissonance of executives or the rhetoric of politicians.

Cigarettes now have low tar, better filters, no advertising, warning signs and plain packaging. The executives selling them must be struggling to keep finding a justification that does not sound ridiculous even to themselves. The solution for them is to just stop doing it! Find something that creates value beyond wealth for shareholders that has purpose and meaning. That allows them to feel as though they are contributing to the world.

'People knew. Governments said they knew. Business knew.'

But this is not all bad news. The challenges faced through these other harmful activities have been addressed despite entrenched interests, lost profits and the need for behavioural change. Some clearly had more imminent peril than climate change and television pictures or knowledge of people dying helps to drive the need for change. Change has happened and there are lessons to be learnt on how we can approach the communication needed to address climate change.

In Opportunities Beyond Carbon, I wrote that:

The comparison between climate-change effects and diseases caused by cigarette smoking has been used by some to create powerful pictures of the 'evils' that may be engendered by big business. I, however, find it more useful to adopt the comparison when considering how scientific knowledge of the health impacts of smoking has been used to facilitate behavioural change. Tackling the problem of cigarette smoking required a range of inputs to achieve any level of success. A price signal was introduced, through increased taxes on cigarettes, together with comprehensive and targeted education campaigns.

The positive outcomes achievable, such as living a longer and more enjoyable life, were stressed in addition to the negative consequences of inaction. Yet new approaches were required and more recently there have been regulations imposing bans on smoking in many places, further reinforcing the messages delivered earlier.

While the warnings against smoking were put in purely personal terms, communities too have benefited from a healthier population and reduced litter. Transitioning to a low-carbon economy is a far larger and more complex issue, but the multi-strand approach to the problems associated with cigarette smoking provides some clues as to the thinking required.

The other good thing is that we do know: a far better situation than we were in forty years ago. We have the knowledge, the technologies and the wealth to be able to make the changes needed. We even have good public discussions on options for a way forward. All that is left now is to get on with it. That will happen. The only uncertainty left is when.

Cleaner, Fairer, Smaller

Rachel Kyte
Vice President and Special Envoy, Climate Change, World Bank
Washington, D.C., USA

The changes came when trees and farms started appearing in every small plot of land in the city. Dining halls became the place to be. No more restaurants with tables for two. On stilts above the wave turbines and under the solar arrays, I remember the academic year when, for the first time, the majority of students sought careers in neither finance or law, but in nexus engineering; food-water-energy. It was the same year that GDP had been replaced with the new wealth index - and despite "Y2K fears" all had gone well. There were no major devaluations and those doubts of a disorderly transition to low carbon growth were faced down.

Did having an all-female G7 Summit ten years earlier have anything to do with the smoothness of the transition? Probably, but with conflicts on the rise, displaced people on the move and air quality choking back progress, it was tough pragmatism that I remember.

Deciding to end income tax and replace it with carbon consumption was the centerpiece of the election platform. Only when three megacities declared bankruptcy after the summer of squalls did soccer mums truly get behind the call. And it worked despite disputes in the courts.

Now, everything has become smaller. Apartments, trains and mobility devices, watches and personal data devices. Veggie burgers. Still, it's cleaner and fairer.

But, I miss some things because we didn't move fast enough. Coral reefs and alpine skiing, anchovies and sardines, having a pet. The coastal paths of my childhood in the UK. The iconic Slip, Slap, Slop campaign seems so quaint now as the summer burns and the winter freezes. So afraid to act, we forgot that not acting was in fact the most dangerous action!

The cost of damages has crippled some economies far more than the costs of adjustment. But those that invested are transformed. Deserts are our new energy super-suppliers from Chile to Morocco to Mongolia.

If we knew then what we know now we would have had more confidence. We could have preserved the cultures of low lying communities from Florida and Tuvalu to the Sundarbans. We could have preserved more of the glaciers and averted the water disputes that have redrawn the political maps. We had the information at our fingertips. We just didn't get everyone to move as quickly as they should have.

On taking up her current role with the World Bank in 2013, Rachel Kyte gave an interview to The Guardian newspaper on her plans. She discussed then the need for a new way of communicating:

> *'so that you can convey urgency in a way that people can respond. There's a long history in the environment movement of fear-mongering and a) not providing alternatives or b) not having those fears realised. So we feel a responsibility to be able to communicate this in such a way that people can say: "OK, so what now?"'*

She went on to say something that fits perfectly with the aim of this book:

> *'...if you're going to paint a picture of the future where it's sackcloth and ashes, don't be surprised if you don't have a long line of people following you. We have to paint a picture of opportunity.'*

Rachel's role at the World Bank is to work across all the development divisions to make sure that their operations integrate climate change and take into account the opportunities that inclusive green growth presents. Her group is also an advocate for global climate action.

Rachel's vision is of a functional world that works well but from which some things have been lost for good. She decries the lack of confidence of the past generations who possessed the knowledge, who knew, but failed to act.

Her comment about an all-female G7 is a fascinating distraction. It presents an interesting parallel with the different approach we have welcomed from Kate's female pain doctor. Men might win wars, get a larger pay rise or a cheaper car but maybe the typical male traits are not suited to more difficult situations. For intractable, insoluble challenges, it is maybe the more female traits that lead to long-term, flexible solutions that better meet the needs of all. In a world of scarcity, the ability to grab a bigger slice of the pie can be critical to survival. In a world of abundance, this strategy is often short-sighted.

From a personal point of view, my psychometric tests have always shown that I thrive on ambiguity and change except when I do not easily see a solution to implement. Insoluble problems such as chronic pain have always therefore been a challenge for me. Maybe the declining few who doubt the science of climate change are actually just struggling with the fact that they cannot see a way through the problem and so, to manage this dissonance, it is just easier to deny it exists.

A 2004 study by Rekha Reddy, then at Princeton, looked at the perceived differences in negotiating styles between genders to see if there was any statistical evidence to justify the stereotypes. The stereotypes explored were that men were 'self-assured, assertive and able to stand firm against compromise' whilst women were 'emotional, relationship-oriented and cooperative'.

Whilst far from conclusive, the study did find some evidence to suggest that, in general, men will secure a better outcome from a more straightforward distributive negotiation whereas women secure a better outcome from more complex integrative bargaining situations.

...some evidence of women being more cooperative and more likely to share information was discussed in the context of this characteristic being a liability. However, in the context of integrative bargaining,

this weakness could be a strength for its contribution to mutual gains. Similarly, if women are more "relationally-oriented" and less likely to be individualistic (a detriment in distributive bargaining situations), this is positive from an integrative bargaining standpoint.

The solution for climate change will not be straightforward and will require an integrative approach to deliver a lasting outcome that takes into account all needs.

Maybe the trigger point for the world's change in direction will be when there are sufficient female leaders to be able to approach the challenge with a different mindset. Clearly this is a simplistic assumption, but is one worth remembering. When we get to that point in time in the coming years, it will be interesting to watch what happens.

In her vision, Rachel also states that we were '*so afraid to act, we forgot that not acting was in fact the most dangerous action!*' Not acting is a fatal flaw in many circumstances but is a natural reaction when confronted with threats. As we saw in Chapter 5, freezing is one of three options taken by mammals when they feel threatened. It is however the option that removes all control of the situation and accepts whatever the future might bring.

In business too, not acting can be fatal. Companies that do not innovate and move forward as their environment changes will be left behind. Classic case studies demonstrating this risk include Kodak's decision to not enter the digital camera market and Nokia's decision to ignore the smartphone market even after the launch of the first iPhone in 2007.

The key to innovation and entrepreneurship is to keep moving forward and to recognise the directions that are not working as early as possible. To create better solutions, for a product, a company or for the world requires risk-taking, creativity and a tolerance of failure. More than anything, in the words of Benjamin Disraeli, '*The secret of success is constancy to purpose.*'

In Chapter 9 we will review how some of the lessons from innovation might be applied to solving an insoluble problem such as climate change to help us accelerate our journey's progress.

★ ★ ★

Rekha Reddy now works as a Senior Economist at the World Bank where she focuses on Latin America and with a focus on Mexico and Colombia. She is therefore the perfect link between Rachel Kyte at the World Bank and the author of our final vision for this chapter.

Claudia Martinez Zuleta is a former Deputy Minister of Environment for Colombia and now works integrating development projects and climate change to build long-term resilient results. When sending through her vision, she added to the email that, '*I would like to live in the world of my vision!*' It is difficult not to feel the same. She has seen a wonderful world that has worked its way through the challenges of a century ago and is inhabited by people with '*an immense sentiment of belonging to a closer world community.*

Claudia works with the high levels of climate risk in Colombia and helps to build the engagement and support for climate opportunities. In particular she works with adaptation planning and vulnerability assessments for cities, agricultural regions and infrastructure development.

A theme that emerges from each of the visions in this chapter is how we measure wealth. Claudia sees that wealth is measured in safe ecosystems, Rachel sees a transfer moment when GDP was replaced and Connie suggests that the world adopted GDP+ to look beyond just dollars to a better measure of human wealth. This theme is repeated by many others in this book as a key step in changing how humans view the world and move to a more effective way of managing this limited resource. The concept is a challenge to those heavily invested in the current system, but the concept remains critical to moving forward.

The weakness of the current world model is explored in the 2014 book by Naomi Klein, *This Changes Everything: Capitalism vs the Climate*. She suggests that it is the system of capitalism that is holding back the action that is required to build a better world and prevent a climate catastrophe. Yet the monetary wealth that has been built through capitalism creates a barrier which cannot be overcome from the top. Instead, it will be at a community level that changes will start and will build to have such momentum that they will become unstoppable.

On considering this challenge, she comments that *"it is our great collective misfortune that the scientific community made its decisive diagnosis of the climate threat at the precise moment when those elites were enjoying more unfettered political, cultural, and intellectual power than at any point since the 1920s."*

This theme is revisited in Chapter 17 as we explore some practical ways the change could be delivered and what might be measured in addition to the creation of money.

We Live in a Better Planet

Claudia Martinez Zuleta
Executive Director of E3-Ecology, Economics and Ethics
Representative for Colombia Climate and Development
Alliance (CDKN)
Former Colombian Deputy Minister of Environment
Bogotá, Colombia

In 2100 some of the world's most important ecosystems like the Amazon have survived. After more than 30 years when cities like Sao Paulo, Rio de Janeiro, Lima and Bogota suffered serious problems for lack of water, South Americans have finally concluded that scientists were right when they spoke about the 'aerial rivers' produced by the Amazon or the Choco forests, and from there spreading rainfall across the continent.

Corporations have realized that regeneration has to be part of the business models. They are competing to be the best companies FOR the world, with social and environmental indices. They also realized that garbage is a problem of design and consumption, and so now there is far less waste.

Solar systems are found all over and massive transport systems are fueled by hydrogen. People have adopted a trading system of consumers and producers of ecosystem services in a bank of 'necessities for all'.

The rich are no longer the ones who have acquired money, but those who live in safe ecosystems. People are better educated with innovative school systems. Food is produced organically with many diverse varieties from natural seeds that were claimed by nations from the Svalbard Global Seed Vault. Poverty is eradicated. Diverse cultures have flourished and are widely appreciated.

My grandchildren still feel Colombian, but with an immense sentiment of belonging to a closer world community.

Chapter 9

NOT RATIONAL

I am heartened to find so much wit in you, that you'd give thought to consequences and choose your way with reason, not passion only.

Deborah J. Lightfoot, The Wysard

The best time to plant a tree was 20 years ago.
The second best time is now.

Chinese proverb.

Chapter 9

NOT RATIONAL

Zero Zero Vision
Sam Bickersteth, Chief Executive,
Climate and Development Knowledge Network,
London, UK

The way people lived in the early decades of this century seems far removed from our world of 2100. Then, as global growth and prosperity began to be shared across Asia and Latin America, economies were addicted to fossil fuels and rampant destruction of natural resources. Inequality was rising in all societies just as the impacts of climate change became more apparent in more frequent and extreme disasters.

Leaders' commitment to a vision of both zero net emissions and zero poverty changed the game.

Eradicating extreme poverty had already become an accepted global norm by this time, but it took further time to understand that climate change hits the poor hardest and undermines development gains if left unchecked. And leaders realised only slowly what we know now: that achieving net zero emissions and avoiding dangerous climate change depends on equitable development – development that benefits all parts of society and not just the few.

It was some of the low income countries that moved fastest towards zero poverty and zero emissions, and built themselves climate resilient, low carbon economies based on renewable energy and smart technologies. Their rapid urban growth and investments in educating their rising populations provided that opportunity. International finance, smart access to new knowledge and visionary leadership took the countries that did this earliest to become some of the most successful countries that we now see in 2100 across all regions of the world.

Rationality is rarely the decisive factor in decision-making. If it was, this book would be irrelevant and the world would be acting rationally on the compelling evidence laid out clearly by the scientists.

In his ground-breaking 1994 book, *Descartes' Error: Emotion, Reason and the Human Brain*, Antonia Damasio, then Professor of Neurology at the University of Iowa, explored the concept of emotions in decision-making. It looked at patients with a damaged prefrontal cortex of their brain and how that was linked to their inability to make simple decisions. This was attributed to the damage removing the '*necessary emotional machinery*' to be able to weigh up feelings about whether a decision was beneficial. This 'gut-feeling' is critical in the assessment of options and brings in many sub-conscious inputs that provide a context for the veracity, relevance and priority of the options. Damasio's conclusion feeds neatly into Professor Susan Greenfield's research discussed in Chapter 3 which looked at how computer games were changing the function of the prefrontal cortex to impact the consideration of consequences in decision-making.

So as discussed already we need to approach problems, and in particular complex problems, with both rational and emotional arguments. The rational is essential as it either provides the starting point for the decision-making that is then assessed emotionally or it provides the business case to justify an emotional decision that has already been made.

Those who have decided not to act on climate change have made this decision emotionally based on its threat to the way they live or how it might discredit their work to date. They will then search for data that provides enough justification for their emotionally chosen position. This is often in the form of 'doubts about the science' so that it would be 'foolish to act before everything was certain'. As we will discuss later in this chapter and also in Chapter 22, entrepreneurship and innovation policy never waits for certainty. Certainty is rarely achieved and where it is, it becomes a challenge that is too late to avoid or change.

The only absolute certainty we will ever have with climate

change is how much damage we have done – after it has been done. Having said that there is incredibly strong and consistent scientific consensus on the impacts that humans are having on our climate. The Intergovernmental Panel on Climate Change brings together and synthesises the views of over 800 climate scientists from around the world. It is comprehensive and compelling and if you happen to be starting with a rational argument in your decision-making then it is a good place to start. There is very little scientific doubt about the causes and potentially catastrophic consequences of what is happening. If you start from an emotional decision on your stand-point that action is required, this then also provides the rational back-up that you need.

If you have stayed with the book through to this point, you are probably already interested in helping your fellow humans to make decisions that will have long-term benefits. What much of the rest of the book is going to provide is some ways in which you can engage with those who are not yet convinced.

Those who have made strong emotional decisions against taking action will not be convinced with ever increasing and compelling data so there is no point arguing with mere facts. There will always be a scientist, even if not a climate scientist and with little expertise, who will provide a contrary position or find a possible hole in any argument. If you are seeking justification for your strongly held beliefs then that will be enough. In my mind, it is therefore not really worth engaging in debate on this front. Pointing out flaws in pseudo-scientific arguments is a useful exercise but direct engage-ment will not change belief.

To some extent, any faith or belief can be put into the same context. Many people have a very strong belief in one or many gods of some description. Their belief cannot be proven or unproven by science so it is clearly not based on a rational decision-making process. Nevertheless, it can be an incredibly strong belief that becomes a core part of the person. Arguing the scientific case against the existence of god is not something that is going to carry weight for someone who believes.

Where there is important work to be done and where this book may help the process is with the many people who are not yet engaged, do not understand and have not yet formed an opinion - whether rational or emotional. This is the middle ground of our global population and forms the majority of your seven billion fellow inhabitants. We have the facts to win the minds once people are engaged. Therefore it is the winning of hearts and getting engagement that will determine the extent of damage we cause to our fragile planet.

This is what the visions in this book might help with. By attracting people to build a better world that excites them will drive the emotional decision-making process. That is what is critical to changing global opinions.

Sam Bickersteth runs the Climate and Development Knowledge Network (CDKN) that is based in London and works globally. CDKN's aim is to support decision-makers in designing and delivering climate compatible development. It does this by combining research, advisory services and knowledge management in support of locally owned and managed policy processes.

Sam's vision sees a world that prioritises '*equitable development – development that benefits all parts of society and not just the few.*' He sees the countries that took this approach earliest will become the most successful countries by the year 2100. The global adoption of a policy of '*zero net emissions and zero poverty*' was the thing that changed our path and built a better world.

The crossover between climate change adaptation and development work is a fascinating area. The impacts of climate change will be felt most by those in the poorest countries that have the fewest resources. We are too late to prevent this happening. We are not too late to prevent it being much, much worse than is already the case.

Whereas a resident of London, New York, Beijing or Sydney might be moderately inconvenienced or suffer a financial impact, maybe even asset damage from extreme storms, those that live in the least developed countries will suffer famines, devastation and mass migrations. The impact of the dislocation of hundreds of millions of climate refugees will ensure that the impacts are not just felt in those suffering regions.

Not only will there be the mere logistical problem of how to prevent the death of hundreds of millions of our fellow humans, but the anger imbued by the suffering will drive disruption that will impact more widely. The climate change induced drought in Syria between 2006 and 2010 caused much suffering and drove the initial uprising against an inactive government. In the chaos that ensued, the Islamic State organisation stepped in and offered an alternative 'solution' to desperate people.

Writing in the Huffington Post in 2014, Charles Strozier from the City University of New York and Kelly Berkell from the Center on Terrorism at John Jay College of Criminal Justice wrote:

> *The drought that preceded the current conflict in Syria fits into a pattern of increased dryness in the Mediterranean and Middle East, for which scientists hold climate change partly responsible. Affecting sixty per cent of Syria's land, drought ravaged the country's northeastern breadbasket region; devastated the livelihoods of 800,000 farmers and herders; and knocked two to three million people into extreme poverty. Many became climate refugees, abandoning their homes and migrating to already overcrowded cities. They forged temporary settlements on the outskirts of areas like Aleppo, Damascus, Hama and Homs. Some of the displaced settled in Daraa, where protests in early 2011 fanned out and eventually ignited a full-fledged war.*

In the early 1990s I lived and worked in Deir ez-Zor, an agricultural city of 200,000 people on the banks of the Euphrates. It was founded in the times of the crusades and is the largest settlement in eastern Syria. I was there working on the oil wells on the Iraqi border. It is now in the Islamic State heartland.

As a slowly maturing and largely ignorant male, my time in Syria was the first time that I thought about systems of governments and their relative merits. Dier ez-Zor and even Damascus were, at the time, entirely safe places to live. People would help when they could, there was not a 'bad' side of town, communities appeared to function and life seemed happy, hard-working and settled. The one thing you could not do in Syria was criticise the Assad regime. Other than that it was a benign dictatorship with a reasonably content population.

Coming from the UK, the thought that liberal capitalist democracy was not the only effective form of government was a challenging proposition. The freedom of cities such as London evidently came with lots of downsides in terms of safety and trust that made things not quite as free as they claimed.

Democracy when first achieved is celebrated with abandon. The queues of people in South Africa for the first post-apartheid elections in April 1994, shortly after my return from Syria, attested to the strength of the hope of control over one's own destiny. Twenty years on, democracy has not delivered on the hope it created, just like the despondency of Obama's first term in office.

Climate change is a challenge to democracy in more than one way. It has a longer lifecycle than even the longest serving politician and is a threat to the way lives are lived today. Countries that are making the quickest progress in the second decade of this century are those under most threat and those that have the undemocratic luxury of effective long-term planning. Whilst driven primarily by reducing local pollution, the Chinese government is one of those taking the most drastic and effective action to reduce emissions.

Strozier and Berkell continue their article by reviewing other areas of the world that are prone to climate collapse and the potential for disaffected populations to look towards radical alternatives. They comment on how glacial melt has caused catastrophic weather in Afghanistan '*potentially strengthening the Taliban and imperilling Afghan girls who want to attend school*'. They also consider Bangladesh and its low-lying areas prone to rising sea levels and storm surges.

In the coming decades, Bangladesh stands to lose up to 17 percent of its land to flooding, displacing 18 million people to overcrowded cities and neighboring states in a region that has seen a recent upsurge in Islamist militarism.

Amin Malouf's fictional book, *The First Century after Beatrice* that I mentioned in the introduction, provides some scenarios of how things might pan out as this sort of climate-induced migration takes hold. The book centres on an ancient Egyptian remedy made from a scarab bean which is used to increase the odds of babies being male. It was found to have scientific merit and was marketed and sold globally. Inevitably, the population in many regions became overly male which challenged or changed almost all of the social structures that had been built for a world with a different gender balance. Whilst initially the impacts were local and small and seen as interesting titbits of global news, the consequences started to build and led to civil and regional wars, a breakdown in global security structures and impacts on every country and every person. The rich of London and New York found their 'perfect' world to be shaken. The impacts were truly global. This will happen with climate migrations.

Malouf includes his own vision of his perfect world in the book:

> *Then, in the space of one walk, I build a different world. A world in which freedom and prosperity have gradually spread like the waves on the surface of the waters. A world in which the only challenge left to medicine, after it has overcome all diseases and wiped out epidemics, is to postpone ageing and death indefinitely. A world from which ignorance and violence have been banished. A world rid of the last patches of darkness. Yes, mankind reconciled, generous and victorious, with eyes fixed on the stars, on eternity.*
>
> *To that species, I would have been proud to belong.*

I unsuccessfully tried to contact Malouf for this book to see if he had written *Beatrice* as an allegory of climate change. Whether he did or not, for me it has provided a vision of the future that is to be avoided.

It is not rational as a race to behave as we are. Like the well-known, if disputed, story of the Easter Island inhabitants causing their own demise by cutting down the last tree, we are merrily living beyond our collective means. On its own, however, rationality is not sufficient to garner action.

Removing the Carbon Mask

Tim Hobbs

Year 12 IB Student, Prince Alfred College

Adelaide, Australia

What sets us apart from other species is the way we can think, reason and act based on the information we have available to us. It was this unique ability that allowed us to recognise the damage that we were causing to our environment.

Mankind has engineered many revolutions over its millennia of progress; the latest chapter in our story being the carbon revolution. For years substances that emitted carbon were integrated into our cities, our economies, our lives. Our world was enveloped by a carbon mask and once we saw the beginnings of the catastrophes that this carbon mask would bring, we changed our ways. Humanity was united in its efforts to bring about global change; promoting a low carbon future so that our children could live a more fulfilled and comfortable life. The change was slow but gathered momentum as time passed on and soon the carbon mask began to fall away.

The result was an enriched society, an expanding economy, a relieved environment and a more mature humanity. The future of our world never looked so bright.

Tim Hobbs is an impressive young man who happens to be one of my son Jack's friends. His vision of how the world comes to its senses is clear and simple. It shows a vision of the way forward that will certainly lead to a better world where the '*future of our world never looked so bright*'.

The rationalists and pragmatists will bristle at this simple vision. I can hear them picking holes in the vision with '*it is not that simple*', '*think of the practicalities*' and '*get in the real world, son!*' '*It is just the naivety of youth and he'll learn how things really work in time.*'

Or maybe Tim speaks with the wisdom of youth before it has been corrupted by the rationalists. Rather than seeing things as being too simple, maybe he is not unnecessarily complicating a simple goal. Tim is more determined and more clear-sighted than those who have been worn down by not achieving their own goals.

It is not something that needs to be dissected; it is just something that needs to be done and will be done. The carbon mask will be removed.

★ ★ ★

To solve complex problems and create improvements in non-linear situations requires trial and error. Whilst research and knowledge building form a critical part of the process, the quickest progress is often made through trial and error to find all the ways that will not work. When experimenting in this way, there is often an even stronger reliance on 'gut-feeling' and the emotional response.

Innovation is defined as the '*introduction of new things or methods*'. It can therefore never be certain that innovation will work. If it was certain, it would be thoroughly proven and so would not be innovative.

Innovation and entrepreneurship is most often linked to founding and growing new businesses. More recently social entre-preneurship is looked at using the same thought process to tackle social issues such as long-term unemployment, depression and dys-functional communities.

The Australian Centre for Social Innovation has delivered some fascinating benefits through applying entrepreneurship principles to social problems. Some of their successes have included the Weavers and the Family by Family projects.

The Weavers project is a new peer-to-peer model supporting carers to address the significant challenges of caring for a loved one. Weavers are people with caring experience who are trained to provide support to other carers in their local community.

Family by Family was developed to reduce the number of families needing crisis services and to help keep more kids out of the child protection system. The program finds and trains families who have been through tough times, matches them with families who want things to change, and coach the families to grow and change together.

These innovative approaches have enabled step changes to participants and provided an affordable and appropriate solution to complex insoluble problems.

The thinking used in innovation is exactly what we need to deliver meaningful action on climate change. The barriers faced by entrepreneurs are also the same. There are therefore many lessons that can be learnt from innovation theory that might help for the world's complex non-linear problems.

Joseph Schumpeter is often referenced as one of the fathers of innovation. In his 1942 book, *Capitalism, Socialism and Democracy*, Schumpeter pointed out that entrepreneurs innovate not just by figuring out how to use inventions, but also by introducing new means of production, new products and new forms of organization. These innovations, he argued, take just as much skill and daring as does the process of invention.

He argued that innovation by the entrepreneur leads to '*creative destruction*' as innovations cause old ideas, technologies, skills, and equipment to become obsolete. This creative destruction enables continuous progress and improves the standards of living for everyone.

Schumpeter wrote that the key to progress was '*competition from the new commodity, the new technology, the new source of supply, the new type of organization ... competition which ... strikes not at the margins of the profits and the outputs of the existing firms but at their foundations and their very lives.*'

To change the way the world lives will require plenty of innovation!

Successful entrepreneurship requires the ability to recognise opportunities, try out possible solutions and to fail as quickly and as cheaply as possible. The 'right' solution is unknown and in fact may never be found. The challenge is to get to a solution that is good enough and will achieve the required outcomes.

In my work helping to commercialise environmental technologies, I often come across inventors who are determined to keep tinkering until they have the perfect solution. For this reason, those inventors will probably never manage to get their products to market, regardless of whether or not the technology is the best in the world. The success stories come from good technologies that get to market as quickly as possible and then continually improve based on feedback from customers. This way they make their product more attractive to potential customers rather than merely perfecting a technology that they later try and 'push' onto uninterested customers.

The best entrepreneurs, whether focussed on money, social challenges or environmental solutions, tend to start with little idea of how they will get to their chosen destination. They know there is a challenge to overcome or an opportunity to take and they start to explore options for what may work. What the consequences will be of their actions are not known and it is only by experimenting and trying different things that the entrepreneur starts to understand the patterns of the system they are playing with.

Donella Meadows rose to prominence in the environmental world with the publication of The Limits to Growth in 1972, and from there she went on to a distinguished career as an author and environmental journalist until her death in 2001. In her 2001 article, titled 'Dancing with Systems', she states that, 'We can't control systems or figure them out. But we can dance with them!' To be able to dance with a system, you have to understand how it works by testing reactions to activities.

When looking at successful entrepreneurs, Professor Saras Sarasvathy from the University of Virginia showed that a very large proportion of successful serial entrepreneurs took an 'effectual' approach when confronted with a challenge. Entrepreneurs often work in a space in which the future is not only unknown, but unknowable. Sarasvathy found that the ability to consistently and successfully navigate through the unknowable focussed on five common techniques used by expert entrepreneurs:

- They know their means: who I am, what I know, and whom I know. Then, the entrepreneurs imagine possibilities that originate from their means.
- They understand their affordable losses. They choose goals and actions where there is upside even if the downside ends up happening.

- They interpret "bad" news and surprises as potential clues to how the system works.
- They build partnerships and co-create the future with engaged partners.
- They focus only on activities within their control and know their actions will result in the desired outcomes.

An effectual worldview is rooted in the belief that the future is neither found nor predicted, but rather made. Creating a future that we want to live in is exactly what the authors of this book want to do.

The final lesson from entrepreneurship that has relevance to our current journey is that of opportunity cost. The opportunity cost is the value of what you have chosen not to do. If you spend money on one product, your opportunity cost is the missed value of what you could then not afford to buy. For entrepreneurs, assessing their opportunity costs is everything. They have limited resources and must use them in the best way to increase the chances of success. If they make the wrong choices they will run out of resources and go broke.

As a race, the cost of choices we are currently making is destruction, loss of assets, loss of species and loss of life that will result from accelerating climate change. Our opportunity cost for delaying action is that we will have to cope with and repair the damaged world later.

Which of the world's assets are we destroying each year we delay? If we knew for sure the answer to this question, maybe we would act differently. Maybe the psychology of imminence would become strong enough.

Dr. Shamshad Akhtar is the Executive Secretary of the United Nations Economic and Social Commission for Asia and the Pacific (ESCAP). The role of ESCAP is to build a resilient Asia and the Pacific founded on shared prosperity, social equity and sustainability for its 53 member states. Established in 1947 in Shanghai, China to assist in post-war economic reconstruction ESCAP's ultimate goal is to lift 680 million people across the region out of poverty.

Dr Akhtar's vision sees the world grabbing the entrepreneurial opportunity to change the view of climate change action from '*burden sharing into opportunity sharing*'. That we grasped this opportunity was the key turning point in building her world which '*delivers holistically on our economic, social and environmental sustainable development goals.*'

To be able to take these opportunities on our journey into the unknown will require many lessons to be learnt from successful entrepreneurs. The bureaucratic structures of government and big corporations were not designed to be able to cope with this challenge. To succeed, we must take a chance, risk some failures and adopt an entrepreneurial attitude to building our future. It is within our control if we chose to take it.

Windows of Opportunity
United Nations Economic and Social Commission for Asia and the Pacific (ESCAP)
Bangkok, Thailand

Climate change tested human civilization. In 2015, we had recognized that it was a global threat and that it must be tackled by global partnerships for a more sustainable future. The cost of inaction was clearly far greater than the cost of acting now, but we needed to rise above our own immediate concerns as individuals to deal with collective challenges. Fortunately, scientific and technological advancements enabled actors, such as the IPCC, to deliver unequivocal and timely warnings to mobilize the necessary global action.

Combatting climate change was also a fight against our own misperceptions that there was no future beyond carbon; that mitigation was an economic burden and implementable only at the expense of our own self-interests. Climate change was a challenge for that generation, evident from the devastating signs that the impacts of climate change were already upon them.

Stretching the time horizon of development planning beyond the era of cheap fossil fuel was the critical step in turning climate change mitigation and adaptation from burden sharing into opportunity sharing. This approach helped us to seize the rapidly closing window of opportunity to shape the future we have created in 2100 that is not only low-carbon, but that also delivers holistically on our economic, social and environmental sustainable development goals. Our world in 2100 is the product of the global partnerships that emerged and the new global climate deal that was forged in Paris at the end of 2015.

Chapter 10

CHANGING THINKING

The only journey is the one within.

Rainer Maria Rilke

Chapter 10

CHANGING THINKING

On the Other Side of the Dark Decades
Paul Gilding, Sustainability Advocate and Author
Formerly CEO, Greenpeace International
Tasmania, Australia

It was at once surprising, yet so predictable, how fast it all unravelled in the period 2015-2025. Despite so many warnings since 1960, it still came as a shock to many. While most focused on climate change as the key threat, in the end galloping inequality brought the system down and triggered the dark decades of conflict and crisis. The conflict and loss of trust in the elites caused by inequality made it so much harder to deal the economic restructuring climate change required. For those born after 2050, it's hard to imagine how society got itself into such a mess.

In 2100 no one questions the imperative of working within ecological limits, nor the need to keep inequality in that balance point between sufficient motivation to strive for better while avoiding the intense resentments caused when it gets out of control and becomes so blatantly unfair.

Of course we still have social issues that require attention and no doubt we always will, as we pursue ever-higher levels of awareness and quality of human development. But the inherent stability of the system today, where the basics of food supply, energy and social cohesion are actively managed to the benefit of the whole is such an obvious idea no one would question the core of our approach. But in the end we managed the transition, despite the challenges, proving yet again the endless potential of people to come together for the greater good and the indomitable nature of the human spirit.

Paul Gilding has been working on environmental and social issues in many different ways for over 35 years. He started as a teenager chaining himself to the gates of the South African Embassy to protest against apartheid and went on to lead Greenpeace International and build a successful international consulting business. In 2011, he published *The Great Disruption*, which set out how he saw things happening over the coming decades. His vision above reflects the content of that book.

Paul's vision demonstrates how thinking changed through the century. By 2100, he sees that no-one questions both working within ecological limits and managing to keep inequality to within acceptable limits. He sees that the ultimate turning point will not be driven by extreme weather events, as many of the authors here suggest, but rather by '*galloping inequality*'. The thinking in 2100 has changed and his future is focussed on pursuing '*ever-higher levels of awareness and quality of human development.*'

The paradigm shifts that are required to take the global population from its current state to any one of the visions included here are massive. It will be no easy task to remove society's underlying assumption that prosperity is created by increasing monetary wealth, owning more stuff and building more things. To date, this philosophy has worked well for the small portion of countries and people that have become wealthy. It is physically impossible for the same philosophy to now be adopted by the rest of the world. This is not a matter of idealism or choice: it is just that the resources available on this planet are not sufficient to allow this.

How paradigm shifts happen is a fascinating area of study. Just like everything else, the process is based more on emotional reactions than on rational thought.

Thomas Kuhn introduced the phrase, paradigm shift, in his 1962 book, *The Structure of Scientific Revolutions*. Kuhn suggested that the progress of science was not steady and cumulative towards greater understanding but instead had major discontinuities. There were periods of 'normal' activity with acceptance of the underlying principles established and 'business as usual' incremental progress. There were also periods of 'revolutionary' thinking when those underlying assumptions are challenged and changed.

Kuhn's thinking was borne of study into how Aristotle had historically approached simple mechanics and why his thought process was so alien to that deemed as obvious in Kuhn's day.

When anomalies in scientific research appear, as they often do, they are generally explained through incremental changes to the current way of thinking or by showing experimental error or uncertainty. In non-scientific circles, it can even lead to the response that 'the exception proves the rule'. Over longer periods, however, unresolved anomalies accumulate to a point where some scientists begin to question the paradigm itself.

This leads to a time of crisis when those wedded to the old way of thinking are under threat and those driving the new paradigm are fighting against the accepted norms. The resolution of this situation is the revolutionary change in the world-view that replaces the old paradigm with one that better fits the world.

It is clear that there will need to be a paradigm shift to adjust to the 'new normal'. The established world view remains that growth is good, consumption drives prosperity and rich countries are happy countries. The people advocating a different future are seen as disruptive, unsettling and even dangerous. Some of the fossil fuel industry reactions to Bill McKibben's divestment campaign are great examples of this.

However, when the paradigm does shift, it shifts irrevocably. People look back on the old way with disbelief. Like Aristotle's view of mechanics, looking back from the year 2100 will lead to disbelief at the accepted norms of the world in the 2010s.

A key part of Kuhn's theory was that a shift only happens when there is something better, which fits the evidence more completely, to move towards. If the only evidence is just that the current view of the world is not perfect, then people will stick with that view. So our visions of the future set out here might provide that better-fitting paradigm that accommodates the accumulating anomalies.

By giving people a world view that fits with their values and what they really want from life, there is just a chance that we can shift thinking before we are forced to.

Gilding does not see this as the likely outcome. Instead he sees the current system collapsing to a point where it is so clear to everyone that the current paradigm is inadequate that they are forced to change.

As we saw in Chapter 6, this is the fall-back position. If we do nothing else, this is what will happen. The challenge is now to try and bring the paradigm shift forward to avoid the suffering that will otherwise entail.

Raising Consciousness
John Harradine
Social Ecologist & Counsellor,
Sydney, Australia

Deciding what we stand for without standing against anyone or anything opens the door to find solutions that benefit all and the planet. Somebody has to start and hold that sentiment, no matter what, for it to take hold. Many have already and we look up to them as inspirational leaders; Nelson Mandela, Mikhail Gorbachev, Mahatma Ghandi, Martin Luther King all with the flaws of their humanity just like ourselves. It is the embracing of these flaws without judgement but using them to course correct our lives that spurs us to our own inspiration, no matter how big or small a difference we can make to our world.

If we predicate change on what somebody else will or won't do we are doomed to powerlessness. Awareness, awareness and more awareness of our unconscious drivers is central to personal uplift-ment. Neuroscience has shown that ninety to ninety-five per cent of our personal strategy is unconscious and the unconscious always wins over the conscious mind. Awareness raises our consciousness so just start there. See what judgements you can suspend about what's 'right' and what's 'wrong'. Replace notions of what's 'right' with 'this works' and what's 'wrong' with 'this doesn't'.

So just get up one more time than you feel ready to and stand for what you believe in. If you must be against anything, be against 'againstness'. Start with the smallest experiments that help you feel successful and build from there.

Delivering change and facilitating paradigm shifts requires standing up against the crowd. It can result in powerful people feeling threatened as their work might be discredited or forgotten. It can take a very long time to go from pointing out the first anomalies to getting widespread community acceptance and support - for the paradigm to change.

To be part of this change, as the authors here are, requires resilience and determination. The trait of stubbornness is one that is extremely useful for this. I am fortunate to having been extremely stubborn from birth, a fact not always fully appreciated by all of my family! The authors in this book that have been active in the sector since the 1970s or 1980s have displayed exceptional stubbornness to stick to the course of what they believe.

To permanently change the long-term thinking of others requires connections at a deeper level than we see in everyday marketing. Stories need to connect with the base assumptions and values of the listener to help them focus on what is important to them. Changing the assumptions and values can however force people into uncomfortable situations where they feel the need to go against the prevalent culture.

Writing in New Scientist in January 2015, developmental psychologist Cristine Lagare from the University of Texas at Austin said, '*Rituals provide a very visible means of identifying who is a group member and who isn't. They help define us as a group, reflect our group values, and demonstrate shared commitment to the group.*'

For a species like us that is dependent on social support, this is crucial for survival.

Lagare has completed work looking at the connection between rituals and the puzzling phenomenon of children copying activities precisely even when some of the steps to a procedure are clearly superfluous - or '*causally opaque*'. Her contention is that the exact copying of behaviour is designed to ensure that they are seen as socially part of the group and not an outsider

This is why it is hard to change thinking. You have to go against the group, break the ritual, proclaim that you are no 'longer one of us'. Like leaving a sect, there is no way back.

I first met John Harradine in 2005 when he was providing executive coaching to managers at the corporate energy company where I worked at the time. He challenged my thinking about my frustrations with the reluctance of others to accept some of the changes I thought were important. He also helped me to start thinking about self-awareness and to better understand my own motivations and behaviours. His input was partly responsible for me starting on my current journey and getting away from what I found to be a toxic and unconstructive business culture. Whilst I am not sure the company considered this to be a success, it was certainly a beneficial move for me! John continues to help others make a difference for themselves and their worlds.

John broke the rules with his vision, but I guess that is his right. His vision provides the means of changing your personal thinking. It takes away the competition, the winning and suggests that to make a real difference in whatever you want to, you need to just stay the course. Adjust the sails as needed as the winds blow from different directions but keep on your journey with a good heart and you will create benefits along the way.

His key lessons are to work on understanding yourself, suspend judgements of others and their behaviours and to keep going – to *'get up one more time than you feel ready to'*.

This is of course easier said than done but it is powerful advice. Whether about climate change or anything else, if you want to change your world for the better, then these principles will stand you in good stead.

An Australia Worth Living in

Jacqui Hoepner, Centre for the Public Awareness of Science,
Australian National University
Canberra, Australia

There was a period where it seemed impossible. I think we were all scared Australia would be left behind. Trying desperately to sell our coal when the rest of the world had moved on. The government had wound back the carbon tax and investment in renewable energy was at an all-time low.

But with a lot of community involvement and protest, we finally started to see a shift. Complacency and uncertainty gave way to long-term commitments and a shared belief in real change. We realised we couldn't keep going the way we were headed - the world we'd created wouldn't be worth living in.

It seemed impossible that we would be able to mobilise so much support from the public and force the hand of policymakers.

Within a few months of the 2019 election, we saw real change. And everyone was ready for it. Efforts of climate scientists, communicators and other stakeholders in bringing the public along this time around were remarkable. They had learnt the lessons of the past. They ensured the public was just as passionate as they were - by providing meaningful reasons to act as well as achievable and practical solutions.

We can be proud of the world we're leaving behind.

The Australian National Centre for the Public Awareness of Science (CPAS) conducts diverse science communication research and science outreach activities. It promotes active communication about science in the public arena, through many mediums from social media to science shows to academic journal papers. Jacqui Hoepner works in the 'Communication and the environment' group and looks at projects such as the best methods for inclusive, meaningful environmental and climate dialogue.

Jacqui's vision focuses on how public engagement was the key to getting meaningful change in Australia. This will be critical in all countries.

Once you have the inner resolve to work towards a paradigm shift, the next challenge is how to communicate this in a way that attracts others to want to join you on your journey.

The challenge for leaders is not only how to tell the story but also how to communicate through the short attention spans of the media.

In the political run-up to 1992 US presidential election, research at the University of California showed the length of the average television sound bite had dropped from 43 seconds during the 1968 presidential election to just nine seconds during the 1988 election. In 2011 a Journalism Studies Journal found that the typical political sound bite had shrunk to just eight seconds.

It is very hard to mount a coherent meaningful argument in eight seconds especially when the topic is one that is complex, long dated and non-linear!

Will Grant, whose vision was included in Chapter 4 is Jacqui's colleague at CPAS. Some of his research is looking at how using 'Long Conversations' might impact the dialogue about climate change.

Grant sees that many scientists and public policy makers do not understand why people are so confused about what they see as obvious. The project took *'leading climate scientists and experts to rural towns around Australia to talk about climate change — discussing the complex science and policy issues. The idea was to build a space where members of the community could discuss climate change with leading researchers. They could ask questions, provide ideas and discuss their needs, fears and desires on the issue.'*

The aims were not only to help provide good information to local towns, but more importantly to help the science and policy makers to better understand how to communicate in a way that will be heard.

Just providing straightforward rational information, which is what scientists are trained to do, does not work. To be heard, understood and accepted the information must be conveyed in the form of engaging stories. The facts are important but they are worthless if they are communicated ineffectively.

★ ★ ★

Effective communication is of course different in different situations. It depends on the composition of the audience and what cultural contexts are in place. Clearly the style of discussion is different if chatting in the pub, speaking with energy managers or with political leaders, even if the core content and the facts used are the same.

To achieve the desired outcome, there is a two-step strategy that works regardless of who the audience happens to be. Firstly, you have to decide how you want your audience to feel. For instance, do you want them to be inspired, to feel confident, committed or excited or do you want them to feel safe and cared for? Once you have decided how you want your audience to feel, you need to design a way of telling the information you have in a way that will inspire these emotions.

I have used this most successfully with entrepreneurs who are going into pitch for investment, for customers or for partners. The emotional reactions you want for each audience is slightly different and it is that which can guide the way the story is told.

For speaking with people about the transition to the low carbon world, maybe you want to make them feel excited about the opportunities that will exist for them, reassured that the changes will be beneficial, safe for their families and engaged in the process of change so they can get the benefits more quickly.

The communication challenge becomes even more complicated when it is also being delivered across different nations and delivered in multiple languages. It is therefore not surprising that achieving a global consensus on a way forward that requires a global paradigm shift is taking some time.

In different countries, the opportunities and threats of climate change are seen very differently. As we have seen, poorer countries are generally more susceptible to the changes that are already happening and so are keen for action but do not have the resources to have much impact. In the rich countries, there are many people who see the changes as a threat and so lobby hard against politicians trying to win popular support.

There is another area of difference between the rich countries and the ones still struggling with poverty. The assumption that all countries aspire to live like Americans is being challenged. The world does not have the resources to allow this to happen. To some extent, this theme has already been raised by Sam Bickersteth and Claudia Martinez in their visions above. Our final vision for the chapter sets out clearly how this might unfold.

The Global Institute for Tomorrow (GIFT) provides insights into how the world will change with the shift of economic and political power from the West to the East and how this will require the reshaping of the rules of global capitalism. Chandran Nair is the founder of GIFT and the author of the 2010 book, *Consumptionomics: Asia's Role in Reshaping Capitalism and Saving the Planet.*

Chandran's vision below builds on this theme. His neatly phrased '*Austerity for All*' focuses on delivering the basic needs to all of humanity, reducing the focus on gadgets and monetary wealth and delivering dignity for all. Freedom as we the rich now know it is challenged but is replaced by a wider meaning that provides freedom from misery for all. This is a very different future to the Green Growth scenario outlined in the next chapter.

This vision certainly challenges the assumptions of many in the West. It will need many stories to be told to be able to gain the emotional support for it to become real. Chandran does not see the change as happening quickly but rather as a slow realisation through the first half of this century.

Changing thinking and the assumptions held by many is a challenging task. It is not something that can be controlled but rather is an example of Meadows' need to dance with the system. Creating and sharing meaningful, positive visions is the only way to engage the wider community and get them to design the future that they want to see.

Austerity for All

Chandran Nair
Global Institute for Tomorrow
Hong Kong

*In 2100 we now have six billion Asians and Africans living lives that
are very unlike the American or European lives of a century earlier.
That was once thought of as something to aspire to but those
who understood resource constraints knew that it could only spell
disaster. Our low carbon world of today began with the premise
that the developing world rejects the old West-promulgated model
of economic growth - one that hinged on promoting relentless
consumption through the under-pricing of resources and the
externalizing of true costs.*

*But what replaced it? Answering that question is what policy
makers in Asia in the first half of the twenty-first century made their
priority. Their answers included the rejection of the fashionable idea
of an 'Asian Century' wherein the region aped western economic
aspirations.*

*During the century, the very idea of prosperity was redefined and
the old economic theories were replaced by what became known as
'austerity for all'. Austerity for all was a political project to create a
collective attitude of "living within ones means" and replaced feel
good slogans such as "inclusive growth" with real commitments
to meeting the most basic needs for all. Among these needs were
a safe and secure food supply, water and sanitation, basic housing
with a minimum access to electricity, healthcare and education. This
was only achieved when polices were put in place where constraints
were respected and the collective welfare was allowed to override
individual rights and thereby even challenges old notions about
freedom.*

This world remains messy but it is one in which billions are now removed from daily misery, empowered and given dignity – thereby becoming free. It is a world far removed from the obsession with technology that, at one stage, resulted in more people owning mobile phones than working toilets or decent homes. It is one where more people are interconnected by sewers and potable water systems than fiber optic cables. It is also one where car ownership is not considered a human right. It is a world more physically prepared to cope with the havoc that climate change has wrought on the planet because the disenfranchised are now more resilient.

Chapter 11

CHANGING BEHAVIOUR

One does not discover new lands without consenting to lose sight of the shore for a very long time.

André Gide

Chapter 11

CHANGING BEHAVIOUR

Green Growth

Yvo de Boer
Director-General, Global Green Growth Institute
Seoul, Korea

In the early twenty-first century, it became clear that the existing model of growth could not be sustained by the planet and its ever-growing population. The consequences of this traditional growth model, in the form of inequality, climate change and natural resource degradation, had created economic and environmental stresses that would soon be impossible to overcome. Taking a step back from the precipice, the global community made the historic shift toward a green growth pathway. Countries chose to pursue development in a way that simultaneously advanced economic growth, environmental sustainability, poverty reduction and social inclusiveness. At the time, this model was referred to as "green growth". Today, in 2100, as a result of the global community's cooperation, conviction and commitment to sustainable development, the model is simply referred to as "growth".

I think of the town of San Vicente on Palawan Island in the Philippines. A century ago, this coastal town, whose inhabitants depended on fishing and farming for much of their livelihoods, was highly vulnerable to sea-level rises, increasing instances of coastal inundation, flooding and drought. In the face of these threats, San Vicente acknowledged the need to 'climate proof' the local economy and implemented measures to modernize its farming and fishery sectors and mitigate disaster risk. The success of these inclusive efforts served as a template to reduce vulnerability and create inclusive, environmentally sustainable growth in towns and cities throughout the Philippines.

In their 2011 book, *Sustainable leadership: Honeybee and locust approaches*, Gayle Avery and Harald Bergsteiner set out a theory of how the behaviour of companies can fall into two camps when considering sustainability: the 'honey bees' and the 'locusts'. This provides an important distinction in the way in which the behaviour of our corporate and civic leaders will need to change to deliver on the visions set out in this book.

Bee colonies consist of a queen, drones and workers who can produce more than 90kg of surplus honey a year. At the same time, the humble bee pollinates the plants that provide much of the food for humans, animals and insects. Honeybees are an essential part of our ecosystem. Through cooperation, the honeybee is highly productive for all.

The locust is usually a benign, solitary insect. However, under the right environmental conditions, millions of locusts congregate into thick, ravenous swarms that devastate healthy crops and cause major agricultural damage. The apparently benign locust can have a devastating impact on its environment causing famine and starvation. 'Locust' leaders play 'hard ball' and get short-term results by being ruthless.

The honey bee approach can deliver transformational change that thrives through working in collaboration with stakeholders and the environment to create long-term benefits for all. The locust approach is more rapacious where every available resource is exploited and, ultimately, the model of existence becomes unviable. Locusts subscribe to the philosophy of short-term returns and bees look to creating long-term 'wealth' in multiple ways.

The concept of Green Growth is similar to that of the honeybee. Green Growth pursues development in a way that simultaneously advances '*economic growth, environmental sustainability, poverty reduction and social inclusiveness.*' The Global Green Growth Institute (GGGI) is an international organization dedicated to supporting and promoting strong, inclusive and sustainable economic growth in developing countries and emerging economies. It was established in 2012 at the Rio+20 United Nations Conference on Sustainable Development.

GGGI's Director-General is Yvo de Boer, who as the predecessor of Christiana Figueres led the international process to respond to climate change in the role of Executive Secretary of the United Nations Framework Convention on Climate Change (UNFCCC) from 2006 to 2010. This included the Copenhagen Conference of the Parties in 2009.

Yvo's vision is one of the transition to green growth, or just *'growth'* as it is known in 2100. The concept here has close parallels with that envisioned by Sam Bickersteth in Chapter 9 where he talked of a Zero Emissions, Zero Poverty strategy. It does not however fit with Chandran Nair's austerity for all and others who believe chasing growth, whether sustainable or not, is not a viable option. My view is that Green Growth is a valuable and essential first step that enables many otherwise reluctant parties to engage.

It is also in stark contrast to some economists and politicians who promote the idea that economic growth does not need to be restrained; we just need to find the right technological 'silver bullet' that will allow us to continue growing without limit. The bullet might be geo-engineering to suck carbon dioxide out of the atmosphere or a single technology that replaces the need for fossil fuels in one fell swoop.

The reliance on technology without an acknowledgement that humans need to change their behaviour is a risky strategy. It is possible that it will work and the 'brilliant' solution will be found that enables unlimited growth. However, in the meantime we will be travelling much further along the road to catastrophe whilst we wait.

The Green Growth Knowledge Platform (GGKP) is a global network of international organizations and experts that is trying to work out the best ways to put the theory of green growth into practice. It is based in Geneva and was established in January 2012 by the GGGI, the Organisation for Economic Co-operation and Development, the United Nations Environment Programme and the World Bank.

In its third annual conference in Italy in January 2015 it considered specific fiscal policies that can assist in the transition. The conclusions are published in a report online and cover topics such as how to use financial policy to increase clean energy investment, water resource management, clean technology development, low emissions transport and biodiversity protection.

There was a session on behavioural change that looked at when and why populations will accept environmental taxes to drive change. A case study of how not to do this was the now-repealed carbon pricing mechanism in Australia. The general population did not understand the need for it and its benefits and so it was open to political attack.

The report recommends that, to achieve support for environmental taxes, policymakers must provide *'information about how taxes work, earmarking revenue for environmental purposes and public investment in environmentally friendly technologies.'* The Australian scheme did reasonable well in the latter two points but failed on the first.

So the key to moving to Yvo de Boer's 'growth' or Avery's 'honeybee approach' is to spread information on the benefits widely and consistently. As Benjamin Disraeli said in a speech at the Manchester Athenaeum in 1844:

> *It is knowledge that influences and equalises the social condition of man; that gives to all, however different their political position, passions which are in common, and enjoyments which are universal.*

This of course comes back - again - to effective story telling of a positive future!

Pilot Vision
Mike Duggan, Sustainability Specialist,
Gladstone Ports Corporation
Gladstone, Australia

My Father has always had a love of flight and some of my fondest memories have been shaped in the cockpit of his Cessna 172. He taught me from a young age to have 'pilot vision': planning, looking and probing the world. In the year 2100 people have learned to use pilot vision to plot the course towards a more balanced and resilient world. Here are my Father's seven principles of pilot vision:

1. *Local Visions: we constructed regional visions that allow us to better manage our local natural and social environment for the benefit of the community.*

2. *Situational Awareness: we became keenly aware of our circumstances that have helped us to understand the impacts of our decisions.*

3. *The Power in Planning: we slowed down to speed up. The slow food, slow life movement has become the norm and we now take more time to evaluate our social, environmental and economic decisions.*

4. *Soaring with Technology: we utilise technology to complement and advance our goals.*

5. *Communication: we learned to communicate with each other using a strong 'ecolect' and understanding of how to make balanced economic, social and environmental decisions.*

6. *The Power of Knowledge: we improved education such that all people now have the ability to engage in lifelong learning and develop core individual strengths.*

7. *Flying with Trust: we learned to trust in ourselves, our wider family units, communities and our 'instruments' to create a just society that values individuality and liberty above all else.*

In Chapter 9, we considered the aspects that were common in expert entrepreneurs. Entrepreneurs change the behaviour of those they deal with. Maybe they change people's buying patterns, or change people's worldview on how things work. A successful entrepreneur will change the paradigm of the sector they work in and will create benefits that can be in terms of investment returns, social returns or environmental returns.

One of the five common traits found by this work by Sarasvathy was that they took a '*Pilot-in-the-plane*' approach where they just focussed on what they could control and did not worry about predictions on what they could not control. This effectual worldview is rooted in the belief that the future is made rather than being found or predicted.

Mike Duggan is a Canadian who now lives and works in Australia. He has spent years working on leading sustainability initiatives including certification and labelling projects. His take on how the world has changed its thinking is based on how his father flew a plane and fits neatly with Sarasvathy's entrepreneurial trait.

Mike's mixture of slowing down and considering all aspects combined with the use of technology and the development of the 'ecolect' provides a wide ranging framework that would clearly be effective once achieved. The challenge is how we enable this change in behaviour to happen.

Professor Dexter Dunphy of the University of Technology, Sydney has researched ways that this can happen. In his 2003 book, *Organisational Change for Corporate Sustainability*, he sets out a comprehensive plan for change agents to start transitioning their organisations. Whilst the title is very dry, the content is still very current and provides an engaging and practical guide to help drive effective behaviour change in organisations.

Dunphy set out six phases that companies can go through on their way to becoming a '*sustaining corporation*'. Starting with rejection and non-responsiveness, the phases then go through compliance, efficiency and enlightened self-interest as companies journey towards providing positive returns for investors, the environment and society.

His advice for change agents is to work like the best butchers and '*work with the grain rather than against it*'. By this he means you have to work within the system of the organisation and influence and educate rather than trying to force people to accept a different way of thinking. He suggests that to be an effective leader of change, you '*need clarity of vision, knowledge of what we wish to change and the skills to implement the changes. But none of these can be fully effective without maturity and wisdom.*' He warns however that '*being a change agent is not for the faint-hearted. Emotional resilience is a fundamental requirement.*'

Dunphy also talks about the important role of creating visioning capabilities within the organisation. It is only through developing a compelling and engaging vision that people are attracted towards the future that is being suggested.

In my corporate career, I dismally failed to achieve the changes I saw as necessary. Looking back at that time, it is clear that I failed on every hurdle suggested by Dunphy. In particular I worked against the grain and lacked much maturity. The battle scars of being a failed intrapreneur have been extremely useful ever since.

Other battle scars are the result of our quest to get sufficient healthcare for Kate. Few organisations in the health industry would come anywhere close to Dunphy's sustaining corporation despite the good intentions of the employees. Whilst effective for trauma cases, the health system in most developed countries is weak when it comes to increasing the well-being of the citizens. It is stuck in the limited paradigm that it is there to save lives rather than the paradigm that it is there to improve the quality of life. There are change agents working hard on this issue. However, changing the behaviour of the entrenched power structures of the medical profession may well be as difficult as to change the paradigm of growth.

★ ★ ★

To me, one of the most impressive leaders that have inspired people towards a goal is not a world leader or even someone who has received any real attention. However, through his words and his actions he has created a large group of people with a world view and a goal to create a better world.

Kevin Tutt was the headmaster at Prince Alfred College in Adelaide for over a decade. Three of his students, including my son Jack, have written their visions here. He created an environment that was focussed on what the boys lucky enough to grow up in a rich country might give back to a world that is less fortunate. As part of the change he created he focussed on being kind to yourself and to others and to work hard to achieve what you can. This was instilled in the culture of the staff and the respect and care engendered in the boys.

Kevin's favourite quote was Zig Ziglar's '*Your attitude, not your aptitude, will determine your altitude.*' In a school where the focus is on finding each student's strengths and helping them to achieve, this is a great mantra.

This is also useful when considering the challenge of climate change communication. Whilst the technical solutions might be seen as the human race's aptitude to solve the problem, it will only be our attitude and emotional response that will enable us to achieve success.

Kevin was a fine role model at the school and, for me, the greatest impact he will have on the boys there was when he resigned from his highly respected post in 2013 to become head of teaching at the Cambodian Children's Fund in Phnom Penh. He is now using these same skills to inspire 1500 orphaned and disadvantaged children to achieve and take their place in the world. After talking so much about giving back it was sad to see him leave but wonderful to see him be true to his beliefs.

★ ★ ★

One of the greatest challenges for anyone trying to change behaviour is how to find the right emotional response to transform resistance into support. If you get it wrong, then the change agent can be seen as difficult at best or unreliable or dangerous. As Dunphy says in his book '*Changing entrenched power structures can be a career-threatening experience.*'

As we have discussed, the rational arguments for changing are clear but business decisions are always emotional, if sometimes also rational. Currently the primary emotion at play for many incumbent businesses and successful people is that change means the loss of profits, loss of power or loss of position. The task of the change agent is to make this dominant emotion one that means change is good and beneficial. Attraction towards the better world is probably the best way to achieve this.

Another way of getting an emotional response is to use the marketer's trick of playing on the fear of missing out. Marketers use this by suggesting that if you do not buy this product you will miss the bargain or not be as cool as your peers. To help people see the benefit of taking action on climate change, stories can be told of how forward-looking companies have already changed and those that do not change are being left behind.

This can be enhanced by sharing stories of success whether in the same country or around the world. Most businesses, politicians and communities rarely want to take the risk of being the first to try something new. Being able to provide reassurance that the transition is underway elsewhere can be highly effective in increasing engagement.

Finally, a communication tool that can also be effective is to position the transition as just normal business evolution. Industries and technologies come and go and a cursory glance at all the companies that have failed provides a great list of case studies for anyone with doubts. Companies that do not evolve and adapt to new environments do not survive. Kodak and Nokia are examples of companies that missed the moment to move into their own futures.

With this message, it becomes critical for business to change to ensure their survival. Those working with the outdated technologies and outdated business models will themselves become outdated. Services will continue to be provided, workers will continue to be employed, but these will be done by new emerging companies that have stayed ahead of the curve whilst the incumbent companies fail. We will look more at the fate of incumbents in our next chapter.

★ ★ ★

One of the assumptions underlying much of the argument in this book is that our resources are limited to what our planet can provide. Whilst a few of our contributors see permanent colonies on other planets, most assume that we are largely stuck with that we have been given.

The classic 1972 publication, Limits to Growth, of which Donella Meadows was one of the authors, set out the thesis that we would be unable to continue to grow indefinitely. The research that formed the basis of the book assessed a number of scenarios for future growth up to 2100. Most of these scenarios saw ongoing growth of both the global population and the global economy until around 2030 when there was a significant decline or collapse. To maintain the levels of wealth and population after that date required '*drastic measures for environmental protection*'.

Limits to Growth was commissioned by a think tank called the Club of Rome. Researchers working out of the Massachusetts Institute of Technology built a computer model to track the world's economy and environment. Called World3, this computer model was cutting edge for its time.

Since its release, the book has been criticised as being overly pessimistic and a Doomsday fantasy. People such as the controversial and largely discredited figure, Bjorn Lomborg, have stated that it should be consigned to the "dustbin of history".

However, 2014 research from the University of Melbourne has found that the book's forecasts have been remarkably accurate when looking at its business as usual scenario. The research undertaken by Dr Graham Turner suggests that, if we continue unchanged, the early stages of global collapse are likely to start appearing soon.

A scenario that was not considered by this study was that we would be able to access and exploit on a significant scale the resources of other planets. This would presumably solve some, if not all of the resource and environmental limits of just a single planet.

In his vision, Professor Barry Brook envisions this future. Barry is a climate scientist at the University of Tasmania and has been a long-time advocate of transitioning to nuclear fuels. His vision does not see a place for renewable energy technologies but rather the continued use of fossil fuels until a time when nuclear is advanced enough to take over. He also sees the move to space and the use of the resources from there as allowing as to 'pull back' from human's impact on the world's environment.

Barry is one of the eighteen environmental scholars who published the 'Ecomodernist Manifesto' in 2015. This sets out an alternative, technology-focused approach to conservation. The manifesto sets out a picture of using technology to reduce the impact on the environment without reducing amenity for humans. As Barry says, '*These processes are central to economic modernisation, improved human welfare and environmental protection. Together they offer the prospect of allowing people to mitigate climate change, to spare nature and to alleviate global poverty.*'

There is much sense to this philosophy and given that I spend most of my time working with amazing cleantech solutions, I certainly understand the sentiment. However, the technology fixes alone will not resolve the challenge of re-designing society to work in a more sustainable, equitable and caring way. It resonates clearly at a rational level but is limited once we consider the emotional elements also at play.

For me, this trust in the technology solution alone feels like a dangerous gamble. Another fifty years of unabated fossil fuel use will put us so far along the road to catastrophe that we will have caused too much irreparable damage.

In addition, the concept of taking the philosophy used to date to exploit all available resources to other planets may well be possible, but destroying other planets in the same way as we are doing to this one feels as though we are not learning from our mistakes.

Barry has a clear and in-depth understanding of the consequences of climate change but appears unable to see how we will be able to change behaviour sufficiently to make the changes needed. His position is that we will have to wait for technology to allow us to keep going on the 'business as usual' path and seek to defeat the limits to growth.

New Resources

Professor Barry Brook, Chair of Environmental Sustainability
University of Tasmania
Hobart, Australia

The great 'power-down' never did happen. Yes, there were short-term supply crises with oil and gas, and increasingly dogged protests as each new coal project was pursued. But the hydrocarbons kept flowing, and stacking up, at least for the first few decades of the twenty-first century, as we found ever more inventive ways of squeezing and milling it out of ancient geological traps.

But set against this dismal 'progress' was an emerging realization of the astounding potential of nuclear fission. When finally done right, it proved to be cheap, safe, massively scalable and inexhaustible. By the 2060s, we had an abundance of zero-carbon power, which was just as well, because planetary rehabilitation was an energy-hungry task.

We geo-engineered, we intensified agricultural production, we built upwards, and virtually. Space—'cyber' and 'outer'—were the vast vistas of the next economy. And it was the visionary entrepreneurs that ended up taking us to space—permanently—opening up a virtually unlimited supply of raw materials and living space for the future of humanity. On Earth, our footprint shrank, as we pulled back from our encroachment of wildlife and habitats and let nature gradually reclaim large swathes of the planet. We simply didn't need it anymore, and it was time to give back.

Chapter 12

THE FATE OF INCUMBENTS

Far better is it to dare mighty things, to win glorious triumphs, even though checkered by failure... than to rank with those poor spirits who neither enjoy nor suffer much, because they live in a gray twilight that knows not victory nor defeat.

Theodore Roosevelt

Chapter 12

THE FATE OF INCUMBENTS

Climate Crimes

Professor Peter Doherty AC
Joint winner of the Nobel Prize in Physiology or Medicine in 1996
Australian of the Year in 1997
University of Melbourne
Melbourne, Australia

The eminent international lawyers who drew up the Climate Crimes Against Humanity Statutes way back in 2045 certainly hadn't made it easy for prosecutors or defense counsel. Even without any Statute of Limitations, most of these cases had to be tried after the real defendants were dead. Those early jurists had, of course foreseen that circumstance in mandating the confiscation of inherited wealth that could be traced back to a culpable individual. But, apart from the difficulties associated with following the money trail, and even with the capacity to penalize complicit bankers and accountants, the basic problem was the unfairness of recovering substantial amounts of money from people who were often completely innocent of any personal wrongdoing.

Still, the level of public rage was so overwhelming that there had to be some perception of retribution against those who had, for example, bought-up promising clean and green technologies to suppress them, or had benefitted from the aggressive marketing and distribution of fossil fuels. And the long-gone politicians who had allowed this to continue had, in the main, not left substantial estates. Apart from the odium attached to their names in the historical record - every school kid can list them – they paid no price.

The year 2100 saw the abandonment of the whole strategy. Prosecuting climate crimes had been a waste of time and effort, with no real deterrent effect or any other obvious benefit. We've learned our lesson and have moved on.

Incumbents have the privileged position of deciding whether they want to survive into the long-term or to maximise profits in the short-term. They do not always understand or consciously assess this choice, but it is theirs to make.

Sometimes it is entirely valid to just focus on meeting a short-term need and to not plan to be around forever. At an individual level, it is like saying you would prefer to live two happy years than to live for ten years in agony. Of course, with health there are complications on how religious influences impact euthanasia debates but that is probably getting beyond the scope of our discussion here.

Incumbent companies have the wealth, control and knowledge to adapt to changing conditions. By doing this, they may cannibalise their own revenue streams for a while but in the end they will have transitioned with the changing environment and will remain in business. Companies are built by pioneers that create new markets and meet unmet needs. Their founding is often a pioneering act. However, like the countries considered in Chapter 7, the pioneering spirit wanes with time and instead can be replaced by constraints and controls that limit the ability to continue to innovate and evolve. The company founders might be horrified by the lack of foresight demonstrated by the CEOs of their now huge corporations.

In 2013, I worked with a group of small Melbourne-based manufacturing companies exposed to the dying Australian automotive industry to help find some cleantech things for them to make. We reviewed over hundred companies and ended up working with ten of them. About half of these ten were already diversifying and were very engaged in the project and keen to make new connections and learn of new opportunities. The other half agreed to be involved but were not that interested saying that they had always worked for the auto industry and saw little reason to change. I found this latter attitude very frustrating as I could not get them to see that there soon would be no auto industry and no work for their businesses. Eventually however I realised that this was just the way business evolves. There is a binary outcome with companies either continually evolving or eventually failing. The companies that stand still and look backwards will go out of business and their employees will move to the forward-looking companies that are thriving. The losers in this are the owners and shareholders of the businesses that do not change.

As we will see later, for countries that do not adapt, the consequences are more severe.

The loss of investment, employment or health can lead to anger and frustration. Similarly, the loss of habitat and other detrimental environmental impacts can drive strong emotional responses. This has been seen in the determined environmental protests against the felling of trees, the building of dams or against polluting companies. Like grieving for a lost loved one, the grief cycle goes from initial denial, through stages of anger, bargaining, depression and finally acceptance.

The different stages of this cycle could be applied to the differing views on climate change. Denial is still evident from those who are unable to accept what science is telling them. The angry protests against fossil fuels companies maybe come from those in the second stage. Those seeking ways that do not challenge the economic growth paradigm by finding technology silver bullets are at the bargaining stage and our pessimists from earlier are sitting in the stage of depression. By 2100, many of our visions here have reached the acceptance stage of grief for the lost world and are busy rebuilding something better.

The anger stage can lead to calls for retribution. Peter Doherty's vision tells the story of how this need for retribution led to the investigation of climate crimes in the second half of the century. The furious search for someone to blame for destroying the climate and the lost way of life is something that can be easily imagined. However, exacting retribution is never sufficient to be able to move on and start again.

Peter Doherty is one Australia's fifteen Nobel Laureates for his work in the 1970s on how the body's immune cells protect against viruses. When not thinking about wider issues such as climate crimes, he continues to work in the Department of Microbiology and Immunology of the University of Melbourne. He also wrote the semi-autobiographical book, *The Beginner's Guide to Winning the Nobel Prize* that was published in 2005.

Renee Lertzman from Chapter 3 talks about the difficulty that people have over grieving about environmental loss. Because it is less tangible than the death of a person, people can struggle to pinpoint the cause and focus of their loss. She terms this inability to mourn as '*environmental melancholia*'.

This type of collective pain is not uncommon. South Africa's post-apartheid Truth and Reconciliation Commission is an example of how this type of grief can be effectively handled. Lertzman says, "*I'm not saying there should be one for climate or carbon, but there's a lot to be said for providing a means for people to talk together about climate change, to make it socially acceptable to talk about it.*"

Maybe instead of Peter's climate crimes, a Climate Truth and Reconciliation Tribunal would provide a more effective way to help the world move forward.

The Regenerative Economy

L. Hunter Lovins
President, Natural Capitalism Solutions
Colorado, USA

Today, in 2100, humanity is settling into the comforts of the Regenerative Economy, an economy in service to life. In contrast to the neo-liberal paradigm that saw every individual as sovereign, governments as evil, markets as perfect and greed as good, our economy now sees finance as a tool to serve the real economy that meets basic human needs, assuring dignity for all and the integrity of the planet's ecosystems as the basis of prosperity.

The fears in the early twenty-first century that humanity would go extinct by 2050 proved legitimate, but concerted action that began early in the second decade of the last century averted the crisis.

Humanity's success in its final exam built on the publication in 2015 of Regenerative Capitalism, by John Fullerton, which laid out the eight principles of place-based economies.

The Chinese led the world in the creation of the Ecological Civiliza-tion, investing billions in simultaneously cutting carbon emissions, reducing air pollution and creating jobs. The Mayor of Shanghai declared that the city would no longer use GDP as a metric of success, but rather job creation. Coal stocks lost 90 percent of their value, rewarding those farsighted investors who had already divested their ownership. Finally, Regenerative Agriculture, pioneered by Allan Savory, showed how holistic management could regenerate the world's grasslands as the second biggest carbon sink on the planet.

In the end, our low carbon future became possible far faster than anyone had thought possible.

L. Hunter Lovins is an author and has advocated for sustainable de-velopment for over 30 years. She co-founded the Rocky Mountain Institute which she led for 20 years and is now president of Natural Capitalism Solutions.

Hunter's vision of a regenerative economy in 2100 addresses how thinking has changed by then and how the currently accepted neo-liberal paradigms have changed. Finance is seen as just a tool to provide dignity and integrity across all our ecosystems and deliver a new form of prosperity. This is a theme that is revisited time and again by our authors as they see the dysfunctions of our current world being replaced with ways of living that consider more of what we really want.

Implied in the change of world view is that the organisations that evolve with this change of thinking will survive and even thrive. Those that continue to operate in the old paradigm will undoubtedly fall away like the automotive suppliers in Melbourne who wake one morning to find there are no customers left.

The incumbents that survive will find new business models with wider benefits. They will collaborate more freely and build more common wealth. By creating new ways of doing business, they will become their own creative destructors.

Similarly, the smart investors will move away early from companies that are reaching the end of their lifecycle and will deploy their capital to the industries of the future. As Hunter sees in her vision, there were many rewards for 'those farsighted investors who had already divested their ownership' of coal before it crashed. There should be no concern reserved for investors as part of the transition as they take the upside risks and wear the downside risks. The focus on incumbents that do not survive must instead be on the employees and to make sure that they able to transition to more forward-looking companies.

China's leadership is also a theme of this vision. I have visited China several times a year for most of the last decade. The support for environmental action there is in stark contrast to the current situation in Australia. There is strong government support at every level, very strong investor interest and many thriving and growing companies meeting the local and global needs. The drivers for this support for action are more around local pollution issues such as smog or polluted waterways but have now extended so that China is also becoming a leading force globally on climate change action.

The end for companies that do not adapt in China can be more sudden than elsewhere. In an effort to reduce smog levels, the government has shut down many factories that are using old technology that was acceptable only a few years ago. The owners of those companies probably feel very aggrieved at their sudden demise but, like all functioning governments, the needs of society as a whole takes precedence over the needs of any one individual.

Nordic Changes

Nina Harjula
Head of Development, Cleantech
Lahti Region Development LADEC
Lahti, Finland

It is year 2100 in Finland, a Nordic country which unfortunately gave in a bit to the changes in climate and has now lost some of its traditional Nordic characteristics, especially in the southern parts of the country.

But many good things have also happened in the last decades. Here's my top three:

1. ***Understanding the value of resources and materials.*** *There is no longer such a concept as waste. Companies which utilized a combination of cleantech and industrial design (cleandesign) survived. These values go through product and process lifecycles to reserve and reuse materials and resources like minerals, energy and water.*

2. ***Digitalization and internet of everything.*** *Machines interact and react to, for example, moving people and material flows. We now communicate at a totally different level utilizing all data to systemize and control transportation, services and production.*

3. ***Circular economy and culture of sharing is everything and everywhere.*** *Circular economy thinking changed whole industries and businesses by turning their business models upside down. We might own less things now but by sharing things and services we actually have more and a better standard of living than ever.*

Finland is known for its innovation and forward-thinking. With its 5.5 million people it is the most sparsely populated country in the European Union. Although the country did not industrialise until the 1950s, it now has one of the highest per capita incomes in the world. The country also is a top performer in more meaningful metrics such as educational performance, economic competitiveness, civil liberties, quality of life and human development.

The reasons behind Finland's need for innovation stem from its small population and limited natural resources. It has had to be innovative and to think globally to survive and it has done this extremely well. In addition to its lauded education system, the country places a strong emphasis on backing start-ups and helping small companies to grow.

Nina Harjula runs the cleantech development initiatives for the Lahti region north of Helsinki. I know Nina through her role as a co-founder of the Global Cleantech Cluster Association. This global outlook is typical and is one of the reasons that the country has been so successful.

Nina's vision of the future sees a more functioning society driven by the disappearance of 'waste', the effective utilisation of data and the adoption of the circular economy concept. She provides a positive view of life in 2100 despite Finland having to 'give in a bit' to climate change.

The concept of a circular economy is one that is gaining traction globally. In China, there have been a number of government policies based on encouraging circular economy initiatives. The concept is now presented as an alternative development model by China's Nation Development and Reform Commission (NRDC). After eight years of trials at different scales, the model is now being rolled out across the country. There is an index for appraising four aspects of the circular economy: resource productivity, waste discharge, resource utilisation and waste treatment. China's leadership in this area is noted by Hunter Lovins above.

Elsewhere, the Ellen MacArthur Foundation in the UK is pushing the concept widely. MacArthur, known mostly for her single-handed round the world sailing, believes that the circular economy offers '*an opportunity to harness innovation and creativity to enable a positive, restorative economy*'.

A McKinsey & Co report in 2014 authored by Markus Zils digs into the practicalities of what the circular economy really means. Zils says that the circular economy seeks to systematically eradicate wastes '*throughout the life cycles and uses of products and their components*' and distinguish itself from the '*linear take–make–dispose economy, which wastes large amounts of embedded materials, energy, and labor*'.

The disruption in this transition will change the way companies operate. Nina notes that it '*changed whole industries and businesses by turning their business models upside down*'. For incumbents that do not understand how this might impact their businesses this might be fatal. More nimble companies that see the opportunities that this presents will thrive.

Similarly, countries that do not act will be left behind. The world is moving relentlessly towards being more resource efficient and low-carbon regardless of how politicians may fiddle. In the long-term, national Governments will have little impact on how we end up living. They do however have a huge impact on which industries will thrive locally and the relative wealth of nations.

Policy positions can drive the best 'efficient technologies' to relocate internationally or might help them grow and thrive at home. Countries such as Korea and Singapore are actively trying to poach the world's best low-carbon, clean technology companies as they see this advanced manufacturing as a great way of growing jobs, investment and trade. So short-term Government whims are incredibly important if you care in which country you live.

The fact that the dominant Kodak company did not transition to the new world of digital cameras did not stop the world changing. It just drove the company into an ever weakening position leading to its eventual bankruptcy in 2012. Decisions made in this decade will determine which countries may have their own 'Kodak moments'. The policy positions will either help industry align with global trends or will precipitate their long slow decline.

Providing incentives that assist new industries to grow and help old industries to evolve provides economic stability. To attract the community and then the government to this vision we need some great success stories and we need to tell them loudly and proudly. The good news is that there may just be some on the way. They will succeed because they have world-leading technologies that also create high value jobs, drive investment and deliver trading opportunities.

Some good Australian examples of this include BluGlass Ltd, a company developing world-leading LED manufacturing technology and RayGen Resources which, in 2014, signed a $60m deal in Shanghai to supply high-tech solar systems to China. Others include Z-Filter, a Perth based company that has developed a filtering technology at one tenth the cost and size of traditional systems, and Enlighten Australia, a Sydney manufacturer of luminaries that can save 93% of energy costs. Each of these great companies are alumni from the Australian Technologies Competition, a mentoring program that helps Australia's good technologies become great global businesses.

★ ★ ★

Big business is often seen as an opponent of action on climate change as they are the incumbents that have much to lose in the short-term. This is not always the case however and the financial might of big business is an important ally on the journey to a better world.

As part of their lobbying efforts to protect current profits, however, there are plenty of examples in Australia, Europe and North America of emissions-intensive industries threatening mass redundancies, relocation of activities to 'emissions friendly' countries and blackouts as a result of the closure of local coal-fired power stations. Big oil companies similarly have fought to protect their businesses from change.

The emotion at play for these businesses is a fear of change and the way to get them engaged to change this to a fear of the status quo; the fear that they will be remembered as the next Kodak; the fear of being left behind. Combined with the fear needs to be the way forward, the opportunities that can be grasped and the new markets that can be dominated.

A key message for incumbents is that this is just economic evolution and it happens all the time. When governments protect or prop up old industries, it doesn't stop progress, it just makes the fall harder when it happens.

Think of how automotive manufacturing cities like Detroit or Melbourne might have evolved if its car industry had led the development of electric vehicles rather than clinging on to making big fat cars that the world did not want. When companies complain that the upcoming changes are unfair, it is often a sign that they have not adapted quickly enough to the changes that are already happening. Those that have adapted just stay quiet and make good profits.

Carina Larsfälten runs the Global Policy division of the World Business Council for Sustainable Development whose members include some of the multinational companies that are leading the transition. These companies can see that the old business models are changing and are seeking ways to adapt to ensure both a better future for their company and for the world. The WBCSD is a critical advocate for change as it represents some of the world's largest companies and holds strong influence with governments globally.

Carina's vision looks back with pride at what was achieved to get through the crisis and create a world that 'is so much better than it might have been'. The key role of how business shaped this future is highlighted and in particular how, through collaboration and part-nerships, it 'supercharged the innovation potential of some of the world's greatest minds'.

Innovation and collaboration both in finding the optimum solutions and in the delivery of a better world are recurring themes throughout the visions in this book. The challenge of innovation policy is an area we will explore later. The concept that we are the entrepreneurs of the world looking for a way to help our venture survive and thrive is a useful analogy when deciding how to set off on our journey of discovery. There are many lessons to be learnt that will determine how quickly we get to some workable solutions.

Uppermost is the hope that we manage to *'fail fast, fail often and fail cheap'* as we try and try again to find the best way to manage our complex ecosystem.

The fate of incumbents as part of this journey will depend entirely on whether they participate in the discussion with an open mind or whether they sit back and cling to their existing business model claiming that life is unfair. Incumbents are therefore in the privileged position of being able to make the decision as to whether or not they survive or become just another historical footnote.

The Power of Collaboration

Carina Larsfälten
Managing Director
World Business Council for Sustainable Development
Geneva, Switzerland

Living in 2100 isn't perfect, but I'm proud to be part of a world that's so much better than it might have been. I'm proud of the progress we made last century. I'm pleased with the way we managed to decouple economic growth from ecosystem destruction and material consumption. I feel good about our sustainable cities and the net zero emissions society we have created.

Looking back, there were two transformative movements that enabled this shift. One was the strong climate change agreement brokered at the COP 21 Climate Change conference in Paris in 2015. Another was the carbon price that world leaders agreed shortly afterwards, which gave us a new lens for viewing true value, true cost and true profits.

I'm proud of the critical role that business leaders played in this transformation. The world's most forward-looking companies put together a resounding business case for tackling climate change, and their action provided support to governments across the world as they entered the climate negotiations. The companies formed partnerships to accelerate technology solutions, and the partnerships supercharged the innovation potential of some of the world's greatest minds. Visionary business initiatives such as Action2020 showed the way forward in real terms, based on real actions and real business solutions - and they delivered real results.

Our biggest lesson from the last century was about the power of collaboration. These partnerships were instrumental in globally transforming industries, infrastructure and behaviour. They show that when we share our ideas, expertise, networks and resources, global challenges can be solved.

Section 4

LIFE IN 2100

Chapter 13

EVOLUTION CONTINUES

The requirements for our evolution have changed. Survival is no longer sufficient. Our evolution now requires us to develop spiritually - to become emotionally aware and make responsible choices. It requires us to align ourselves with the values of the soul - harmony, cooperation, sharing, and reverence for life.

Gary Zukav

Chapter 13

EVOLUTION CONTINUES

We're not Afraid Anymore!

Adam Bumpus
Environment, Innovation and Development, University of Melbourne
Co-Founder, Apidae Development Innovations
Melbourne, Australia

In 2015, we were afraid. We were late to the climate game and we knew it.

We also knew that information connectivity would provide the mechanisms for a decarbonized industrial revolution, just as canals helped facilitate the first industrial revolution in England. But we hadn't figured it out yet. We were more technologically connected, but still obsessed with trivial status updates.

As connections online became connections in reality, we left behind the narcissistic elements of social media, and instead used technology to tell stories of resilience, pride and courage.

By 2025 new generations of businesses – decentralized and productive, creating shared value and wealth facilitated by connection – challenged and overcame entrenched interests. People had chosen to buy differently because they saw benefits to others and themselves. They created a swell for new ways of sharing, working and being. The political economy of high carbon was fully dismantled as people reconnected with their environment.

Overcoming psychological difficulties of long-termism, we adapted to be flexible, and fostered care and compassion with friends and faraway places alike.

Earth Day in 2062 celebrated the centennial of Rachel Carson's Silent Spring, and marked the point of a fully decarbonized global economy, created through smart systems, connectivity and will power. The world celebrated, connected together, in real time.

Today, in 2100, we are not afraid anymore. We are flexible and have overcome our fear of the future. We tell stories of transformation, of overcoming the challenge, of freedom and of building a safe climate, together.

We have set the scene, discussed the complexity of dreams and fears and travelled on a bumpy journey over the years to the end of the century. Now we have arrived in the year 2100 and you get to find out what the future holds. There's a catch of course but we'll get to that later.

The year 2100 will see a world that is now living within its means and starting to repair the damage caused by earlier generations. The unexpected bonus will be that it has also been re-designed to improve the quality of life, enhance communities, enable meaningful employment and reduce inequality. This vision makes the short-term transitions seem like minor inconveniences in the evolution of the human race.

Adam Bumpus sees this in his vision. Adam's research and project work has sought to connect business, innovation, communication and policy to create sustainable development solutions. He also convened the Decarbonise Asia Pacific Roundtable in 2015, a high-level business, policy, and research forum to address key issues for decarbonisation.

Adam's vision sees that the human race continues to evolve in the way it thinks and behaves through the coming century. People have started to behave differently because connections have enabled greater benefits to be generated through sharing rather than owning. This echoes the vision from Nina Harjula whose vision of a circular economy has the same outcome.

The biggest evolutionary change in this vision however is that the residents of the year 2100 will have overcome their '*psychological difficulties with long-termism*'. Given all that we have read on the current state of human psychology, this would be a significant change and one we will explore further in this chapter.

Adam's vision, like so many others, is compelling and attractive. I want to live in this world too! The one addition I would add would be to have the story-telling not only about '*resilience, pride and courage*' but to also include stories of hope and visions of what we really want.

The evolution of the brain is a fascinating topic. Researchers look at how the brain has and could change and whether it is possible to predict anything at all about what might happen next.

Not surprisingly, predicting the future of human evolution is not a straightforward task. Whilst many here envision a world where humans think and behave differently, that does not mean it will happen that way.

In his 1989 book '*Wonderful Life*', the late palaeontologist Stephen Jay Gould assessed the potential to accurately predict evolution.

The book looks at the Cambrian explosion, a flurry of evolutionary innovation that took place more than 500 million years ago and saw the first appearance of vertebrates. Gould's position was that, even if you knew everything about life on Earth at that time, it is highly unlikely that you would predict the evolution of humans. He argued that as life is constantly buffeted by random evolutionary gusts, prediction is impossible. He writes, '*Our continued existence is the result of a thousand happy accidents.*'

There are others however who believe prediction, at least in the short-term, is more possible. Michael Lässig from the University of Cologne is studying the annual evolution of flu strains and forecasting which strain will be most prevalent in any one year. By forecasting accurately, the annual flu vaccine can be developed and distributed in advance to provide a greater level of protection than if it was developed after the strains have taken hold.

Manufacturing a new season's flu vaccines takes several months. In the Northern Hemisphere, vaccine manufacturers must decide in February which strains to use for the flu season that starts in

October. Worldwide, flu kills as many as 500,000 people a year so any advantage can be significant in terms of lives saved.

This physical evolutionary process is of course very different to the evolution of the mind and how it makes connections, manages emotions and treats apparently rational inputs.

In his BBC documentary, Brian Cox from the University of Manchester (and former 1980s pop star!), explored a paper published in 2014 entitled 'East African climate pulses and early human evolution'. This paper correlates periods of rapidly changing climate with rapidly increasing brain size.

The Rift Valley in East Africa has areas of unusual geology and climate that 'created periods of highly variable local climate'. The long-term drying trend in East Africa was punctuated by episodes of 'short, alternating periods of extreme humidity and aridity'. The paper suggests that it was this variability that drove evolutionary changes as humans had to change quickly to survive.

Maybe the struggle to survive over the next decades will force another jump in the development of the human brain. The physical change in brain size discussed by Cox is not something that will happen so quickly but maybe the re-wiring of some of the preferred circuits within our current brains might be possible.

Survival of the Species

Caleb Rice
Year 12 IB Student
Prince Alfred College
Adelaide, Australia

With ten billion people on the planet, Earth is practically on the threshold of substantial species extinction. We eat a lot of fish, because ocean farming is more efficient than terrestrial methods. Resource consumption is higher than ever, and the protection of biodiversity is no longer the priority; instead the survival of our species is at the top of every government to-do list.

Our scientists managed to pull off nuclear fusion about 30 years ago, but reactor plants are so expensive that only a handful of developed countries can afford it. We have come to a greater knowledge of genetics and can design food more suited to human health, which is also easier to produce. Water is scarce, and very expensive.

With years of low birth rates in developed countries, there have been serious political, social and cultural shifts throughout the world. In more developed countries, there has been significant economic strain due to the rapidly ageing population, as well as the increasingly smaller working-age population. The tiny working population demanded an increase in immigration, and this meant that countries began to fight for immigrants. Multiculturalism became the norm all over the world, and assimilated European societies were forced to change, or risk economic ruin. With an influx of different cultures, societal unrest has been common.

In Caleb Rice's vision, science has provided many effective solutions to help ease the world's problems but this has not delivered the harmonious and happy world hoped for by so many others. This view of the future might act as a counter-balance to the views of groups such as Ecomodernists we discussed in Chapter 11.

Caleb, another of my son Jack's friends and an excellent pianist, sees that in the year 2100, '*survival of the species*' is the highest priority of governments everywhere. He sees a '*business as usual*' approach with a reliance on technology to get us through but leading to resource consumption continuing to grow. The world is on the point of collapse because we are living in the same paradigm that worked so well at the time of the industrial revolution.

One idea that does particularly appeal to me from this vision is the thought that countries will be competing to get the best immigrants. Coming from Australia and its appalling recent record on the treatment of refugees, this is a refreshing concept. Countries do currently compete to get rich investors, but there is little current active competition to get the best minds and the best workers. To me, it would seem that any government that adopts this approach would create many benefits for their local economy.

To avoid Caleb's vision being the one future in this book that comes to fruition, the operation of human mind needs to change and a new '*business as usual*' needs to be created.

Doidge's review of case studies in neuroplasticity that was discussed in Chapter 3 is worth revisiting here as it may hold the key to how this re-wiring might happen. We have already discussed the treatment of chronic pain through *competitive plasticity* by Michael Moskowitz in Sausalito.

Another case study in the book was about a sufferer of the degenerative Parkinson's disease who has stalled and has even reversed the progression of symptoms through walking and walking and walking. John Pepper has had Parkinson's for over fifty years but has not followed the standard path of neuro-degeneration. Through a regime of three '*conscious*' walks of five miles each week, John has stimulated the brain growth that has repaired some of the damaged dopamine-producing neurons, the cells that die off in Parkinson's. The '*conscious*' part of the walk is to focus on every movement to ensure that it is not being affected by the Parkinson's degeneration. Doidge suggests that the conscious thinking unmasks '*existing brain circuits that had fallen into disuse*'.

One of the side effects of the limitation in movement, seeing and hearing that comes with Parkinson's is that there is less brain stimulation and, as Doidge puts it, '*their brains begin to atrophy from the lack of stimulation*'. It is not clear whether the cognitive deficits so common with late stage Parkinson's are caused directly by the disease or from the lack of stimulation but they are certainly the result.

John Pepper now shares his experience helping other Parkinson's sufferers. A lot of the message that John imparts is that the patient has far more control over their symptoms than the medical profession might suggest. Parkinson's is a disease that is not fully understood and there is little progress on finding the root cause. The symptoms and what is causing them is understood to some extent and medication can be prescribed to treat or retard these symptoms but there is as yet no treatment for the unknown cause.

Chronic pain fits into a similar idiopathic description of a condition. The medical profession is very good at prescribing drugs to dull the symptoms. Sometimes these drugs simply dull the patient's ability to tell anyone about the ongoing symptoms so it appears to others that they have reduced. There are theories of how pain is amplified and pain receptors over-react to become neuromas. Neuromas are a bit like the mythical Hydras of the pain world in that if you cut them out they just grow back larger and angrier!

The challenge with any of these apparently miraculous cures – curing chronic pain or reversing Parkinson's symptoms – is that by passing control back to the patient, there can be very negative impacts if this method does not work. The patient may think that they have failed, that they did not think hard enough or that they are not strong enough. It is their weakness that has failed to deliver this cure. In the communication of this type of cure, it is therefore critical to stress that it *may work* and that it is just another option worth investigating. Like an entrepreneur looking for solutions to a challenge, it is something worth giving a go

I know this feels like we're getting a bit off topic, but keep going; there is a link back to climate change coming.

One of the things that happens to Parkinson's sufferers is that their dopamine levels reduce dramatically and this then leads to the restriction of movement. The standard treatment involves a dopamine replacement drug that can have serious side-effects including hallucinations and other symptoms that mimic paranoid schizophrenia

Dopamine also has a role to play as a natural analgesic or pain treatment. In a 2008 paper, Dr Patrick Wood from the Louisiana State University linked the pain of Parkinson's to dopamine depletion and goes on to '*suggest a role for dopamine in chronic regional pain syndrome and painful diabetic neuropathy*'.

In Chapter 3, we also looked at the work of Susan Greenfield at Oxford on the impacts of video gaming on the development of young minds. Her work looks at the over-stimulation of the prefrontal cortex. This causes a high release of dopamine which desensitises the brain leading to a loss of empathy, reduced assessment of consequences and risk and a desire for instant gratification.

Dopamine is an important chemical. It provides the desire for unexpectedly good outcomes, enables complex problem-solving, focuses attention and facilitates movement. Dopamine is released when you experience the expectation of something pleasurable and it gives you good feeling. The released chemical then helps you to focus intently on the activity so that you do not miss a moment.

When my son Jack was very young, he used to focus so intently on an exciting activity that he would look completely miserable. As new parents it took us a while to understand that the anticipation and experience of the steam train was so good that he had no choice but to be entirely focussed on it. The three year old Jack had clearly just had a huge hit of dopamine.

Dopamine release is about craving, wanting and seeking. When a rat's dopamine system is wiped out, it will still love the taste of sugar if you give it to him, but it will not actively seek it out. Dopamine is what spurs us to focus on working towards what we think will make us feel good.

So here's where I demonstrate that I am not a neuroscientist!

Envisioning something that we really want is pleasurable, especially when we see, hear and smell our virtual world. If we envision on a regular basis, then we can come to crave this to give us a regular dopamine hit.

Once we have got in the habit of doing this however, it is easy to let the process move away from the conscious brain and so will not provide as much motivation or anticipation. Like John Pepper and his conscious walking however, if we force ourselves to think clearly and consciously about our envisioned world, then we will continue to get pleasure.

If we then share it with others and talk about our future, we can anchor the thought more firmly into the conscious mind of ourselves and others. By doing this all towards a positive world with benefits for all, we might just be able to start changing the prevalent paradigms of our society.

As I reread the last three paragraphs, it all feels a bit 1960s and hippy-ish: '*If we all love the world man, the world will love you back!*' Yet, there appears to be at least a partial scientific logic that dreaming and sharing your better world will help take the world towards that vision.

The trick is to do it in a way that is actually heard by your audience. If it is heard in a way that provides a threat to the listener's way of life, it will be dismissed.

"*My idea of an agreeable person is a person who agrees with me,*" said Hugo Bohun a character in Benjamin Disraeli's 1870 novel, Lothair. This is why people feel more comfortable in groups of like-minded people who are less likely to argue and maybe fight. By being with those you agree with, there is less likelihood of conflict and so our caveman instinct is keeping us safe. The use of language to convey messages in a strong and yet non-threatening way is a great skill. But as a skill, it is something that can be learnt and with practice can come more easily.

A challenge to the argument of getting a chemical reward from thinking about a better world is that, given the choice, a teenager will more often choose a war game that they can win than over a nice game where you build a better world. I know myself that the one time I went shooting pest rabbits on the farm of my best man Jimmy in Scotland, I got a huge dose of adrenalin and dopamine despite my misgivings about what we were doing. Similarly, the thrill of doing the big deal, getting the big sale, winning the sports match or outdoing your peers will quickly drag people back to 'business as usual' thinking.

The rewards from 'winning' and killing have been bred into our race as part of what we needed to survive from our time living in caves. They are natural, particularly for men, and still offer short-term benefits for individuals. However, to be able to make the transition to a stable climate as early as possible, they are natural traits that need to be challenged. The practice of envisioning and sharing your goals for a better world might just deliver that.

★ ★ ★

Despite once holding the title as the 'smallest altar boy in the world', I am not a religious man. I have strong views about how the world could work better and am certain that science has only started scratching the surface of what will be known in 2100 by my grandchildren and their contemporaries.

So to move from sounding like a hippy to talking about religion is uncomfortable for me at all points. My outwardly rational, organised, slightly-perfectionist self is cringing a bit at the prospect but they are both important areas so bear with me.

Spirituality and the religion that can go with it are important parts of being human. It is the emotional sides of our beings finding nurture in things that are not just of this world. I am not so comfortable with the parts of religious organisations that are overly hierarchical, behave in a dictatorial manner or see their particular brand of religion is superior to the other available brands. The vast majority of religious people are just good people seeking spirituality and the local religion offers that service.

Mainstream religious organisations have very large followings and can wield enormous influence over world affairs in ways that governments cannot. This is partly because they are global organisations but more importantly because they connect with people at their most fundamental level. The relationship is not a rational one in the same way as that of a government, but rather an emotional one. A religious organisation can therefore have significantly more influence over the decision making of its followers than, say, a government advertising campaign.

The Catholic Church leads a global congregation of 1.2 billion people, 5,000 bishops and 400,000 priests. Pope Francis has continued the position of his predecessor saying that climate change is a 'moral imperative'. He encourages his congregation to take action on moral and scientific grounds. The message is that it is incumbent on Catholics to look after the environment which they have been given. His June 2015 Encyclical, Laudato Si, supports strong environmental action '*On Care for Our Common Home*'.

Archbishop Bernardito Auza is originally from the Philippines and is now the Permanent Observer of the Holy See to the United Nations in New York. His vision below echoes this message from the Pope.

The Archbishop's biblical reference to wise farmers '*who carefully planted, patiently cultivated and joyfully reaped*' is a strong analogy for those seeking to guide the world towards an improved state. Having an aim to sow seeds that '*blossom in shared prosperity for the edification of the common good,*' is one that can only lead to a better world.

Another example of religious groups exerting global influence is through an organisation called OurVoices, which was originated by Tessa Tennant who spoke of peace and plenty in her vision in Chapter 4. Our Voices is a non-denominational organisation that provides a forum to unite people of faith in a call to action on climate change. The movement's ambassadors come from all the main religions around the world to combine to provide a joint and powerful voice.

The challenge of climate change, combined with a burgeoning population and resource depletion, is going to test the mettle of humanity. If we choose to continue on our current path we will be betting everything we have on technology that does not yet exist. As the population of the world grows it will drive further inequality and poverty, both exacerbated by climate change impacts, which in turn will drive many global social problems.

By changing the thinking accepted as a societal norm and over-coming the caveman instinct to want to win, we have a chance to lessen the hurt we cause and joyfully reap our crops. The telling and re-telling of visions can provide a way of using our essentially caveman psychology to further evolve our ways of thinking to be more suitable in our current world.

Wise Farmers

Archbishop Bernardito Auza
Permanent Observer of the Holy See to the United Nations
New York, USA

Looking back from 2100, I saw creation flourishing in all its splendor and goodness for everyone to enjoy and contemplate. The human person, its crowning glory and steward, did everything possible to care for it, love it and use it responsibly and equitably. I rejoiced to see my generation and those after were faithful stewards, not slash-and-burn exploiters. They made healthy changes in their lifestyles, joined in collective efforts to reject unbridled consumerism and excess, and weaved a network of solidarity among societies across generations. They lived responsibly to assure themselves of resources that they could use and bequeath to future generations, and to act on the moral imperative that loving and caring for the environment flows ultimately from the will of the Creator.

Learning from the parables of Jesus Christ to describe the Kingdom of God, they imitated the wise farmers who carefully planted, patiently cultivated and joyfully reaped. Avoiding scattering seeds of a throwaway culture, they sowed seeds to blossom in shared prosperity for the edification of the common good.

Looking back through a healthy ozone layer, I saw a beautiful world out there. Rather, should I say: It's one beautiful day in 2100, and I see a wonderful world down there!

Chapter 14

FUTURE CITIES

It was the best of times, it was the worst of times, it was the age of wisdom, it was the age of foolishness, it was the epoch of belief, it was the epoch of incredulity, it was the season of Light, it was the season of Darkness, it was the spring of hope, it was the winter of despair, we had everything before us, we had nothing before us, we were all going direct to Heaven, we were all going direct the other way – in short, the period was so far like the present period, that some of its noisiest authorities insisted on its being received, for good or for evil, in the superlative degree of comparison only.

Charles Dickens
The opening paragraph of A Tale of Two Cities.
The two cities referred to were London and Paris during the
turmoil of the French Revolution.

Chapter 14

FUTURE CITIES

The Rise of Homo Urbanus

Jonathan Woetzel
Director, McKinsey Global Institute
Co-Chair, Urban China Initiative
Shanghai, China

2100 marks a milestone in the great urban journey that reached a takeoff velocity in the second half of the twentieth century. With the urbanization of China and then India and now Africa, we have become homo urbanus - the creature that lives in cities. And not just any cities but shining archipelagi, multifaceted in their diversity of economic, social and spiritual life, and the launching pads for even greater fields of human endeavor in the stars.

Along the way it is true that some clusters failed due to economic stagnation, or social or environmental externalities. We learned to recognize the warning signs of an economy out of balance with its natural and human resources, although this was sometimes regrettably after the fact.

Rising sea-levels and acidifying oceans threatened all life even as waves of social instability roiled cities and infrastructure strained to catch up to the influx of migrants. But the ingenuity and resilience of humanity proved enough to the task as we developed new mobility systems, cleaned up our energy supply, vastly accelerated our capacity to learn, redefined our centuries-old building technologies, and finally learned to value the collective benefits of being a twelve billion strong set of unique individuals.

When I grew up in the UK, one of my favourite television pro-grammes was called Tomorrow's World. This appealed to the technical nerd side of my personality and was well-hidden from my sporty and party friends. When I arrived as an undergraduate at Oxford, it was wonderful to find that there were other sporty nerds that enjoyed a few beers!

Tomorrow's World introduced me to many of the things that are now standard global technologies. I clearly remember thinking that bar codes were unlikely to take off, that brick-sized mobile phones in 1979 were interesting if impractical, CDs in 1981 were amazing and the 1991 touchscreen technology seemed set for great things. Of course some of the technologies showcased there were rightly destined for the historical oddity collection: the fold-up car that fitted into a suitcase and collapsible knives and forks were two of the more bizarre.

In the 1990 twenty-fifth anniversary edition when our global population was only five billion, the programme took a global look forward a further 25 years to 2015. It featured many city focussed predictions including home automation, mobile video confer-encing, GPS navigation, future transport systems and urban forests and farming. It particularly focussed on how climate change was going to impact food production in unstable weather conditions. Interestingly, the science of climate change was presented as con-clusive in 1990 - it was then just a question of how we solved the problem. The programme suggested the novel idea of taxing the emission of carbon dioxide and using the money raised in aid packages to help the developing world! Whilst the presentation style is very dated, the discussion on climate change solutions seems almost unchanged.

In a pessimistic piece from Charles Ouko in Nairobi, Kenya from his envisioned 2015 in the programme, he reports riots, mal-nutrition and the extinction of elephants caused by the onset of climate change. Ouko saw then that Africa's climate vulnerability meant that, by 2015, crops would have collapsed leading to societal collapse.

It is amazing to think what has changed in the last twenty five years and how foreign today's cities would seem. Taking the leap forward to 2100 will undoubtedly see changes that are unimaginable to even the wisest commentators. Maybe the science fiction writers such as Arlan Andrews from Chapter 5 might provide a better source of ideas for what might be possible. Some of the authors have however given the challenge their best shot in this chapter and they provide some interesting thoughts for the world in which your great-grandchildren will live.

Jonathan Woetzel is heavily involved in the strategy to develop Chinese cities in a way that will deliver environments that are functional, effective and sustainable for the growing urban population. As well as having been a Director in McKinsey & Company's Greater China Office for the past 25 years, he is co-chair of the Urban China Initiative.

The Urban China Initiative is a joint initiative between McKinsey & Company, Columbia University and Tsinghua University that aims to find and implement effective solutions to China's urbanization challenge.

Jonathan's future has cities that are '*shining archipelagi, multifaceted in their diversity of economic, social and spiritual life*'. This would certainly be a wonderful future and a very significant improvement on the growing cities as we see today. The concept that the human race has also effectively worked out how to flag '*an economy out of balance with its natural and human resources*' is also something that would stand the world in good stead for its future and is certainly not something that we have yet managed to do to any great extent.

Re-defining '*our centuries-old building technologies*' will be one of the critical steps to re-designing city life. I designed buildings for a few years in my twenties and I was very disappointed to find that my years of studying differentiation and finite element analysis (readers who happen to be proud nerds will know what I am talking about!), were of no use whatsoever as I was handed the books on standards and rules of thumb and told not to do anything too clever! The building technologies of London in the 1990s seemed little different to those used for the pyramids.

To create urban environments that function more effectively for the megacities of the future requires a different way of thinking. Materials, designs and living habits will change significantly and the paradigm of city living will change dramatically in the 'Today's World' of 2100.

Cities are growing through the promise of jobs and prosperity. By 2050 two-thirds of the world's growing population is expected to live in urban areas, up from around half today. Growing cities have many problems including poor air and water quality, insufficient water availability, waste-disposal problems, high energy consumption and grid-locked traffic. All these problems are exacerbated by the increasing population density that results from rapid and uncontrolled growth. The role of strong, long-term city planning is essential in managing the level of dysfunction created. This is why programs such as the Urban China Initiative are so important in helping advise on ways that will work most effectively in overcoming these challenges.

Writing in Forbes magazine in 2014, Jacob Morgan, described the 'Cities of the Future'. He took the city of Songdo in Korea as an example of what is coming. Close to Incheon Airport, Songdo was built on a greenfield site and first opened in 2009. It features sensors throughout the city monitoring everything from temperature to traffic. Rubbish is sucked directly from kitchens to a processing centre, telepresence is fitted in schools, the buildings are eco friendly and there are plenty of open spaces.

These types of technologies are available now and are being rolled out gradually across the globe. The step change to the city of 2100 is however going to be far more significant. It will require effective planning to make urban communities more connected with each other and their environment. If successful, Jonathan's vision of a settled, functional and respectful race of 'homo urbanus' may well be the result.

Achieving ZeroWaste

Vaughan Levitzke
CEO, ZeroWaste SA
Adelaide, Australia

It was predicted in the early 2000s that solid waste generation rates were going to more than triple to exceed eleven million tonnes per day by 2100.

Today, however, the concept of 'waste' does not exist: we only have resources. By necessity, we have developed a truly circular economy, deriving value from materials formerly termed wastes that we did not previously know how to efficiently recover. In this circular economy, GDP is no longer the main measure. The focus is instead on how efficiently we utilise our limited resources.

All products are now designed for reuse, disassembly, repair and easy upgrade. Products of a high cost nature such as housing or transport are leased to users, then taken back and refurbished or re-manufactured for lease again. As an additional benefit, this has provided for more skilled, high value jobs.

Food is better packaged and stored, preventing waste and feeding more. New energy coatings, laminates and even packaging that changes colour when food begins to be unfit for human consumption, are widely used. The little food that is wasted is used for energy recovery and as a composted fertiliser. Landfills are a thing of the past and are now being mined for their resources.

Vaughan Levitske set up and runs ZeroWaste SA, a small South Australian government agency that has led the step change thinking in how 'waste' is a concept that does not have a place in the twenty-first century. Vaughan's success in changing the 'paradigm' of waste for business, government and the community has led to projects advising many international city governments on ways they can benefit.

Vaughan sees his vision of a 'wasteless' society in 2100 as having many benefits. Not only do we use our limited resources more carefully but we have created high value jobs, can feed more people and have removed the need for landfills.

In practical terms, ZeroWaste SA has delivered its success to date through a mixture of education, incentives and driving collaboration. This work has been targeted at local governments, at industry and in the community. Its goal has been to remove 35% of waste from landfill and to date it has reduced landfill volumes by 20%. The mix of regulation, education and incentives has proved to be a powerful recipe to get engagement and to change behaviours.

To deliver the changes to date has required the agency to take some risks in programme delivery, something rarely found in government agencies. The fact that the group was small, flexible and innovative, that it was given ambitious targets and was allowed to design and experiment was why it has succeeded. This may well provide some guidance for governments everywhere to deliver step changes in waste policy and other areas going forward.

In all aspects of designing our tomorrow's world we will need to step into the unknown and we will need to take risks on what might deliver the best outcomes. To be able to take the opportunities that arise on this journey will require many lessons to be learnt from successful entrepreneurs. The bureaucratic structures of government and big corporations are not designed to cope with this challenge. To succeed, we must take a chance, risk some failures and adopt an entrepreneurial attitude to building our future. It is within our control if we chose to take it.

As the populations of the world continue to grow strongly and the urban populations are growing so quickly, we have a window of opportunity now to start to change how people will live in the coming century. As we delay, we continue to build on the cumulative mistakes delivered to date making them harder and harder to unravel. In the words of Mark Twain:

> 'Twenty years from now, you will be more disappointed by the things that you didn't do than by the ones you did do, so throw off the bowlines, sail away from safe harbor, catch the trade winds in your sails. Explore, Dream, Discover.'

This is a challenge for city governments but it is one that is critical to be overcome.

★ ★ ★

Twenty-second Century Food

Dr George Ujvary, The Foodologist
Managing Director, Olga's Fine Foods
Lecturer in Gastronomy, Le Cordon Bleu
Adelaide, Australia

After the food shock of the mid twenty-first century created serious global food shortages, step changes in attitudes towards food waste and a sustainable food and water supply has led to a recovery of our food supply in the early twenty-second century. Whilst increases in the global population has led to an increased demand for protein, advances in food technology, agricultural productivity and the use of plant based protein has led to sustainable global protein sources for all. Meat and fish meat are still an important part of the diet, but eaten less frequently and treated with reverence as opposed to a commodity due to increases in cost and attitudes towards its ongoing sustainability.

Our economy is still global, but global collaboration has optimised our food supply to ensure that appropriate foods are grown in areas with the most suitable climates, which are now significantly different to what they were. Our seas are now being used to grow sustainable aquaculture on a mass scale for both plant and animal based produce.

At a local level however, food is grown in our increasingly large cities in 'urban farms' which are able to mass produce staple foods, highly efficiently, all year round for local communities. This is made possible largely due to the move towards sustainable and cheap energy sources and recycled water.

We still face significant challenges but our outlook is more hopeful due to changes in our attitudes and our wishes not to repeat the mistakes of the past.

Not only will the cities of the world have to house and support the growing populations, but all these extra mouths will have to be fed. As people get richer they also expect more nutritious diets so the demand for food will be even greater than the growth in population. At the same time as the demand is increasing, the supply side is going to come under pressure from adverse climate change impacts, from tighter environmental regulations and from land degradation from over-production. Supplying food for our world in 2100 is going to be a major challenge.

The scale of this challenge is of course going to be determined by the global population in 2100. Looking through the predictions made in this book, there is not much consensus on where this might end up.

At the top end, Ian Chubb sees nearly sixteen billion and Jonathan Woetzel twelve billion closely followed by Rohan Hamden and Campbell Gemmell at eleven billion. Mary Robinson and Christiana Figueres sit in the middle ground of nine billion and several people including Chandran Nair and Tony Wood see that the population will drop back to six billion after the climate catastrophes of mid-century. The outside forecasts included John Gibbons' fifty million and, the even more extreme 'few dozen survivors' from Arlan Andrews.

In their song, Seven Deadly Sins, The Dubliners sang,

'Some say that gamblin's a sin,
but I'll bet you fifteen-to-one
that gamblin' has been in this world
since horses and greyhounds could run.'

So while, it seems inappropriate to run a 'book' on the outcome of these population estimates, if I was a betting man, I would put my money on a bit over the six billion of Chandran and Tony and maybe around the seven billion mark.

Cormac, my younger son, will turn a hundred in the year 2100 and he can assess whether I would have made him any money if I could have found a bookie to take the bet.

Feeding seven billion increasingly wealthy mouths in a climate-stressed world is still going to be difficult. One of the likely reasons for the population reducing to seven billion from its peak of maybe nine billion will be that we failed to provide adequate food. As the populations grow in poorer countries just as the traditional cropping areas fail from climate induced weather events, there will be major famines. This will cause much disruption in those areas and throughout the world as hundreds of millions of people have to relocate. These events will change everything.

By the time we get to 2100, whatever the population is, we will be growing and eating very differently from today.

George Ujvary runs his family's small goods factory in Adelaide, lectures at the Cordon Bleu school, runs a highly successful global food blog called the Foodologist and played rugby at Oxford. Needless to say he is great fun at a dinner party and a good friend.

George's view of future food is insightful. He sees a shift away from meat and fish and an increased use of plant based proteins. We will have specialised areas producing the most productive crops and will be utilising the oceans for farmed aquaculture.

We will have failed the challenge of feeding the cities in the middle of the century as agricultural growing patterns changed. This failure will lead to the growth of urban farms that will be major suppliers of year-round food in the cities. The advantage of highly efficient, hydroponic urban farms is that they can produce predictably regardless of the season and that they can be located close to the point of consumption, reducing costs and wastage.

The breakthrough in economically viable urban farming will remove the variability of climate and disease from food production. Once adopted globally, this could eliminate famines and the inevitable consequential wars and unrest. This would create a more stable and settled world and could even lead to improved global collaboration on solving other complex problems.

★ ★ ★

Personal Assistant

(Joe) Hyunbum Cho
Partner, Australian CleanTech
Seoul, Korea and Sydney, Australia

10ᵗʰ Jan 2100, 6:30am, current temperature is 18C, highest temperature today will be 30 (winter in Korea is becoming warmer). Your Energy Storage System has 80% power and you have 500 litres recycled water ready for today's use. No further supplies from outside needed today.

Your first meeting is at 9:30am with the Mayor of City of Seoul to discuss for building more residential buildings for aging population. Driverless Electric Taxi will collect you at 9:00am. It is 20km from home to City of Seoul and takes 15min and costs 100 APD (Asia Pacific Dollar). Korean Rain Control Centre has just announced that, as there has been no natural rain for 15 days, it will manufacture rain in the Seoul area today, so you need take your umbrella.

This afternoon, you have a meeting at 2:30pm in Pyongyang to discuss the redevelopment of Pyongyang Stock Exchange building and you need to get on the Super-fast Euro-Asia Rail (connecting Europe – Russia –China – Korea – Japan) at 1:30pm. It is 195km from Seoul to Pyongyang and takes 20 minutes. At 5pm, you need to attend the opening ceremony of the world's most environmentally friendly Disneyland and Resort in DMZ (Demilitarized zone) as part of the 70th anniversary celebrations of the Reunited Korea.

You are the major property developer in Korea.

Who am I? I am your personal assistant robot.

Sometimes when I visit Korea, it feels like I am visiting the future. The rapid adoption of technology often means that there is widespread adoption there several years before Australia.

Seoul in 2100, as envisaged by Joe Cho, is not surprisingly at the leading edge of technical innovation. Joe has given us a picture of a day in the life of his grandson who is a major property developer living in Seoul. The personal assistant robot has arranged the day fully and even warned of the scheduling of manufactured rain. Transport is fast and efficient and the reunited Korea seems to be thriving.

Joe is one of my colleagues at Australian CleanTech and manages our work in Korea. He is a finance expert and will soon complete a PhD in real estate investment trusts across Asia. We have funny conversations sometimes where I end up defending seemingly unreasonable Korean behaviour whilst Joe is excusing apparent Australian rudeness.

Our work connecting Korea and Australian businesses is all about interpretation and communication. Just like the challenge of communicating long-dated complex problems to the community, international trade often fails because of misunderstandings or mis-communication. Having a translator is rarely sufficient to enable a full understanding of meaning between different cultures. There is also a need to explain what lies behind the words, the context for why each party is worried about particular things and what is accepted as normal practice.

This complex challenge is no different to communicating the need for action on problems such as climate change. Whilst the individual words are usually understood, there are often misun-derstandings between the different cultures of the speaker and the audience. The scientist talks about the rational responses and the community hears nothing that they can influence in the short term.

When working with international companies and governments, the reason for all the effort is that they can see opportunities and can see a future with a better outcome. There are many challenges and many reasons that seem to make it all too hard but the persistent vision of success is what makes the effort overcoming the barriers worthwhile. The communications challenge discussed in these pages can therefore be similarly applied to international trade negotiations.

★ ★ ★

Chandran Nair's vision in Chapter 10 set out how he saw 'austerity for all' being the only way that the population of the world could build acceptable living for all its communities. It is not possible for everyone to live in the way that Americans and Australians have done in recent decades.

Balanced against this is the growing expectation of those pulling themselves out of poverty and wanting to adopt more comfortable lifestyles. More people want to live in nicer environments, with less pollution and less inconvenience. Fewer people will tolerate the 'cheap' end of town.

All of this will have a huge influence on our future world. The Copenhagen Cleantech Cluster published the *Global Cleantech Report 2012* that explored the determinants of future urban environments. The report focussed in on the largest and fastest growing cities to see what trends might be adopted more widely. The growth cities in developing and emerging countries were seeking to avoid the mistakes made by others in urban planning, resource allocation and utility development.

The report analysed the top 200 growth cities in terms of their GDP growth and population growth. This analysis showed that there are thirty cities with abnormal growth patterns in terms of either absolute population and/or GDP growth. The report concludes that it is these cities that will provide the largest global markets for clean technology solutions and will be the leaders in future city design.

The list of thirty includes already wealthy cities such as New York, Beijing, Tokyo, Shanghai, London and Seoul. It also includes rapidly growing cities such as Tianjin, Guangzhou, Shenzhen, Hong Kong, Sao Paolo, Moscow, Mexico City and Bangkok.

As an example of this rapid growth, in 2014 I took a group of Australian cleantech companies to Shenzhen, a very modern city close to Hong Kong. We were there to meet with investors and local partners to help facilitate market entry into the booming Chinese cleantech sector. Shenzhen was made the first of China's Special Economic Zones in 1979 when it had a population of only 30,000. In 2014 the population topped fifteen million. We found that the demand for new ways of growing the city, including the integration of many cleantech solutions, was creating a very different environment to that found in older cities.

Our last vision for the chapter is from Remo Burkhard who runs the Future Cities Laboratory at the Singapore ETH Centre. He focuses on how to solve the problems of cities with a focus on South East and East Asia. He is however looking beyond just technical solutions and exploring ways to design collaborative forums that allow the existing technical solutions to be financed and widely adopted. The mechanism of solution deployment is at least as important as the invention of the technology. As we will see in the next chapter, there are many amazing technologies that never leave the inventor's shed because of a lack of understanding or ability of how to turn a good technology into a great business.

In the same way that technologies turn into businesses, the success of future cities does not just depend on putting in place suitable local laws. To deliver constructive sustainable outcomes that deliver value across the whole community requires a holistic approach. It needs technology solutions but these must be supported with education, infrastructure and regulatory programs to guide the complex system towards the desired outcome. Developing a 'Growing Green Cities' program is essential to this success. This type of program includes innovation programs, community engagement initiatives, ongoing education and the long term commitment of elected officials. There are successful examples of some of this globally and developing holistic programs that provide a solution framework for local adoption are available.

Of course, the art of prediction is far from precise and so whilst we may seek to be the midwife of change, there will undoubtedly be many unexpected twists along the way in the creation of our future cities. As Benjamin Disraeli, the nineteenth century British Prime Minister wrote in his novel, Henrietta Temple:

'What we anticipate seldom occurs; what we least expected generally happens.'

The one certainty is that our future cities will be very different from those of today. A rational person would expect that the chaos, congestion and pollution of today's growth cities will have been addressed to provide environments that are more habitable and more efficient. If we are lucky, then maybe our future cities might even house Remo's vision for *'happier, more connected communities.'*

Future Cities

Dr. sc. Remo Aslak Burkhard
Managing Director, Singapore ETH Centre
Future Cities Laboratory
Singapore

With rapid urbanisation at the beginning of the twenty-first century, cities like Jakarta and Beijing faced huge urban challenges, such as traffic congestion, pollution, flooding, housing, sanitation and lack of access to clean water. Despite the urgency to solve these problems with severe negative social, environmental, and economic impacts, it was not clear then how to "fix" these problems.

The first step towards building our functioning and sustainable cities of 2100 was to establish an 'Impact Platform for Future Cities'. This was initiated by organisations such as ETH's Future Cities Laboratory that brought together academics, industry and government to find workable solutions to overcome the challenges of cities.

In parallel, attractive impact investment opportunities for innovative joint ventures with a city focus were co-designed to meet the needs of institutional investors.

By 2035, these schemes were driving the following significant benefits that expanded by the turn of the century:

1. *city governments benefited from the inflow of talent, know-how and solutions; the creation of new value jobs, increased GDP and improved quality of life;*

2. *investors backed products with investment-grade returns that also contributed to the ultimate benefit of cities and society;*

3. *joint-venture companies gained access to capital for implementing their growth strategies and their pilot projects.*

In 2100, cities are more functional, more efficient, more resilient and ultimately contain happier, more connected communities.

Chapter 15

TECHNOLOGY REVOLUTION

Unprecedented technological capabilities combined with unlimited human creativity have given us tremendous power to take on intractable problems like poverty, unemployment, disease and environmental degradation. Our challenge is to translate this extraordinary potential into meaningful change.

Muhammad Yunus

Chapter 15

TECHNOLOGY REVOLUTION

Distant Memories
Jules Kortenhorst
CEO, Rocky Mountain Institute & Carbon War Room
Boulder, Colorado, USA

It's amazing to think how a century ago coal and natural gas fuelled our electricity and oil fuelled our cars. That was such a dirty, expensive, antiquated way to power our world.

Thankfully, rooftop solar got so cheap it became economically irresistible, causing widespread investment that made customer adoption of smartphones look slow. Utilities that shifted to this new energy paradigm survived and now run today's resilient, reliable, affordable, low-carbon grid. Those that clung to the old model of big central power plants perished. Coal and natural gas couldn't compete, which is why America's fracking boom of the early 2000s busted as badly as it did.

Meanwhile, superefficient electrified powertrains took our cars off oil for good. The oil crises of the previous century will never happen again. Gasoline pumps are not even a memory for today's generation; they're found only in 20th century movies and the Smithsonian. EV charging stations, on the other hand, are as ubiquitous as the USB plugs of our tablets and laptop computers.

All of this happened not only because the world's major powers finally rallied to address climate change at the eleventh hour before it was too late to act, but because today's clean, prosperous, secure energy reality marshalled the private sector to rapidly rally capital behind the economic opportunity that supports today's wealth.

In The Witches of Eastwick by John Updike, Darryl Van Horne, the character played by Jack Nicholson in the movie, goes on a rant about how the world is changing. He tells Sukie that energy will be, *"Clean, abundant, and free. It's coming, honeybunch, it's coming!"* When Sukie complains that solar panels are ugly, he tells her, *"That's Model T stuff. I'm talking about paint."*

"A simple paint you brush on with a brush and that turns the entire epidermis of your lovely home into an enormous low voltaic cell."

Solar paint and many other incredible technologies are certainly coming. By 2100, we will be using our resources very differently. Several of our visionaries have talked about there being plentiful, free energy and how that has changed the way the world behaves. Without having to fight economically and physically to protect or secure energy reserves, global diplomacy will change.

The potential for every roof, every window on the sunny side of a building and every car to have built-in solar photovoltaic cells would mean that energy generation was everywhere and easy. There would of course be a need for energy storage for dark times but the need for big power stations, whether coal, solar or nuclear, would be entirely removed.

Companies such as Dyesol in Australia and PowerFilm Solar in Indiana have been developing ways to build solar panels in a different, more adaptable way. There are already products on the market from backpacks with built-in flexible solar to camping gear and mobile phone charges that utilise similar technologies. Taking the next step, research organisations such as the CSIRO have developed organic polymer solar solutions that will further increase the potential to deploy solar onto every sunny surface. Within a decade, this type of technology is going to be fairly ubiquitous and over the rest of the century the efficiencies and costs will continue to improve.

Another technology currently only in its experimental stages and that is likely to be in use by 2100 is the wireless transmission of power. Once proven, this opens up many possibilities that are otherwise technically or practically unfeasible. If power can be transmitted by laser beam, then space-based solar power stations are possible. The same technology could be used to make a 'space elevator' a reality and a much easier way to get to space stations!

LaserMotive, a Seattle-based company, is one of the companies seeking to develop this technology. The company was launched when it won the 2009 NASA Centennial Challenges Power Beaming Challenge. The company sees near-term uses for the technology to include powering underwater sensors and drones to launching rockets. The company has demonstrated the technology through a record breaking drone flight for 150 times battery life.

The Japan Aerospace Exploration Agency (JAXA) has demonstrated a similar technology. Researchers used microwaves to deliver 1.8 kilowatts, enough to run an electric kettle, through the air with pinpoint accuracy to a receiver 55 meters away.

There are of course limitations to sending energy in this way and my guess is you would not want to accidentally walk into the laser beam, but this certainly appears to be a step change technology that will redesign our energy systems in time.

Nuclear fusion is another technology that may well redefine global energy. For decades it has promised unlimited cheap power without the radioactive waste issues of the existing nuclear fission industry. So far however, demonstrating the theory in a way that could be deployed has proved elusive.

Nuclear fusion was co-discovered in the 1930s by Sir Mark Oliphant, who started school at the same primary school in the Adelaide suburb of Goodwood as my sons (no pressure lads!) and whose daughter-in-law, Monica, provided her vision on *Our Fragile Plant* in Chapter 5. Fusion energy is the process that powers the sun and is released by joining light atomic nuclei (typically deuterium and tritium, which are isotopes of hydrogen) within a high-pressure, extremely high-temperature "plasma" contained by magnetic fields. Oliphant went on to work on early radar technologies and on the Manhattan Project to create the first atomic bombs.

In 2014, the aerospace company Lockheed Martin announced that fusion technology could be in commercial production within a decade and this saw a wave of interest around the world. The progress is however disputed by scientists who have seen little evidence of practical progress. The main challenge with fusion is that it requires an optimal temperature of a hundred million degrees Celcius, six times hotter than the core of the Sun. The energy required to generate this temperature, even momentarily, is currently far higher than the energy released.

The best hope for fusion currently is the new experimental fusion reactor, called the ITER (originally an acronym of International Thermonuclear Experimental Reactor) being built by an international consortium in Cadarache, southern France. The project was launched in 1985, the designs finished in 2001 and the site finally agreed in 2006. The project is scheduled for commissioning in 2020. If successful, it could drive further work towards deployable solutions.

There is also a lot of global interest in a new generation of nuclear fission reactors. Generation IV reactors will probably use thorium rather than uranium and promise to deliver greater energy output with greater safety and less waste. They also hope to be built at a smaller modular scale for wider distribution. Much work is underway in the development of this as a practical option for widespread deployment after 2030.

Jules Kortenhorst runs both the Rocky Mountain Institute and the Carbon War Room and is a key voice in the global discussion on climate action and the potential for a beneficial transition to a lower carbon world. Since his days in the Dutch parliament, he has been the founding CEO of the European Climate Foundation and then led an entrepreneurial company developing solid biofuel solutions.

Jules' vision of the world in 2100 looks back with bemusement at how the world used to be. It is hard to imagine the use of the dirty fuels that were once prevalent. He notes how the incumbent companies that did not evolve and innovate '*perished*' as the world changed. His transition occurred through both government action and private sector investment and innovation that created '*today's wealth*.' The technology innovations discussed in this chapter will form part of this future.

A Solar Powered Earth

Prof Stephen Lincoln
Research Centre for Climate Change and Sustainability
University of Adelaide
Adelaide, Australia

Whilst, admiring the beauty of Earth's sunbathed curved horizon from the vantage of the three hour suborbital flight from London to Sydney it is easy to muse on how from the earliest times of Homo sapiens the sun was central to life, and is even more important to us now. Captured solar energy drives photosynthesis and plant growth which recycles and purifies air and water whilst feeding us at the same time. It also provided our first sources of energy released through fire; dry grass and wood. Later we discovered coal which initially powered the Industrial Revolution and was later joined by oil and natural gas, each of which provided huge supplies of stored ancient solar energy and increasing prosperity.

However, by the early twenty-first century rising carbon dioxide levels and the consequent global warming stimulated the search for alternative energy sources. Once again we looked to the sun and derived electricity from solar cells and wind power which together began a decentralization of electricity supply. A little later came the solar powered technologies which split water into oxygen and hydrogen through imitation of the first stage of photosynthesis. These provide abundant cheap hydrogen fuel which on burning generates both energy and water. The generation of biofuels from sea-grown algae and other sources also grew in parallel.

Then the sun came to our aid again through a major breakthrough in the middle of the twenty-first century; nuclear fusion. Solar physics taught us that the release of the huge energy generated by hydrogen fusion which powers the sun reproduced on Earth on a small scale could provide a massive electricity supply without the long-term waste generated by nuclear fission. Now with our energy supply secure and plentiful, and our eight billion population in slow decline, we have the ability to tackle the residual problems of global water and food supply and an aging population.

In 2006, Professor Stephen Lincoln published a book titled *Challenged Earth: An Overview of Humanity's Stewardship of Earth*, which reviews options for population, water, food, biotechnology, health, energy and climate change. He is also a long-time advocate for the potential of nuclear energy in Australia.

His vision includes a three hour flight between London and Sydney, something all Australians dream of, and abundant energy from solar, hydrogen, algae biofuels and nuclear fusion. Like Jules Kortenhorst above, Stephen sees that the energy challenge will have been solved by 2100 and this will have a profound impact on the world.

An area that is less addressed in all of the visions here is how to solve the challenge of global water supplies. Many parts of the world are already under significant water stress with organisations such as China Water Risk profiling and analysing the impacts that this is having. Stephen sees that, in 2100, with plentiful energy it will then be time to resolve the remaining water and food supply problems.

The crossover between energy, water and food is a growing area of discussion globally. In its Global Risks 2011 report, the World Economic Forum stated that, '*Any strategy that focuses on one part of the water-food-energy nexus without considering its interconnections risks serious unintended consequences.*'

Over the last five years, I have had the privilege of working with many of Australia's emerging technology companies delivering solutions to these challenges. The Australian Technologies Competition finds, mentors and celebrates the technology companies that are delivering resource efficiency solutions to industry and communities. The aim is to help take good technologies and make them into great global success stories. Over a hundred companies have been through the program to date and some of these are going to leave a significant mark on our future world.

Five of the many companies that are likely to be successful are described below. Each of these seems likely to deliver significant benefits to all of their stakeholders. Looking back from 2100, it may be that each of these will be seen as being major contributors to the global transition that occurred through the century.

RayGen Resources has developed a concentrating solar photo-voltaic system that is easily transportable, quick to install and commission, relocatable and has inbuilt storage. They commissioned their full-size demonstration plant in Australia in 2015 and will be building their first plant in China in 2016. The technology has the potential to deploy many gigawatts of capacity across the world as it provides a low-risk, low-cost way of delivering centralised solar power.

Nano Nouvelle has a technology that increases the energy density of lithium batteries by up to 50%. This would be a step change in the global economics of energy storage and would drive rapid change across all energy systems. The company has developed a Tin Nanode™ from its conductive membrane technology that enables batteries to operate in a far more efficient way. If proven, the technology could be adopted globally to change the battery industry and enable the rapid uptake of renewable energy such as wind and solar.

BluGlass has developed a way of manufacturing Light Emitting Diodes (LEDs) that are cheaper, of better quality and have less en-vironmental impact. The same technology has the potential to also produce solar cells that are more than sixty per cent efficient as compared to the current world record efficiency of forty-four per cent and the standard roof top panel of seventeen per cent.

CINTEP has developed a recycling shower that saves seventy per cent of the energy and water when compared to a regular shower. It has a niche market in new apartments and off-grid locations but also has the potential to redefine how water is used and reused in houses. The company is set to launch its first products in 2015 and seems likely to grow rapidly after that.

Carnegie Wave Energy is one of the world's leading wave gen-eration technologies having commissioned its first grid connected system in 2015. There will only be a few successful wave technolo-gies and Carnegie is well positioned to be one of those. The market for wave energy will be a significant global niche and Carnegie, after many years of development, is now set to grow rapidly as it rolls out its technology.

These and other companies that have been through this program have a good chance of becoming global success stories and to being part of the technology story that builds the world of 2100. The companies that do will fit well into Jules Kortenhorst vision in becoming the holders of '*today's wealth.*'

With the success of this program in Australia, we are starting to also deliver programs to help find and grow the best technologies in other countries such as Korea, China and Singapore. The potential to deliver returns to a city, regional or national economy through backing emerging technology firms is highly attractive for any government. Whilst grant programs can deliver individual demonstration plants, a structured mentoring program can deliver multiple success stories for less than the cost of a single grant. The Australian program to date has assisted over a hundred companies to generate over $250 million of economic value.

Design-led Revolution

Susan Gladwin
Sustainability Lead, Autodesk,
San Francisco, USA

Many forces helped us reach the carbon-neutral world we finally achieved. Over the last century, the power of design has been embraced in a significant way. Designing within planetary constraints, such as our finite carbon budget, moved from being a novel concept to the way things are done. Engineers, architects, makers and others using design rose to the challenge of creating net zero carbon supply chains and transportation. When the first net-positive buildings and cities were developed, we knew we were changing for good.

This design-led revolution made our modern lifestyles viable. Historians note how technologies such as the cloud, 3D printing and simulation empowered designers, their collaborators and stakeholders to connect on local and global scales. These platforms helped us see and work within whole systems so we were able to understand the effects of our choices and select the best ones. Idea generation was no longer limited to what we could think ourselves but supported by the massive number of iterations our tools let us test.

We're still restoring what was lost back when there was not as much awareness but now we know living well within the limits of the planet is possible. It is an exciting time to be designing the future.

Autodesk creates and sells design software around the world and is a supporter of the Australian Technologies Competition discussed above. They have also recognised that, as a multi-national corporation, they have a role in assisting the transition of the world to a place that is more functional. Through its Clean Tech Partner Program it is selling its design software to eligible cleantech companies for only $50 – a huge saving for the companies that are creating the future.

Using digital prototypes, cleantech pioneers can design, visualize, and simulate groundbreaking ideas. This ability allows them to test multiple concepts and reduce costly errors, getting to market faster.

By enabling the forward-looking companies to commercialise their concepts more quickly and at less cost they are playing a part in their success. The challenge of getting widespread acceptance of new technologies is daunting. Not only are there the normal challenges of start-up businesses in financing and resourcing rapid growth, but there is also often the challenge that the technology is challenging the status quo: that it is seen as a threat by incumbent companies.

Most large companies will fight hard to protect their profits as they should. Their CEOs are paid a lot of money to protect the investments of their shareholders. When seeing a threat from new technologies or from changes to government policy, it is a sensible use of funds for them to spend significantly against the change. BHP Billiton, Australia's largest mining company, spent over $8 million in lobbying and advertising against a proposed new mining tax in 2010 and the Koch brothers in the USA have reported spent nearly $80 million on funding climate change denial groups.

It is not however just in the energy sector where incumbents seek to resist the emergence of new and profit-threatening policies and technologies. The health industry too has many large profitable companies that seek to protect their profit streams. This can lead to the blocking of new treatments or the discrediting of treatments that are not perceived as fool proof.

The drive for profit makes it worthwhile spending large sums on research to find the next potential profit stream and this has resulted in many societal benefits. The entrepreneurial spirit can lead to wonderful innovations and to fiercely competitive behaviour to ensure that one solution succeeds over all others. So the fact that big companies seek to block competing technologies is not inherently bad and is largely understandable. In the language of economics, it is however a classic market failure and is the point where good government steps in to ensure that the overall good to society is balanced and optimised.

So our visions of a changed world will happen despite the defence of the incumbents. Changes may be delayed and individual technologies may not succeed but change is the only certainty whether it is to how the energy systems work or how the health system evolves. By 2100, fossil fuel powered technologies will be largely forgotten and replaced by better technologies.

Maybe by 2100, the mechanisms for pain in the body will also be finally understood and there will be ways to block unwanted pain signals and cure the sources of errant pain.

★ ★ ★

In all the technology innovation that will happen between now and our future world, science and technology will be a key required skill. These alone are not sufficient as we have discussed already, but the creation of technical solutions as options to change the world are absolutely necessary to enable change to occur.

The decline in focus and investment in science, technology, engineering and mathematics (STEM) is of great concern to Australia's Chief Scientist, Professor Ian Chubb. His vision below sees that we will pull ourselves out of the bind we are in only through increasing the focus on fundamental and applied research to develop *'solutions to make our world better'*.

The technologies discussed above are all the result of extensive research and may well deliver substantial benefits for society.

To deliver the greatest benefit from the investment envisioned by Ian, there also needs to be an increasing focus on technology transfer and application. This is not a choice between delivering applied research that has immediate application or fundamental research that increases knowledge of how things work. To deliver the best outcomes, fundamental research must be allowed to explore into new fields with no obvious immediate application and, along the way, spin-off applications must be aggressively pursued.

This balance is a difficult one to achieve especially under increasingly tight funding constraints being set by the governments of richer countries. To achieve the best outcome for humanity however, Ian's vision of an ongoing commitment to research spending is critical.

World Saving STEM

Professor Ian Chubb AC
Chief Scientist for Australia
Canberra, Australia

Many decades ago I proposed a strategy for Australia to address the day's main societal challenges – living in a changing environment, promoting population health and well-being, managing our food and water assets, securing Australia's place in a changing world, and ensuring our productivity and economic growth.

Today, in 2100, with the global population now at 15.8 billion*, we face many of these same challenges. However, thanks to the century's advances in science and technology, our responses to these problems are more sophisticated and more effective than ever before.

Driven by our capabilities in science, technology, engineering and mathematics (STEM), we have developed solutions to make our world better. We moved from the fossil fuel-based economy to embrace renewable energy sources providing cheap, reliable energy to the overwhelming bulk of the population. We now meet the energy demands of a growing population with minimal impact to our surrounds. Innovations in agriculture, food and water security, and medical science mean that the world's population is healthier than ever before.

The journey to 2100 has been made possible through an ongoing investment in both fundamental and applied research. The benefits are clear – increased productivity and growth, and a generation of cutting-edge, socially responsible technologies. Through STEM, we have achieved sustainability for ourselves and the generations to come.

*: United Nations, Department of Economic and Social Affairs, Population Division (2013), World Population Prospects: The 2012 Revision, New York.

Chapter 16

A DAY IN THE LIFE...

There are two great days in a person's life - the day we are born and the day we discover why.

William Barclay

Chapter 16

A DAY IN THE LIFE...

Awake!
Kristin Alford,
Futurist, Bridge8
Adelaide, Australia

Mid-morning sun streams through my glass windows. I've forgotten to reset the blackout timer after yesterday's early start. Or it could be faulty again. Our community compound was the best of its kind when my family moved in twenty years ago - all nanoglass, certified wood and low energy concrete - but now it's tired around the edges, these materials quite outdated. I daydream of more resilient kinetic floors and a smaller water recycler that gives me space in the bathroom. I doze, but the emu-wrens are trilling softly amongst the purslane on my balcony and I don't get back to sleep.

I run my fingers through my hair and my iWall fades into focus. Yesterday's stats say profit from sharing my flat's solar energy is up 7% on normal daily rates, probably because I was out most of the day. I check the forecast. Might be worth going out for dinner as spot prices will be lower. I press on the fridge app and activate the lower half so it will be cold when I get back from the markets. I'll need to make lunch for NannaJ before class. This is our fourth year teaching together even though she's nearly 100. She's not stopped advocating for art as essential for change since she was a youth activist in the 20s. She still has a good eye for trouble, even if it is bionic.

The last few chapters have all got a bit rational, technical and dull. Sure it is important to understand the 'what' and the 'how' of the journey to 2100 and what technologies will be in place. What is most important however is how we will live and how we will feel.

What will it really be like to wake up in January 2100? Will it really be no different other than having fancier gadgets or will the world be so fundamentally changed that it will be hard to reconcile any connection with the world back in 2015?

This chapter might help. We take a step away from all that rational stuff and get back to some real story telling. Stories that can make people really feel what it might be like to live in this future world. Suspend the pragmatist in you for this chapter, more than any other, and choose to live in the worlds on offer.

Eighty-five years is a long time for humans. Can you imagine living in the year 1930? Cars were just starting to become common, radio gaining popularity, television had just been invented, the internet had only been predicted in an improbable Mark Twain story published in 1904 and a journey to Australia took six weeks. The pace of change however is not static.

The mathematician Vernor Vinge popularized his ideas about exponentially accelerating technological change in the 1986 science fiction novel *Marooned in Realtime*. He foresaw that technology development would continue to accelerate and would go beyond human comprehension as technology designed the next technology. This theme has been expanded on by Ray Kurzweil's 2005 book *The Singularity is Near* in which he talks about the merging of humans and technology: '*singularity*' as he calls it.

Whether these predictions have any merit, it does seem certain that the changes over the next eighty-five years will be greater than at any other time. The authors here who have envisioned a day in the life of your great grandchildren have therefore had to be bold in their predictions.

My guess is that they have not been bold enough. The world will be so different and our lives will be so unrecognisable that I do not think we would recognise the real future if it was shown to us. Maybe it would be like dropping a pre-industrial revolution farmer into Times Square today. Cars, trains, planes, lights, mobile phones, crowds and crowds of busy people would seem like a nightmare or maybe a Shakespeare play gone very wrong. Would we really recognise our world of the future? What technologies will be a regular part of everyday life that have not yet been thought of? This is maybe where we need to rely more on the science fiction writers and the futurists and less on those too stuck in the reality of today.

Kristin Alford is a futurist who works with governments and industry to help them think differently about what the future might hold. She challenges assumptions of how things 'always' work and allows organisations to create their own different futures that can be far from incremental or business as usual outcomes. I first met Kristin in 2008 when she was heavily involved in communicating the potential and opportunities from nanotechnology. I was doing an almost identical task for cleantech so we explored ways to collaborate and jointly ran a forum looking at environmental applications for nanotechnology.

Later we both learned much about commercialisation from setting up a company together to demonstrate and sell a very smart nanotechnology enabled biosensor for water monitoring. The initial target uses for the technology allowed for real time online testing of phosphates and nitrates in water and sulphites in wine. The potential customers we spoke to were very excited about the potential to improve the management of both rivers and wine-making.

We managed to demonstrate that the great success in the laboratory failed dismally in the field. We also learnt that University commercialisation departments do not always act in a commercial manner! To my knowledge the excellent technology is still sitting on a shelf in Melbourne after we walked away from the venture.

It was a very frustrating process to see a valuable technology left unused. The technology had been proven, had a significant market need and was actively courting investment. It appeared to have all the parts in place to be a successful business. Whilst still risky, a rational view of the chances of success would have rated it higher than most.

The technologies that do become successful are not always the ones that seem most likely. Conversely, some that do succeed seem highly unlikely. A computer game that involves 'crushing candy' in a mind-numbing way makes money. Solar powered cockroaches were one of the most profitable investments for an Australian venture capitalist! These are not the outcomes of a rational world. So predicting the future requires creativity and insight. The only certainty with prediction is that it will be wrong – some predictions are just less wrong than others.

Kristin's future world is interconnected and proactive. NannaJ, a real teenager today, will still be teaching at the age of 100 with her bionic eye. Food is local, although it is not clear whether the lean emu-wrens are pets or dinner! It feels to me as though life is more compact, people are more connected both with each other and the resources they use and lives are more fulfilling.

Late Again!
Ketan Joshi,
Research & Communications Officer, Infigen Energy
Sydney, Australia

In the distance, Hanne spots a car stuck in queued traffic creeping forward. The vehicle behind it inches forward, and the effect ripples back through the traffic-- as though the cars of Berlin were an invisible pull-toy. The electric motor clicks on. Hanne feels a pathetically small moment of relief as his car automatically whirrs forward fifty centimetres. The ETA displayed on the dashboard indicates a miniscule change: 8:09pm changes to 8:08pm. "Scheiße", he mutters. He's late.

Hanne flicks on his display headset and flickers over to the traffic display. A fierce, deep red all along the Berlin Inner Ring Road up to Invalidenstraße indicates stand-still traffic. The traffic is caused by the 'Entelektrifizierung', or 'de-electrification' - the long-delayed removal of the vestigial and archaic electricity network.

In the distance Hanne sees workers lowering dilapidated telegraph poles. Lennox Film coats the rooftops. The thin, flexible technology, invented in China and commercialised in the 2080s, can soak up a megawatt-hour each day, per rooftop, quickly filling a bank of basement batteries with energy. The government made Lennox hybrid systems compulsory for every single building in Berlin a few years back - most people barely noticed the change, but Hanne had read about a few angry, near-violent objectors, mostly paranoid loners who saw the rise of Lennox Corporation as some sinister Chinese plot.

An Elektroauto Authority message pops up in the corner of his vision. It suggests there will another half hour of delays, with autonomous vehicle routes being re-programmed to maximise flow. Hanne sighs, leans back in the orange dusk light and slides off his headset. He is temporarily transfixed by the dark, shimmering apartment rooftops. As his eyes followed the curve of the street, a single block stands out-- a red, tiled rooftop, oddly devoid of generation technology. A crude, painted sign hangs from the window, written in German: "My mind is clear, you pigs". As the sun drops below the horizon, Berlin seamlessly switches to battery power. Hanne's car whirrs - another fifty centimetres closer to home.

Ketan Joshi is, amongst other things, the Communications Officer for Australia's only listed wind generation company, Infigen Energy. With a degree in neuroscience and psychology, he works extensively on how to effectively communicate possible futures. He is also the co-founder and co-curator of The Yeah Sessions, informal and entertaining talks on science, technology, life, the universe and almost everything, held regularly in Sydney.

Ketan's traffic jam in Berlin in 2100 feels as though we have not progressed very far in some things. He has plenty of new technology with the autonomous vehicles, compulsory solar film and batteries. His world is certainly not perfect and the rise of globally dominant companies worries the citizens of 2100 as it does today.

Historically, the largest global companies do not last for very long at the top of the list. Only 12% or sixty-one of the Fortune 500 companies from 1955 were still on the list in 2014. These survivors include Boeing, Campbell Soup, General Motors, Kellogg, Proctor and Gamble and IBM. Of the 439 that have disappeared many are long forgotten.

According to Stephen Denning, author of *The Leader's Guide to Storytelling*, fifty years ago the life expectancy of a firm in the Fortune 500 was around seventy-five years. Today, it's less than fifteen years and declining. It is therefore likely that very few, if any, of today's companies will still be dominant in 2100.

One company that seems to have the potential to become a significant multinational at some point in the near future is Tesla. Tesla has not only changed the global thinking on how electric vehicles can achieve significant market penetration market but are also now entering the energy storage market with their 2015 launch of their Powerwall product. The company has open sourced its designs and is building very ambitious production facilities to meet the demand that they are busy trying to create. The company's products are good technology and very smart design but it is the innovation in both the business models and the marketing that have the potential to propel the company towards global success. With both its cars and its batteries, the company has sought to connect with customers at a very emotional level. There are other battery systems that are superior in terms of specifications, such as those being produced by Korea's LG Chemical, but none are currently comparable in the minds of the consumers. Tesla communicates at a very different level from its competitors.

The essence of successful marketing, whether it is for a car or for a change in the way the world approaches environmental issues, is about getting its message heard and exciting the hearer into action. It is all about communication and connection with the target audience at an emotional level.

Maybe Tesla will eventually be listed on the United States of Europe Stock Exchange in 2100 and will be featured in one of Anne McIvor's 'USESE Results Round Up' reports. Anne founded and edits the international Cleantech Investor magazine and website and is based in London. For many years she has been at the forefront of financial reporting on the companies that provide the solutions to the world's environmental challenges. Her vision from 2100 tells the story of how the corporate world might unfold.

Anne sees a combined GE-Tesla company being the global leader in energy storage, which will be one of the world's largest industries. Her 2100 also has nuclear fission energy decommissioning all but completed, nuclear fusion taking off and AppleEnergy's iWave as a major supplier of data centre power. The integration between software and energy also appears to be a major theme as the management of energy has eventually progressed from the nineteenth century business model that remains prevalent in 2015.

USESE Results Round-Up, 15 January 2100: Energy stocks dominate USESE (United States of Europe Stock Exchange) results

Anne McIvor
Editor, Cleantech Investor
London, UK

Storage underpins AS

USE energy equipment giant AS, formed from the 2082 Siemens-Areva merger, reported 40% sales growth underpinned by contracts for three CAES (Compressed Air Energy Storage) systems. AS is the world's second largest energy storage equipment supplier (offering CAES and Power-to-Gas technologies), after GE-Tesla of the USA (which is focused on liquid air energy and battery technology).

AS nuclear equipment sales fell by 40% as decommissioning revenues decline. MSNuEquip, the nuclear fusion systems company, majority owned by not-for-profit multinational conglomerate, Gates Trust, is rumoured to be eyeing the AS legacy nuclear client base and to be considering buying the division at a nominal price.

DSPCity sees further strong African Group

African distributed solar power shone brightly at DSPCity, with 40% revenue growth. Africa now dominates sales at DSPCity, formed from the merger of Solar City (USA) and Solar Century (USE) in the 2060s. The mature US businesses of DSPCity, which is 51% owned by GooSau, the Saudi Solar-Google energy fund, grew at just 2%.

AppleEnergy's iWave continues

iWave, the AppleEnergy innovation which revolutionized datacenter energy economics back in the 2050s, continues to dominate results. Royalties on sales to third party energy generators overtook generation revenues in the 2080s, but generation from East Atlantic iWave installations (including the original Galway site next to the first Apple USE datacenter), supplies one third of USE and 10% of African energy.

The Energy Silk Road

Andrew Affleck
Managing Director, Armstrong Asset Management
Singapore

In 2014, out of South East Asia's six hundred million people, over 130 million people did not have access to electricity and more than fourteen per cent of the population was living on less than $1.25 per day. Over a few decades, the region's socio-economic landscape evolved as aggressive electrification programs and changing energy dynamics allowed for higher standards of living and greater distribution of wealth. Currently, all 758 million people in South East Asia have ready access to electricity through local and rooftop solar installations.

The role of public utilities has gradually diminished over the years as power generation has become localized with large scale community ownership. The region is now a net exporter of solar energy.

The historical correlation between rapidly growing cities and pollution has been broken as the benefits of energy commoditization have caused a boom in the electric transportation industry. Electric cars, buses and trains, equipped with solar panels and powerful energy storage systems, are now the main mode of local transportation.

On a broader scale, governments across the region have collaborated to invest a portion of their solar tax revenues to create a new Energy Silk Road. The 3,000 kilometre route starts in Singapore, passes through Malaysia, Thailand and Burma before linking with the energy-hungry giants China and India. Bullet trains, which utilize magnetic levitation technology powered by solar energy, ply the routes at lightning speed, facilitating not only the distribution of energy but more importantly, the distribution of opportunities in the region.

Andrew Affleck founded and runs a private equity fund in Singapore that invests in renewable energy and resource efficiency projects in South East Asia. He works with project developers across the region to help them fund utility scale renewable energy and resource efficiency projects.

Andrew's vision sees democratisation of energy across the region such that all its residents in 2100 have ready access to locally generated solar energy. The ability to generate cheap and abundant electricity is a recurrent theme throughout this book. Energy access is a critical factor in lifting communities out of poverty.

According to the United Nations Industrial Development Organisation, there is a '*strong positive correlation between direct access to electricity and per capita income in terms of the percentage of population living on or below US$2 per day*'. As an example there are over five hundred million Africans without access to modern energy. To build a world that shares its wealth more effectively across its regions, it is therefore critical that energy provision expands.

It was for this reason that the then Australian Prime Minister, Tony Abbott, said that coal is "*good for humanity*" at the opening of a new $3.9 billion coal mine in 2014. The energy of the future will however be provided with less harmful side-effects. It can be comforting to realise that there are always those who misjudge progress and, where there is any memory of them, they are seen as being 'mere blips' on the journey to the inevitable future.

Transport and energy are central to Andrew's vision of the future. In addition to these, our final vision of the chapter discusses the critical role of food and agriculture. Fred Chang from Shanghai tells of how the collapse of traditional agriculture led to the '*Great Climate Catastrophe*' but that the '*resilient agriculture and 3D printing-like real-time nutrient delivery*' now meets the needs of the world's population in a way that is sustainable.

Fred Chang is Managing Director of Unicorn Capital, a China-based private equity firm investing in cross-border and global sustainability companies. He has also worked with Chrysalix Clean Energy Capital, GE Equity and McKinsey & Company and is the founder of the China Cleantech Collaboratory.

Fred's vision creates a sense of a world that is more grown up, settled and living happily within its means. He sees '*self-sustaining and thriving ad hoc networked communities*' in a world that has achieved '*ecological balance and rejuvenation.*' When I take a moment to visit Fred's future world, I see a world that respects the individual, that provides an environment where people feel connected, can contribute and have meaningful lives. Self-worth and happiness are widespread and the world is a better place. Fred is '*blissful*' in his future world and what a wonderful thing that will be.

Tourist Destination

Fred Chang, Managing Director
Unicorn Capital
GCCA China Cleantech Collaboratory
Shanghai, China

Looking out my portal towards the Milky Way and then back to the view of Earth below, I am amazed how similar the millions of tiny lights flicker Brownian motion-like across our planet. The view from this space station reminds me how lucky we were to avert the Climate Catastrophe of the mid-century leaving this orbiting station no more than just a historic tourist destination today.

As inhabitants of planet Earth we have now found how to live in harmony and in equilibrium with Mother Nature. But we were lucky. Only a few decades ago the Great Climate Catastrophe devastated coastal cities and inland metropolises alike, as much from rising sea levels as from the near collapse of the world's food and agricultural ecosystem.

Fortunately early in the century breakthroughs in nuclear fusion, the hydrogen economy and other sustainability technologies created cheap, clean, ubiquitous power, enabling us to create self-sustaining and thriving ad hoc networked communities across previously uninhabitable parts of the world like lichens colonizing barren land. Complemented by advances in food sciences, the resource intensive livestock farming methods of yesteryear gave way to resilient agriculture and 3D printing-like real-time nutrient delivery to meet the world's ten billion plus population.

Today with nearly unlimited, low-cost, distributed, clean energy sources, our productivity of the Earth's resources has increased many-fold, yet without depleting and damaging our environment. We went through the Great Energy Transition to achieve ecological balance and rejuvenation.

Ah! How blissful am I as my family and grandchildren await the next shuttle back to Mother Earth!

Section 5

THE BENEFITS

Chapter 17

MEASURING WEALTH

In a country well governed, poverty is something to be ashamed of. In a country badly governed, wealth is something to be ashamed of.

Confucius

Chapter 17

MEASURING WEALTH

Defining Growth
Tim Jarvis AM
Sustainability Lead, Arup
Expedition Leader, Shackleton Epic Expedition
WWF Global Ambassador
Founder www.25zero.com
Adelaide, Australia

Looking back from 2100, the year 2015 seemed to hold much promise and much concern. There was much positive work being done by WWF and others in the sustainability field. The World Parks Congress in Sydney showcased the conservation commitments made by the many governments attending. Their commitments were as great a cause for optimism as the pronouncements made at the parallel G20 Summit in Brisbane were cause for major concern.

Perhaps the key outcome of that G20 Summit was its most potentially worrying: the commitment to ensuring that the global economy grows at 2%. This growth fixation that was held in those days was unhealthy at best and caused many of the problems we faced through the remainder of the century. At the time, it seemed unbelievable that governments were promoting more of the business as usual practices that had already contributed to accelerating climate change, biodiversity loss and the widening gap between the haves and have nots.

At the most fundamental level we needed to remind ourselves of what economic growth actually meant – the increase in the market value of the goods and services produced by an economy over time. Put more simply the global economic growth those leaders so yearned for was simply a running total of all things that were bought regardless of their merit. Case in point was the UK being chased by the EU in 2014 for an additional €2.1 billion contribution for its undeclared earnings from the drugs and sex industries.

The reason for economic growth that was then cited by those beholden to it seemed to be the notion that a buoyant global economy would somehow miraculously combat climate change and lift the poorest out of poverty like a rising tide lifting all boats. This was disingenuous given that much of the growth up to that point had so often been the major contributor to these things. At the same time, the global system of perverse subsidies for many unsustainable sectors seemed designed to get precisely the wrong environmental and social outcomes.

We now have a definition of growth that maintains the future world we want - a resource efficient, de-carbonised, equitable global economy where the value of ecological services and environmental externalities are taken into account and where 'growth' is not synonymous with borrowing from our children to destroy the legacy we leave them.

A society that recognises and measures the things which are of greatest value to its members is one that will have many benefits.

Gross Domestic Product has provided the measure for the world to pull itself up to a level of wealth that provides all of the primary needs of food, shelter and security. As the world transitions to consider the elements that really make us human, the measures will change from pure economics to the quality of the life. Many changes will occur to our social, technological and economic systems through the transition to a low carbon world. The way we measure the important things will have a direct correlation to how we design our future.

Peter Drucker, the Austrian management consultant, academic and social ecologist, famously first used the phrase '*what gets measured gets managed*' in his 1954 book The Practice of Management. This has been a strong management mantra for decades and has led to much analysis and performance monitoring. The full quote from Drucker tells a different tale however:

'What gets measured gets managed - even when it's pointless to measure and manage it, and even if it harms the purpose of the organisation to do so.'

Until his death in 2005, Drucker called for a healthy balance between short-term needs and long-term sustainability; between profitability and other obligations; between the specific mission of individual organizations and the common good; between freedom and responsibility.

Another management guru was Henry Mintzberg who suggested that starting *'from the premise that we can't measure what matters'* gives managers the best chance of realistically facing up to their challenge.

If we *'can't measure what matters'* and we do what is measured, it is no surprise that the world of today does not deliver as many benefits to its inhabitants as it might. Our contributors suggest that by changing what we measure, we will be able to build a better future world.

Gross Domestic Product is the measure used by almost every government to show their worth. It is measured very carefully, reported publicly and provides the guiding themes for many hustings' speeches. As our civilisation continues to evolve, it seems highly likely that we will start to measure things that will matter more.

Tim Jarvis is best known for his epic journeys to some of the world's most remote locations. He has undertaken unsupported expeditions to the South and North Poles, across Australia's Great Victoria Desert and in retracing the polar journey of Sir Douglas Mawson using 100 year old gear and equipment and starvation rations.

Tim's most recent expedition in early 2013 was the first authentic retracing of the journey of polar explorer Sir Ernest Shackleton. He sailed a replica James Caird boat 1500kms across the Southern Ocean from Elephant Island, Antarctica to South Georgia and climbed over South Georgia's mountainous interior, all done using only the same rudimentary equipment, period clothing and technology as Shackleton.

Tim uses his expeditions to promote change in the areas of climate change and biodiversity loss and emphasises solving problems by action not advocacy. As an environmental scientist, Tim also works as a sustainability adviser on multilateral aid projects in developing countries for organisations including the World Bank and the Asian Development Bank and is also Global Ambassador for WWF-Australia.

Tim's vision of a future is about how we value our world and measure wealth. He points out that the current fixation with growth is just a measure of '*all things that were bought regardless of their merit.*'

His 2100 has wealth measured on its merit. He sees a world that no longer borrows '*from our children to destroy the legacy we leave them.*'

This theme has appeared in many of the other visions and is critical to how we build our future world. What we measure we manage so the goal must surely to start measuring what we value.

Connie Hedegaard in Chapter 8 talks of the adoption of GDP+ that started to include consideration of both '*the impact on the environment*' and '*the consequences for future generations*'. In the same chapter, Rachel Kyte saw GDP being replaced with '*the new wealth index*' without '*major devaluations*' or '*a disorderly transition to low carbon growth*'.

In Chapter 12, Hunter Lovins noted that the Mayor of Shanghai declared that the city '*would no longer use GDP as a metric of success, but rather job creation*' and in Chapter 14, Vaughan Levitzke foresaw GDP being replaced by a measure of '*how efficiently we utilise our limited resources*'.

The Better Life Index is one measure that might be used in the future. Launched by the Organisation for Economic Co-operation and Development (OECD) in 2011, the Index focuses on aspects of life that matter to people and that shape the quality of their lives. The Index measures the eleven dimensions that it views as essential to well-being, from health and education to local environment, personal security and overall satisfaction with life, as well as more traditional measures such as income.

The Better Life Index is an interactive web-based tool created to engage people in the debate on well-being and, through this process, learn what matters the most to them. The Index website allows individuals to create their own index on what is most important to them. In this way, different priorities between countries can be highlighted.

Other alternatives include The Institute of Policy Studies' Genuine Progress Indicator (GPI) and the New Economics Foundation's Happy Planet Index. Each of these considers financial activity as a means to an end rather than the end itself.

Unconstrained growth as the solution to the world's ills is a paradigm that seems unbreakable. But like all paradigms, it will change and, when it happens, it will probably be swift. The important thing will be to have alternatives already developed that can be adopted in its place.

Everything knows Everyone
Nigel Lake
CEO, Pottinger
Sydney, Australia

Looking back over the last thirty years, futurists from the early twenty-first century might think we would marvel at the many extraordinary technological innovations in energy and transportation, manufacturing, telepresence and healthcare. The truth is that these have been incrementally and seamlessly absorbed into our daily lives. Ubiquitous low-cost renewable energy and micro-manufacturing may have transformed some of the largest industry sectors, but it is the social changes which have been most profound.

At some point in the 2020s, the better-educated and more talented realised that they didn't need a nationality any more. They could live and work in any city, and their employer – and indeed their choice of employment – gave them far more back in return than any country could offer. This led to some dramatic trans-continental shifts in the major population centres – you wouldn't believe which are the largest and most popular cities to live in today!

Healthcare became really expensive for a time – many children from the swinging sixties suffered terrible deprivation in their 80s and 90s, unable to afford the dramatically increased cost of medicine. But as all the patents expired, prices collapsed and health treatment automation exploded. The medical profession is still complaining, but it's now health statisticians which save lives. And because nearly all the costs of healthcare were fixed, the technologies were progressively shared around the world – and health standards and life expectancies have more or less evened out.

The other really fundamental change is that the journey to total transparency is more or less complete. Everything knows more or less everything there is to know about everyone. The children of today have no understanding at all what "privacy" means. Perhaps ironically, this has allowed more individuality to flourish, as tiny communities with unusual shared interests can find each other much more easily – and Device Video-presence (DV) means they can connect seamlessly in real time wherever they are in the world. But despite all this innovation, long distance travel remains constrained at sub-sonic speeds – there is no answer to the energy cost of flight.

Of course passports, wallets, credit cards, mobile phones and driving licenses have all become weird anachronisms. Think about it – if every device knows who you are and where you are, and most things can be fabricated when and where they are needed, you really don't need to take much with you. This has had one effect no-one saw coming – most people have more or less given up sending all those electronic messages.

Nigel Lake sees profound social changes in his future. The technology is there to support it but its adoption was not what mattered most. He sees a world in which nationality is not so important, healthcare is global and individuals are seamlessly connected.

Nigel is a corporate advisor and entrepreneur with a passion for diversity, innovation and environment. He has lived and worked in most of the world's top thirty economies and has advised hundreds of major companies and governments. He also leads Pottinger's participation in the Global Council of the Corporate Leaders Group on Climate Change, joining some of the world's largest companies and brands in advocating for strong and effective action on climate change.

The change in how societies across the world function will of course be critical to designing our future. The measurement of factors that are deemed important will be one part of this but we also need to define what goals we want to achieve.

Some of the authors here are playing a critical part in designing our future and their thinking here will be reflected in their guidance delivered elsewhere. However, it seems unlikely that any of the visions here, whilst most are worthy of becoming global goals, will be adopted on a standalone basis.

An initiative that encompasses much of the thinking provided by our authors here is the United Nations' Sustainable Development Goals (SDGs).

Jeffrey Sachs, the director of the Earth Institute at Columbia University, sees how the SDGs might change the way the world thinks of itself in the future. Writing in The Guardian, he states that *'Sustainable development offers not only a new analytical frame, but also a new way of choosing our common future.'* He continues,

> *'At this advanced stage of environmental threats to the planet, and in an era of unprecedented inequality of income and power, it's no longer good enough to chase GDP. We need to keep our eye on three goals – prosperity, inclusion, and sustainability – not just on the money.'*

The sustainable development goals will aim to eradicate poverty by 2030. Economist David Woodward wrote in the World Economic Review that eradicating poverty through our existing economic model was *'a structural impossibility'*. So the existence and adoption of the SDGs presents an immediate and significant threat to the current paradigm.

Commenting on this challenge, Jason Hickel from the London School of Economics noted that, under the current economic paradigm, global average per capita income would have to be US$1.3 million to ensure that the '*poorest two-thirds of humanity could earn $5 per day. It's completely absurd, but shows just how deeply inequality is hardwired into our economic system.*'

Hickel does not believe that the SDGs will be sufficient to deliver real change because they are tied so closely to the current way of thinking. They will make people feel good, they will make some incremental improvements, but they will not change the system. This connects back to Renee Lertzman's hypothesis in Chapter 3 that inaction on climate change is caused by the dissonance between understanding that there is a problem but not being able to let go of all that has led to current wealth and lifestyles.

My view is that the SDGs are certainly not perfect but they are a significant step in the right direction and they indicate an intention of where we are heading. They do not provide all the answers and will undoubtedly suffer failures and setbacks along the way. They are however continuing to move the conversation in the right direction.

In our entrepreneurial experiment on whether we can live with eight billion people on a little fragile planet, the critical thing is to keep innovating, to keep trying new ways of doing things, to endlessly search for innovation that will provide sustainability. If we sit back and say that nothing is good enough, then we are casting our own fate of destruction. If we start on our journey and keep pushing ahead then we have the best chance of averting the dark days to the greatest extent possible. For me, the Sustainable Development Goals are an important step in our journey to measuring wealth in a more meaningful way.

Rebuilding a Thriving City

Tina Perfrement
Future Proofing Geelong
Geelong, Australia

Back in 2015, Future Proofing Geelong was considered to be ahead of its time. If only we'd known then what we know now...we might have been a little more demanding of its vision. Back then, the collaboration between the City of Greater Geelong and nine other partners meant their collective vision, that Geelong be internationally recognised as one of the world's most sustainable cities, became a reality far sooner than we'd thought.

When that vision was created, Geelong faced challenges like climate change and transforming the traditional manufacturing base of its economy. In 2100 it is a thriving, prosperous place known for its collaborative and innovative approach to economic regeneration. The city has been far more resilient than other coastal cities, adapting to the implications of climate change and economic adjustment seamlessly. In Geelong we've seen the rise of industries manufacturing zero waste health care products, creating sustainable jobs in the process. We've also seen the development of precinct scale processing technology for food waste which has built skills and attracted manufacturers to our city. The boom in sales of electric vehicles powered by renewable energy has re-invigorated our workforce and our economy. While our local population has continued to grow exponentially over the decades, these new industries have continued to expand their market share in Australia and globally, providing those much needed jobs which have kept our city thriving.

I never met my great, great grandmother, but the legacy of her work and those in her profession has certainly stood the test of time.

As part of the economic transition that is already underway, traditional industries will decline and be replaced by activities that meet the changing needs of the world. As noted previously, this is of course nothing new. Industries and activities constantly change as technology and demand patterns evolve. A key to building and rebuilding communities the world over that meet the needs of their residents is an understanding of what is valued most. The GDP replacement measures discussed above are a good place to start. Clearly, economic wealth is necessary to some extent but it is only the means to an end in providing real wealth.

When designing a program around 'Growing Green Communities, Cities or Industries', the value is in building a community of people with meaningful lives that challenge and fulfil them. Like the spoilt, unhappy children of a billionaire, just giving people lots of 'things' will not facilitate lives well lived.

Surveys of what makes people happy at work reveal that once a certain level of salary is achieved, it is necessary but not sufficient to keep employees engaged. The key elements that regularly rate higher than salary are being valued, listened to, contributing and working towards a common purpose.

The Society for Human Resource Management provides profiles of US workers and what is important to them. The top contributor to job satisfaction is '*Opportunities to use skills and abilities*'. Salary comes in at number three and others at the top of the list include job security and communications and relationships with managers and supervisors. Employees want to have an impact and they want that impact to be acknowledged. Personal fulfilment is the number one aspect of employee satisfaction.

Moving from jobs to lives in total, the same principles apply. In his book *The Good Life*, Hugh Mackay analyses Australians' attitudes about their lives, loves, hopes, ambitions, fears and passions. He concludes that a good life is not measured by security, wealth, status, achievement or levels of happiness. A good life is determined by '*our capacity for selflessness and our willingness to connect with those around us in a meaningful and useful way*'.

The application of this to building 'good communities' is explored further in Chapter 19. It is also addressed to some extent in Tina Prefrement's vision of a rebuilt city. Tina has been at the forefront of reimagining what the Australian industrial city of Geelong could become and putting into place initiatives that start the journey. By replacing declining industries with emerging ones that contribute to a better world, Geelong is seeking to create meaningful work for a growing population. It seeks to become a place with residents proud of the community in which they live and its role in the world.

To be able to participate in work or community to the full extent requires a reasonable level of health. Good health therefore provides the option of pursuing a meaningful and fulfilled life. Poor health does not preclude life being full, but it does reduce the options and requires greater thought to achieve. Kate's poor health has taken away her options of achieving fulfilment through work, through academic achievement or through an active social life. It can be hard to feel fulfilled when the day can pass without leaving bed.

Those who have poor health and those who care for them know that what is of greatest value to humans is their health. Providing healthy, liveable workplaces and environments and high quality, accessible healthcare is therefore also a requisite part of building all of our future communities.

★ ★ ★

Another area of redesigning the measurement of wealth is in the way that the global financial system functions. It has been designed to date to drive growth and boost the all important GDP figures. If the politicians, bankers and regulators want to ensure that economic growth is achieved then the key lever to ensure this is the financial system.

Omar Khan envisages a new financial system emerging from a time of financial collapse. He notes that with the Second Global Financial Crisis, we managed to learn the lessons of what went wrong, something that seems to have been largely ignored first time around. Omar notes that the first GFC was treated *'like it was simply a misnomer in an extended period of 'prosperity'.'*

Omar has played a key part in building Australia's first Islamic finance group. Islamic banking is based on the principles of Shari'ah Islamic teachings that promote a sense of cooperation, to help one another according to principles of goodness and piety. In essence, it aims to eliminate exploitation and to establish a just society by the application of the rulings to the operations of banks and other financial institutions. By effectively disallowing excessive or unfair profits, it claims to provide a more stable, ethical and sustainable financial system.

Omar's world sees all finance being 'ethical' and providing the greatest value to the world as a whole. Finance is just used as a tool in the delivery of a better world.

The Second Global Financial Crisis

Omar Khan
Director, Strategy & Development
Crescent Wealth
Sydney, Australia

As I look back, 2030 was a significant year, Australia's then Prime Minister Tony Howard tried to convince us all that it was simply "a financial crisis we had to have." I don't think that's how the millions that lost their jobs or thousands that were injured in the ensuing riots saw it. Sometimes the past is so easy to forget. The bankers and regulators had somehow forgotten all about GFC I; like it was simply a misnomer in an extended period of 'prosperity'.

However, unlike GFC I, the people of Australia were not going to stand for it any longer; nor were the rest of the world. Riots, unemployment and crime hit unprecedented levels, which proved to be a catalyst for a paradigm shift in financial practices. A grassroots movement ensued, with people seeking out a more balanced and ethical financing model which served the financial needs of its stakeholders and shared risk equitably.

It is the seventieth anniversary this year of GFC II, and unlike GFC I, we celebrate the fact that we learnt from it. We no longer distinguish between conventional financial services and ethical financial services; an ethical and equitable banking system is the norm. Many of our service models were taken from Islamic banking, which now represents some of the largest banks in the world.

Retail banks also look very different now. The traditional retail banking model of the early 2000s has largely been disrupted. They are largely now facilitators or payments companies, those that survived anyway. My house is financed by a Shanghai based peer-to-peer (P2P) lender, my super is managed by a diverse group of companies based in Shanghai, Cairo and Karachi and I personally help co-fund loans for not-for-profit social enterprises.

Unchecked capitalism certainly got a lot of things wrong during the twenty-first century, but we have since corrected many of these short-comings and I feel positive about the twenty-second century and for those who will live through it.

Chapter 18

TIME

Know the true value of time; snatch, seize, and enjoy every moment of it. No idleness, no laziness, no procrastination: never put off till tomorrow what you can do today.

Philip Stanhope, 4th Earl of Chesterfield

Time is the system that must prevent everything from happening at once.

Cees Nooteboom in *The Following Story* (1993), Harvill

Chapter 18

TIME

The Time Thieves
Paul Dickinson
Executive Chairman, Carbon Disclosure Project (CDP)
London, UK

2100 is a very beautiful time in many ways. We have incredible technology, but far more importantly, humanity has learnt to work together. The wars of history look ridiculous now. Most of humanity now knows the enemy was never each other, the enemy was instead ourselves. We have discovered the extraordinary truth that we must work together or perish.

But there are also many disasters. People who have known nothing but the Great Climate Crisis (GCC) now have grown-up children themselves. Our best and most ambitious young people all want to work on this supreme challenge. Everyone knows extreme weather cost lives today, many lives in fact. But the generations born in to the GCC feel an acute responsibility to their descendants, something the mums and dads born in the twentieth century could not - or would not - face up to.

The news media keep us focused on the Next Greatest Threats and each generation have their own. I love how we work together and know we will triumph. Sometimes people speak of the 'Time Thieves', that generation that gave us this terrible legacy. But they had not learnt the greatest lesson of love through time. Our lives are not easy but I am glad we have moved on.

Time, like health, is precious. Yet we take both for granted until they are taken from us. In the words of William Penn, the founder of the Province of Pennsylvania, *'Time is what we want most, but what we use worst.'*

Imagine a world where we had more time and life was not so frantic, not wrapped up in running around in circles, chasing whatever it is we think we need – or maybe running from what scares us. Where sitting here at midnight writing Chapter 18 could be done in a more leisurely way. Could we really be happier with slower, more contemplative, less stressful lives?

Paul Dickinson considers time in his vision. He sees a world looking back at the generation that did not act calling them the '*Time Thieves*'. They were the generation that stole a world that could have been different and that could have avoided the 'Great Climate Crisis' that led to lives that '*are not easy*' in 2100.

Paul founded the Carbon Disclosure Project in 2000 with an ambition of creating a global economic system that operates within sustainable environmental boundaries and prevents dangerous climate change. In the same year he also published *Beautiful Corporations*, a book that examined the harnessing of corporate personality and style for competitive advantage in sustainability.

As an aside, I first came across the CDP when the gas pipeline company I was working with received a request for its emissions data. With around 2.5% of gas leakage from its system, the company had a major emissions profile. However after only brief consideration, it was decided that it would not be in the best interests of all concerned to be transparent on the issue, a decision which did not sit well with me. Later the reporting became compulsory under Australian law.

The concept of how we spend our time is closely related to how our economies work. If we strive to buy more stuff, having a bigger house and driving a faster car, then the likelihood is that we will have little time left to enjoy any of them. If instead, we strive for the selflessness that, as we saw in the last chapter, has the greatest chance of making us happy, then we are likely to have more time to enjoy that happiness.

Working hours vary significantly around the world. Figures compiled by the OECD in 2012 looked at the average annual hours worked per person in selected countries. South Korea was the country with the longest with 2,193 hours per year followed by

Chile on 2,068. British workers clock up 1,647 hours and Germans 1,408 - putting them at the bottom of the table.

Commenting on the figures to the BBC, Jon Messenger of the International Labour Organization said, *"Asian countries tend to work the longest, they also have the highest proportion of workers that are working excessively long hours of more than 48 hours a week"*.

"Korea sticks out because it's a developed country that's working long hours," he says. *"Normally it's developing countries like Bangladesh, Malaysia, Thailand, Sri Lanka - countries like this that are working long hours."*

Time off also varies significantly across nations as well from an average of nine days in the US to Germany and Denmark with thirty. He also notes that the US is the only developed country that has no legal requirement to provide any minimum amount of annual leave.

In Japan, long working hours are often still the norm for those that work full-time. The word *karōshi*, or *'death caused by overwork'*, was coined in 1993 to refer to extreme stress caused by working more than 60 hours per week.

The business culture in many Asian countries also leads to longer hours even if they are not spent in the office. I have worked on many projects in China and Korea and have found that colleagues there will eat at home maybe two nights a week and will have evening business meetings or dinners every other night.

There is much evidence that long working hours reduces both productivity per hour and the health of employees. For instance, a 2012 study by the Finnish Institute of Occupational Health found that the risk of experiencing coronary heart disease increased by about 40% in employees that worked long hours.

If we use our precious time carefully then it will lead to comparatively more healthy lives and being healthy provides the opportunity to be fulfilled and happy. Creating environments that enable smarter working is therefore one way to start to build our better world.

The End of Automobile Dependence

**John Curtin Distinguished Professor of Sustainability,
Curtin University
Director, Curtin University Sustainability Policy (CUSP) Institute,
Perth, Australia**

*By the end of the twenty-first century, 200 years after the invention
of the automobile and its fuel – petroleum - cities and regions have
overcome automobile dependence. Technological innovations in
vehicles and fuels mean that zero oil can become a reality but only
because the much deeper issue of automobile dependence was dealt
with from the early twenty-first century.*

*Cities were built around walking for 8000 years, then trams and
trains from the 1850's to 1950's then the car. All cities have all
three city fabrics but those that developed mostly around cars
had increasing economic, social and environmental issues. Finally
climate change required all fossil fuels be phased out – 80% by 2050
and 100% by 2100.*

*The twenty-first century immediately began showing that all
developed cities were reducing their car use and even more their
oil use. By 2015 it was clear that China and India were following
suit. Most significantly the more that car use was reduced the more
economic growth was achieved. Thus the Paris Convention back in
2015 was able to make global commitments to achieve the kind of
reductions in oil needed as the big economic driver was no longer
there.*

*Cities began to restructure and build quality transit lines into the
car dependent suburbs and focus urban development in small
cities around stations. The low carbon, low car use polycentric city
became the basis of all city growth.*

*Cars still exist but are all electric powered by renewables and have
become part of a mobility package that families can access along
with bikes and transit via their smart phones. Our renewably-
powered cities not only have electric cars, buses, trains and trucks,
but also biofuels and renewable natural gas for regional transport,
including aviation.*

One area of our current lives that can steal much of our time is the daily commute. In cities with grid-locked traffic or sprawling suburbs, many people can spend over two hours or ten per cent of the day making their way to and from work. In my office in London in the mid-1990s, my colleagues were jealous of my quick 45 minute journey from Clapham Junction to Trafalgar Square. When I then moved to Adelaide, the same 45 minutes got me out onto our rural property and was derided as madness by my fortunate workmates. My hours spent stuck in traffic in Seoul has only been topped by the three kilometre journey in Beijing that took well over an hour.

Poorly designed cities cause immense amounts of wasted time. Current thinking would measure the economic impact of lost productivity. The thinking in 2100 might instead measure the human impact of wasting valuable time that could instead be used to achieve goals, refresh souls or spend with loved ones.

Peter Newman has spent many years researching the alternative transport solutions and on how to build resilient cities. In 2008, Peter founded the Curtin University Sustainability Policy (CUSP) Institute which researches sustainable cities, sustainable regions, sustainable global development and sustainable politics, policy and economics. Peter was also a contributing author to the IPPC on transport solutions.

Writing in Opportunities Beyond Carbon in 2009, Peter saw a central role for transport planning in the transformation to more liveable cities. He saw the need to reduce emissions as a way to resolve many other problems that beset the urban environment:

The advantages of this broader approach may be seen when considering a theoretical review of one city's vehicle emissions. When confronted with reducing such emissions, the relevant community faces change of some sort. A relatively quick and easy 'solution' would seem to be the creation of bus lanes throughout the city and its suburbs. Yet the need for change presents an ideal opportunity for the community and its leaders to question the whole structure of the environment in which they live. Is it easy and pleasant to walk or bike ride within and between suburbs? If not, what can be done to make it so? Town-planning philosophies that design suburbs that exclude industrial areas force residents to travel long distances to work—is it possible to create jobs nearer housing or vice versa? How might the urban transport system as a whole be a positive influence in strengthening the community? It does not take much imagination to see how the implementation of projects answering each question may result in both optimum emissions reduction and a healthier, happier, stronger and more connected community.

Peter's vision for 2100 is of cities that function more effectively without the need for every house to have a car. By using effective public transport and shared vehicles through a '*mobility package*', the cities of 2100 will be more productive and resilient and have inhabitants who are able to use their time more wisely.

★ ★ ★

Good news, every day

Professor Ove Hoegh-Guldberg
Director, Global Change Institute
University of Queensland
Brisbane, Australia

*My son and daughter were told that they would live well into their
nineties as the century closed, and so they did. Improved health
care, technological innovation on steroids, and a stabilised climate
all contributed to a vastly improved human well-being. Sure, the
century had its ups and downs, with the climate catastrophes of
2020 and 2021 affecting people everywhere and causing a short
and disastrous global economic meltdown. This time, however,
world leaders – who had learned from the events of the global
financial crisis of 2008 - moved rapidly to intervene, using economic
stimulation packages not only to restart the global economy
but also to rapidly phase out the burning of fossil fuels. Driven
by unprecedented international outlay and collaboration across
people, industry and governments, global emissions of greenhouse
gases were close to zero by 2040.*

*Cities and towns rapidly replaced centralised power generation with
distributed renewables, and transformed the roar of petrochemical
motors into the silent whir of electrical motors within communities
that were otherwise bathed in sweet and unpolluted air.*

*Within this happy utopia, the daily news went from being
dominated by highly pessimistic stories about the loss of
ecosystems or conflicts over oil, gas and coal, to optimistic stories
about the recovery of ecosystems and the regeneration of human
communities. It almost became tedious to read about how corals
on the Great Barrier Reef, or other organisms and ecosystems, had
increased yet again.*

*Citizens like my children, however, were quite willing to put up with
this optimistic monotony given their personal experience of how this
century had begun in pessimistic decline.*

Ove Hoegh–Guldberg is the inaugural Director of the Global Change Institute at The University of Queensland following academic positions at UCLA and Stanford. The work of the GCI addresses the impacts of climate change, technological innovation and population growth through collaborative research in the areas of clean energy, food systems, healthy oceans and sustainable water. Ove has done extensive research on the impacts of climate change bleaching on coral reefs and was a contributing author to the IPPC on oceans.

Ove's vision sees the world correcting its course after the '*climate catastrophes of 2020 and 2021*' that led to an economic meltdown. In the same way that Omar Khan saw the second Global Financial Crisis, Ove sees this as the moment that world leaders realised they had no choice but to act strongly on fossil fuels and emissions. By 2040, Ove's world is well along the path to low pollution cities with '*sweet unpolluted air*'. From then it all gets boringly happy with '*optimistic monotony*' as the world recovers.

This vision could have been included with our optimists in Chapter 4. Why this is included here however is that this vision sees the transition happening earlier than almost any of the others. If the global mindset changes in the early 2020s and we have largely decarbonised the world by 2040, then by 2100 the world will be thriving on its new path. If we wait longer, then maybe we will still be trying to recover from the increased damage that will be done, as is the case in Paul Dickinson's vision. The importance of the timing of action is an element that is being pushed globally by many but is yet to be captured in the wider community psyche. The difference between building a world in which '*our lives are not easy*' and '*this happy utopia*' may help people to understand the consequences of this generation's choices.

★ ★ ★

I listened to Dr Mike Lee speak at TEDx Adelaide in 2013 on evolution and how there have been step changes that are caused by specific events. For example, the meteor that wiped out the dinosaurs 65 million years ago spawned a mass of mammals that took over the world.

Mike noted that the world is now changing at the most rapid rate in history. He sees that we currently live in a unique time that he calls the '*paleo-digital*' age. This period will last from 2050 to 2150 and is the time where we have '*discovered digital technology but [don't] really know how to use it yet*.' He goes on to talk about, in the event that we should ever meet aliens, it is very unlikely that we will be at the same stage of development so either they will seem like bacteria to us or vice versa. He suggests that when meeting aliens, you should therefore '*be afraid or be very bored!*'

The concept of the paleo-digital age offers the potential for us to use the digital age far more productively. Rather than the primary use within the community being to post pictures of dinner, play games and tweet, by the end of the century we will have harnessed all this data to be able to live better lives. Cities will function more effectively, we will have more time to spend on fulfilling activities and humans will find that '*they can achieve so much more*'.

Stephen Yarwood sees this as his future world. Data is used to make our lives '*ubiquitously organised, effective and easy*'. Stephen's Information Ecology has moved beyond the paleo-digital age and into the next stage of human evolution.

Stephen is a former Lord Mayor of Adelaide and now works globally as an urban futurist helping city governments to imagine and deliver their own city of the future. In his time in office Stephen oversaw many projects that made the city more accessible for bike, pedestrians, electric vehicles and public transport in an effort to increase the vibrancy and activity within the central area of the city. Stephen's prior career as an urban planner stood him in good stead when seeking to design a better functioning city.

Changing the way we design our cities or solve any complex, non-linear problem requires creativity and thinking about the problem in different ways. Entrepreneurs trying to build the best outcome for companies, cities or planets need to find creative answers to the problems they face. Creativity takes time, it cannot be rushed. It does not happen in the middle of a busy week or in time for an approaching deadline.

In an article in the Harvard Business Review, Teresa Amabile and her colleagues looked at whether it was possible to produce creative solutions to complex problems under time pressure. Whilst there were examples of when this happened, they were a rarity.

'When creativity is under the gun, it usually ends up getting killed. Although time pressure may drive people to work more and get more done, and may even make them feel more creative, it actually causes them, in general, to think less creatively.'

Creativity steps away from the rational known outcomes and allows unexpected connections to be made. The psychological process of creativity is not fully understood but seems to involve the brain trying many new connections between apparently unconnected thoughts. To do this effectively requires time to select useful concepts, time to try them out in different combinations and then time to analyse whether the outcomes might be useful. Cities and work environments that have everyone in a mad rush all the time will not produce the creativity that we need to build a better world.

On a personal note, my most creative times are either late on a quiet evening or when I am out running. I try and go for a run for an hour or so every weekend to clear away the last busy week and get ready for the next. I have found that, once my mind has cleared after about twenty minutes of running, I often have some of my best ideas through making connections that I had not seen before. Interestingly, this happens much more so when running than when I have been cycling or swimming for the same length of time. The idea for this book came from a run, although whether that really adds weight to my argument probably depends on whether you are enjoying your read! I thought this was one of my unique traits until I found that this is not uncommon.

David Hindley, writing in The Guardian about his own same experience wrote, *'running for me helps to create a productive space for "mind wandering", where creative thoughts crystallise and ideas incubate. On a long run, mentally I am able to envision whole sentences and paragraphs with a cognitive flexibility that I rarely have when sitting behind a desk.'*

He also listed authors that have a similar experience including American novelists Louisa May Alcott and Joyce Carol Oates and the philosopher Henry David Thoreau. Like me, Hindley also has experienced the need to write down all the thoughts on sweat-soaked paper as soon as he comes in the door.

Redesigning our cities in a way that enables people to spend less time travelling and have better environments to connect with fellow residents will free up time to work on even better solutions. Incorporating good tracks for running may even boost the level of innovation and entrepreneurial spirit. If we do all of this and do it soon, then maybe we will avoid being remembered as the generation of 'time thieves' who failed to act in time.

The Information Ecology

Stephen Yarwood
Former Lord Mayor of Adelaide
Urban Futurist, Cities 2050
Adelaide, Australia

Time management is no longer a skill; it's a product of our artificially intelligent companion running almost infinitely complex calculations. My timepiece is smarter than me and takes the term "watch" to another level. It knows what I like, who I want to be with, where they are, how to connect with them and when they are available.

Life is seamless. No waiting, no rescheduling, no sitting in traffic. The global language of binary digits communicating via technology embedded in everything means that life is profoundly fluid. The information ecology that makes living ubiquitously organised, effective and easy.

Whilst the world may move faster, time is relative to your life and has effectively slowed down. With global average life expectancy now at over 100, my fellow humans find that they can achieve so much more and without the rush.

It is however comforting some things today remain exactly the same. The world still spins on its axis and around our sun at the same speed. It is also still up to you to decide if you want to have a good time too. The best times are still to be had with the one you love.

Chapter 19

COMMUNITY

What is the point of being alive if you don't at least try
to do something remarkable?

John Green

Chapter 19

COMMUNITY

The Great Crash of '29
Christian Haeuselmann
Chairman, Global Cleantech Cluster Association
Co-Founder, swisscleantech
Del Mar, California, USA

After nearly 200 years, the steady global urbanization trend peaked. Decades of trust in the "magic economics" were gone in an instant with the global meltdown of the financial markets in 2029. It turned out that negative interest rates, money printing schemes and the design of ever increasing complex monetary instruments by leading financiers was not sustainable after all. The total system collapse wiped out banks, corporations, pension fund savings and whole states. Governments could not afford the massive subsidies for fossil fuels anymore, which only accelerated the decentralization and restructuring process.

Medium sized, human friendly Greenvilles began to form offering a quality of life and trusted community networks reminiscent of small rural villages of yore. The renaissance of local currencies went hand in hand with this trend, allowing for resilient regional economies. Fossil fuels became abundant since demand simply vanished. The global price on carbon, true cost advantages of renewable energies and energy efficiency gains led to a total transformation of the centralized utility and energy landscape that used to be state-of-the-art until the 2030s. Nature turned from being exploited as a resource perceived free of cost to being the highly protected key treasure trove for sustainable innovation and human development.

A wave of bold pioneering and innovation rippled across the world - touching technology, business models and finance systems alike. The new consciousness and understanding of resilient local structures transitioned the concept of profit-maximizing stakeholders towards the concept of shared value and impact oriented worldholders. Being regionally anchored but globally connected became the new norm for individuals and communities. There is reason to believe that this balanced system should allow for a prosperous century ahead – welcome 2200!

History is littered with failed societies. The reasons for the failures differ to some extent but they are often are connected with either over-using the available resources or becoming complacent about change and sticking to outdated ways of living. It is easy to argue that our current civilisation is pushing the limits on both of these factors.

In a comprehensive book on how societies fail, *Collapse* by Jarred Diamond, many case studies are reviewed with a conclusion that a combination of environment change, environmental damage or the action of neighbours is almost always involved. Not all factors affect every failed society but at least one is in play every time. The critical aspect however is not the cause of the problem but how the society chooses to react to the threat. As an example, different countries have reacted differently to deforestation. Japan, Highland New Guinea and Tonga *'all developed successful forest management and continued to prosper, while Easter Island, Mangareva and Norse Greenland failed to develop successful forest management and collapsed as a result.'*

Diamond is careful to point out that many societies collapse without any environmental problems occurring such as the Soviet Union in recent history and Carthage in the more distant past. However, the reaction to the threat was still the major contributing factor to the outcome.

One of the case studies included in the book is the often told story of the collapse of the Mayan society on the Yucatan Peninsula of Central America. To me this is the story that is of most interest.

This is partly because I travelled through the region in my twenties visiting the lost jungle temples but also because the rise and fall was documented by its inhabitants. The records are not complete but they do provide good historical insight. Diamond concludes that the fall of this sophisticated and rich society was due to the combination of environmental damage caused by the growing population, a series of debilitating droughts and increasing infighting that led to a focus on temples and wars rather than overcoming longer term challenges.

Diamond concludes the Mayan case study wondering why someone did not do something to avert the crisis.

> '..we have to wonder why the kings and nobles failed to recognize and solve these seemingly obvious problems undermining their society. Their attention was evidently focused on their short-term concerns of enriching themselves, waging wars, erecting monuments, competing with each other, and extracting enough food from the peasants to support all those activities.'

Christian Haeuselmann, like Omar Khan and Ove Hoegh-Guldberg, sees that our current society will collapse as the pressure of environmental damage, declining resources and growing populations take hold and those in power behave like Mayan or 'Neroan' nobles.

Chris' great crash of 2029, on the centenary of the Wall Street crash, wiped out both financial institutions and 'whole states'. After getting through the crash, Chris sees self-sufficient 'Greenvilles' emerging as a new way of living that went back to a time of localisation, trust and a real sense of community. Other authors have seen the rebuilding of more functional communities within cities as critical to the redesign of the world to better serve the needs of humans. Chris takes the vision further in that his communities also appear to be separated into geographically distinct 'resilient regional economies'. The challenge with achieving this outcome will be the extent to which our human population is reduced at the time of the crash. With a global population of seven or ten billion, it is going to be unavoidable that we will need to live in big cities.

The cities can however be designed to instil a sense of community within, in the words of Professor Peter Newman, well designed mixed-use Transit-Orientated Developments (TODs) or Pedestrian-Orientated Developments (PODs).

Chris's Greenvilles bear a remarkable resemblance to Schumacher's vision of Buddhist Economics discussed in Chapter 6 with its '*multitude of vibrant, self-sufficient villages which, from their secure sense of community and place, work together in peace and cooperation*'.

Chris is a man with a powerful vision of change and a good sense of humour. He is the founder of Swiss Cleantech, which is been politically influential in Switzerland, and the co-founder with Chapter 12's Nina Harjula, of the Global Cleantech Cluster Association. On a shoestring budget, the GCCA has pulled together fifty cleantech clusters and their 10,000 member companies into a consolidated group that has the potential to drive change around the world. It has engaged with the world's biggest pension funds through the P80 group to enable the financing of projects and is developing demonstration villages that will showcase the world's most efficient technologies.

Chris started his journey to global influence by backing electric bicycles in the early 1990s. Luckily for the world, Chris is a stubborn non-pragmatist. He dares to dream and might just achieve some extraordinary outcomes that any self-respecting pragmatist would deem unthinkable. I have challenged and been defeated by Chris' enthusiasm on stage at conferences in North America and Asia. One day I have a vain hope of at least scoring a partial point against his strength of character!

Greenvilles are so far removed from our suburban commuting lives that they do not seem sensible. But imagine communities in every suburb that have an element of self-sufficiency and a strong sense of community. Imagine what is important about having neighbours who know, care about and look after each other. Communities that provide local meaningful employment and shared visions of the future. Communities that work together to deliver important local initiatives that increase the quality of life for all who live there. To me it feels like a vision worth at least dreaming about.

Self-Determination

Fraser Bell
Partner, Thomson Geer Lawyers
Adelaide, Australia

Here in 2100, we wonder why a centralised energy generation and distribution model had been adopted in the major developed countries. Energy is now generated on a distributed basis with people taking responsibility for their own energy generation and consumption. The notion of 'off the grid' is not used because the old concept of the 'grid' no longer exists. The 'grids' that do exist today relate to information technology rather than the movement of 'electrons'. The world now shares information and is focused on energy efficiency in terms of the carbon footprints.

'Self determination' is the hallmark of a society in 2100 so that small communities take responsibility for their own carbon footprint in the energy space. Some larger communities have been unable to reconcile the competing interests that exist between various members and this has led to a recognition of sub groups of the communities managing their own risk profile in terms of carbon. The efficiencies of scale that underpinned the earlier generations in the energy space have passed. Instead, the focus on 'scale and efficiency' is the province of education and information transfer.

One of the joys of compiling the visions in this book is realising what a wealth of talent comes from the little city I have ended up calling home. Excluding my son Jack and his two fellow student contributors, who have no choice but to live in Adelaide, fifteen insightful visions come from this city of a million people that, if known at all, is famed for its red wine and picturesque cricket ground. When I met my Adelaide-born wife, Kate, I knew absolutely nothing about Adelaide.

I often feel that this little city, whilst having a quality of life that is difficult to match, provides its inhabitants with such a sheltered view of the world that it limits their thinking. I arrived from London to find the news headlines featuring a service station being held up with a man armed with just a screwdriver and felt as though I had travelled back in time. With this as the greatest challenge, how can locals really step up to contribute to global solutions? The shortest international flight is of seven hours duration to Singapore. The closest big city is Melbourne which is an eight hour drive. As a consequence, the majority of residents are only connected with their local communities and have little knowledge, understanding or care about the worlds of Sydney or Melbourne let alone anywhere more 'exotic'!

So I am always pleasantly surprised when I find that there are plenty of insightful people with world views that have lived in this town. Fraser Bell is one of those, in addition to the likes of Tim Jarvis, Kristin Alford and Sam Wells. Fraser was born in Rhodesia, as it was then called, and moved to Adelaide as a child. He is one of Australia's leading environmental lawyers, travels extensively and our sons happen to have played rugby and tennis together.

Fraser's vision for life in 2100 has communities taking responsibility for their own power generation and footprints and utilising education and information transfer to enable 'self determination'. The inhabitants of the communities of this world feel as though they are more connected with each other, with their resources and with their environments. With connection comes responsibility and so, as a result, the communities act in a more responsible and respectful way.

A study by Susan Rans from the School of Education and Social Policy at Northwestern University has looked at the key aspects required to build strong, resilient and effective communities. Rans looks at how being inclusive within a community, even with those that are seen as too old, too young or too disabled, is a requisite factor to make the community and all its members strong. The connections within a community help it to overcome challenges and find innovative collaborative solutions that better meet the needs of all. *As Rans says, 'At core, a deeply connected community – a community in which every member is valued and challenged to contribute – is a strong and healthy community.'*

In building these communities and in particular in ensuring that no members of the community are left out, Rans highlights a number of key elements that she found from her research into successful case studies. These include the presence of '*Connectors*', those people who are so well networked that they can make things happen quickly, and through having dedicated '*Citizen space*' within the community to allow neighbours to interact, build relationships and find the Connectors.

Communities with their strong and valued connections are central aspects to many of our visions throughout this book. The challenge is how to build these envisioned village-like communities with the trust and belonging of good neighbours in an increasingly crowded and resource constrained world.

Good Neighbours

Anna Skarbek
Executive Director, ClimateWorks
Melbourne, Australia

Australia in 2100 is harnessing its abundant renewable energy resources and enjoying the comparative advantage eventually established in response to the global transition to a net-zero green-house gas emissions economy, despite being slower than some to drive the transition in the early part of the century.

The energy security this provides, along with Australia's vast carbon forestry assets and CCS technologies and expertise, enhances our economic prosperity and our vibrant regional communities. Community leaders, corporate leaders and entrepreneurs of the 2020s are celebrated as the pioneers of the expansive energy networks that connect Australia's population centres with regions previously thought to be too remote to attract investment. The emerging renewable energy, energy efficiency and electrification technologies of the early twenty-first century are now the foundation of mature Australian industries, upon which our regional neighbours also rely on to decarbonise their respective economies.

Australia's contribution in transitioning to a low carbon economy has been recognised by our regional neighbours who feared the worst effects of climate change. This has helped enhance Australia's reputation as a constructive and compassionate member of regional and global communities.

Electronic technologies enable cleaner transport and buildings responsive to their occupants' needs, while eliminating wastage. These ubiquitous devices not only help overcome the various market failures that previously hindered sustainable economic development but also enhance the day-to-day activities of billions of the world's inhabitants.

The traits of being a good neighbour do not of course just belong in small communities discussed above. Nations also have a role to play in being good neighbours by supporting each other for their common good. Anna Skarbek sees Australia as evolving into a strong global citizen and a good neighbour to those that are geographically closest. Whilst the country has historically been seen as a good global contributor, this reputation has been eroded significantly in the debate on climate change. From the negotiating ploy that gave the country a 'win' in its Kyoto targets allowing an 8% increase whilst other countries decreased through to its recent protectionist stance over its fossil fuel export industry, Australia rightly earned the title of 'Fossil of the Day' no less than four out of ten times at the 2013 UNFCCC Conference of Parties meeting in Warsaw.

Anna runs ClimateWorks Australia, a philanthropically funded organisation that is affiliated with the US-based ClimateWorks Foundation and is an independent advisor on Australia's transition to a prosperous low carbon future. It has built a reputation as a trusted, credible and fact-based broker by working in partnership with leaders from the private, public and non-profit sectors. Anna often presents a voice of reason in the debate in Australia. Climate-Works provides specific practical guides as to how the transition can start and grow in a way that enables it to happen without causing the crash envisioned by so many of our authors here.

Despite Anna's good work, Australia is not currently acting in a way that would make people want to 'move in next door'. Whilst national governments must look after their own people and economies in the first instance, those that do so at the expense of others deserve little respect. It is like an unruly neighbour justifying their selfish actions by saying they are securing the best outcomes for their family. There are social norms that exist to make communities and societies work. The same philosophy applied between nations will create a world that will be to everyone's benefit. Unacceptable behaviour is not tolerated in your street and nations that are unwilling to work towards the common global good should also not be tolerated.

Australia is of course not alone in this stance but it receives global criticism for its position because it is so much below the bar it has set for itself on prior issues. I travel though Asia on a regular basis and am repeatedly asked why the Australian Government is behaving as it is and why the people of Australia tolerate it. My hope, and clearly that of Anna, is that Australia regains its reputation as being a good neighbour and, once over the current set of 'mere blips', takes a leading role in working within its region to build a prosperous future for all.

★ ★ ★

The challenge for civic and public leaders is to build communities that work within the current cities. A community does not necessarily have to be a physically separate village or 'Greenville', but rather has to have elements that help build connections and trust amongst its members. These 'urban villages' contain areas of shared experience, contain people that are proud to be associated with their community and hold people who look out for their neighbours. Professor Peter Newman's TODs described in the last chapter can provide an element of this type of community with mixed-use developments close to transport hubs. Where local jobs are also provided, then the community will move to another level with people being able to build their lives around their community infrastructure and utilise the local facilities for all their needs.

The 'Growing Green Communities' program is something that I have been working on for several years. Bringing together all the elements that allow for a community spirit to emerge is a challenge but one that is well worth the effort when it succeeds.

Keith Smith from Ohio State University has detailed the nine *'key elements of the good community'* that he has found through his work in building and researching communities. Good communities include access to safe housing and required goods and services. They also need a *'commonalty of values and goals that helps residents pull together'* and to provide *'sufficient opportunities for growth and fulfilment.'*

Smith suggests that the implications for leaders is that, to create a good community, they not only have to ensure that the area functions effectively but must also ask the tougher question of *'What could we do to really improve our collective lives?'*

Being the youngest of seven siblings and with innumerable cousins, my family provided a community for me when I was growing up. Whilst we did not live in the same place, there was always a sense that, if needed, they would provide a safety net for each other. I felt this same sense of community when I first moved to Australia and lived on a five acre property near a small town. You knew that if one of the neighbours needed help, everyone would jump in without hesitation, no matter what time of day or night it was. It is rare to have that same feeling living in big cities. Neighbours are hopefully not unpleasant and everyone keeps themselves to themselves. Communities that work have gone beyond this and have enabled residents to make connections with each other. This then allows conversations to start, joint local projects to be conceived and common values and goals to be built.

The employment patterns of the future will be a key element of these communities. As industries transition, it will be important to look after the workers and enable their transition into new jobs. As discussed in Chapter 12, shareholders have taken their risks in trying to make money and should not be protected in situations where the transition has been clear for some time.

Sharan Burrow has spent her whole career looking after the rights of workers. After nearly twenty years working in education unions, Sharan was elected as the President of the Australian Council of Trade Unions (ACTU) in 2000 and then as the General Secretary of the International Trade Union Confederation in 2010. The ITUC seeks to be the global voice of the world's working people.

Not surprisingly therefore, Sharan's vision includes a consideration of how the workers of the world experienced a 'just transition' to the industries of the future. Her world also includes other good aspects of common spaces and the 'common good' of shared technology.

The rise of the 'sharing economy' is an interesting phenomenon that we are just starting to explore. With smart control systems, there is no need for every house to own every gadget as long as they can get hold of one when they need it. This stems from the out-of-date concept of borrowing the neighbour's lawn mower, something that the untrusting and rich developed countries no longer seem able to do. Instead, every shed has a lawn mower rusting away that is used for only several hours each year. Sharing cars, bikes, spare rooms and gadgets is starting to emerge and, in Sharan's future, is just the normal way of accessing stuff. It will be cheaper, offer a wider choice and will not need to be stored. It will also enable a greater sense of community to be constructed. Our descendents will laugh at the current obsession with owning things that are not used every day.

Good communities offer many benefits to their inhabitants. As we redesign our world to live within its limits, the building of strong, interconnected communities will be a critical element. They enable resources to be used more effectively, people to be better supported and an environment to explore and deliver innovative local solutions. Communities will be a central part of your future and so thinking through and supporting what is important in your community is a good way to help create the future that you want.

A Just Transition

Sharan Burrow
General Secretary, International Trade Union Confederation
Brussels, Belgium

Our climate at the turn of the twenty-second century has stabilized around an average increase of two degrees. While this has quite dramatically changed the pattern of live and livelihoods for many people, with changing seasons and loss of low lying lands, it has offered opportunities for others. The overwhelming number of people now live in mega cities where mobility depends on mass transit systems that are powered by clean energy. Our houses are smaller and connected through 'the Internet of Things' to smart grids that predict patterns of energy use and reduce consumption of wasted energy. Our commons, parks and green verges are re-afforested and make for easier breathing, less respiratory disease and longer life spans. And our workplaces are green waste centres where what can be reused is without question integrated into production and daily lives. Technology is shared as a common good.

The key to sustainability was established in 2015 when the world's governments took a decision to act in concert to stop climate change. It took courage and conviction, but by 2050 the world had achieved massive decarbonisation. Coal is no longer burnt for energy and the majority of fossil fuel reserves will never be used. Renewable energy, re-afforestation and closing the loop on production and waste have made it possible to see a future that survives within planetary boundaries. Many of the industries of today evolved from those of the last century and unions fought for and won the protections for workers to ensure a 'just transition'. Our children and grandchildren can look forward to jobs on a sustainable planet.

Chapter 20

ELEGANT SELF-SUFFICIENCY

Interdependence is and ought to be as much the ideal of man as self-sufficiency. Man is a social being.

Mahatma Gandhi

Chapter 20

ELEGANT SELF-SUFFICIENCY

No Island Left Behind

Dessima M. Williams
Diplomat, development and rights advocate
Grenada

Small Island Developing States successfully championed for universally high ambition in order to arrive at today's highly productive low carbon world. We have survived!

Led by a sustained surge in the transition to affordable, accessible renewable energy, the removal of subsidies, the introduction of appropriate technologies and political will and leadership, the world has brought greenhouse gas emissions down to net zero. This has made possible successful models of inclusive, sustainable, wealthy and resilient island societies and populations world-wide. Despite a rise in sea level, the vast majority of coastal ecosystems and regions are secure. Oceans are healthy. Forests and freshwater sources are intact. We are healthier and more food secure because terrestrial and marine activities are more relevant to island needs.

Islands did not drown. People are not climate refugees. Our sovereignty has remained intact. Development financing reflects a healthy balance between national ownership and international cooperation. Industrial activities no longer threaten, sicken or destroy; rather, they enhance nature and humanity.

It was not always like this. Like girls and women rights and gender equality, the journey took over one hundred years from when the negotiating coalition, the Alliance of Small Island Developing States, AOSIS, launched and remained steadfast to this global vision: re-arranged political, environmental and financial commitments for greater equity, led by a legally binding climate change protocol, and a 'no island left behind' policy.

Today, we are developed islands, oases of paradise. Do you doubt? Then come to Grenada—and see for yourself!

The island nation of Grenada gained independence on 7 February 1974 after 211 years of British control. The island's culture is uniquely Caribbean with a mix of Amerindian, French, English, African, East Indian and Caribbean influences. With a population of only 110,000 and a land mass of 344 square kilometres, Grenada is also known as the 'Island of Spice' because of the significant production of the world's nutmeg and mace crops.

The nation gained notoriety in 1983 with a US invasion, condemned at the time by the United Nations, to overthrow a revolutionary regime. It is now known for its friendly welcome to its many tourists that provide the backbone of the economy.

Grenada is a member of the Alliance of Small Island Developing States (AOSIS) which is a coalition of small islands and low-lying coastal countries that share similar development challenges and concerns about the environment, especially their vulnerability to the adverse effects of global climate change. It functions primarily as an ad hoc lobby and negotiating voice for Small Island Developing States (SIDS) within the United Nations system.

AOSIS has a membership of 44 States and observers, drawn from all oceans and regions of the world. Together, SIDS communities constitute some five per cent of the global population. AOSIS's first chairman was Ambassador Robert Van Lierop of Vanuatu who served in the position from 1991 to 1994. Grenada held the chairmanship from 2009 to 2011 through its Ambassador to the United Nations, Dessima Williams.

In addition to her UN role, Dessima founded both the Grenada Education and Development Programme and HAITIwomen. Prior to her appointment as UN ambassador she was a professor of Sociology and Social Policy at Brandeis University in Massachusetts.

Dessima's vision of a thriving Grenada that did not suffer from any climate catastrophes places her firmly as an optimist. She sees that island nations will be stronger and more resilient having adapted to the changed climate. 'Islands did not drown. People are not climate refugees.'

The UNFCCC Fifth Assessment Report assessed the specific challenges for small islands and low-lying coastal regions. It provides sobering reading for any inhabitants in these areas.

Because of their low elevation and small size, many small island states are threatened with partial or virtually total inundation by future rises in sea level. In addition, increased intensity or frequency of cyclones could harm many of these islands. The existence or well-being of many small island states is threatened by climate change and sea-level rise over the next century and beyond.

Many small island nations are only a few meters above present sea level. These states may face serious threat of permanent inundation from sea-level rise. Among the most vulnerable of these island states are the Marshall Islands, Kiribati, Tuvalu, Tonga, the Federated States of Micronesia, and the Cook Islands (in the Pacific Ocean); Antigua and Nevis (in the Caribbean Sea); and the Maldives (in the Indian Ocean).

The threat of climate refugees is real. Permanent inundation of a low-lying island means that it is no longer an island! Kiribati is one of the most vulnerable of islands and is forecast to lose much of its inhabitable land. One of my high school friends used to spend summer holidays in Kirabati with his father and it remains a place in which I have a strong interest.

It was reported in 2012 that Anote Tong, the Kiribati president, was in talks with Fiji's military government to buy up to 5,000 acres of freehold land on which some of his 113,000 countrymen could be housed if needed.

The potential for climate refugees does not just exist on small islands. Much bigger groups of people might start to migrate if crops fail, droughts persist or large low-lying regions of countries such as Bangladesh become uninhabitable. With large populations on the move or under strain, the crowded world will become a far more troubled place.

Anote Tong sees that there is still time to avert this future, but only if we take action soon. As has been discussed before, the decision not to take action on climate change is a conscious decision on the fate of these countries. A decision to take action in the near term is to allow these populations to retain their homes.

Dessima does not see that the change will be quick and that it requires resilience of purpose from those driving the communication process. Her eloquent comparison with the slow progress to treat all humans with equity shows that global standards can take a long time to change. The challenge will be whether the change in attitude comes before the islands have been abandoned.

The question of equity is one that is becoming more prevalent in climate discussions. There is a growing recognition that the poorer countries are likely to suffer the most yet have done least to contribute to the problem. Amongst her other roles, Dessima Williams is a High Level Advisory Committee Member of the Climate Justice Dialogue which is supported by the Mary Robinson Foundation-Climate Justice (MRFCJ). The MRFCJ defines climate justice as:

> *Climate Justice links human rights and development to achieve a human-centred approach, safeguarding the rights of the most vulnerable and sharing the burdens and benefits of climate change and its resolution equitably and fairly.*

To Mary Robinson, back in Chapter 1, the result of climate justice will be:

> *So now, poverty is eradicated. Every child goes to school regardless of sex, race, religion or place of birth. Every woman enjoys equality with every man. Every household has access to energy; energy sourced from renewables that has enabled the development of nations, communities and families while protecting our planet.*
> *In 2100, the world is just.*

As I write this chapter I can hear the whispers of the pragmatists starting get a little louder. We are back to building a perfect world, a world that has self-sufficient communities with everyone educated and equal and happy. They will tell you that human nature, as it is, will never allow this to happen. Maybe the 'nature' they refer to is actually just a reflection of their own fears. If enough people dare to dream of a better world, then we might just find that we created one.

What could possibly be wrong with dreaming for a world that protects its most vulnerable and allows everyone to thrive to the best of their potential. Clearly it is not easy to achieve and none of our dreamers here would for moment think that it is. But what is the harm in aiming for that as our goal?

If one does not dream of a better world, what is the option? For this reason, one of the working titles for this book was simply, '*Or What?*' Do you instead dream of more of the same but just gradually getting worse? That is not a dream I want to share.

Dessima's elegant vision of small islands being self-sufficient, resilient and thriving in an equitable world is a wonderful place to head towards. Given her successes to date, I would not dare to doubt that her future of '*developed islands, oases of paradise*' will not fail to be achieved. I look forward to my first visit to Grenada to see for myself!

Collaborative Culture

Dr. Martin Blake and Sarah-Jane Sherwood
Global Sustainability Strategist, Blue Aus
Singapore

After the evacuation of many cities due to water-borne diseases from flooding, dangerous pollution levels and food and water shortages, mankind transformed its existence.

Many countries bankrupted themselves and currencies failed. An asset-backed currency was introduced and the economy was restored to pre-stock exchange simplicity.

Fossil fuel subsidies were removed and heavy levies placed on extraction and use of carbon. Levies funded climate change adaptation and mitigation. With fossil fuels too expensive to extract, scientists soon discovered a way to mimic photosynthesis.

Today, the grid no longer exists. Everything we build generates energy; roads, vehicles, even homes.

Tax-funded education has reduced poverty, eliminating high salary requirements for fees and debt. Salaries are more equal and people are happier because they have careers they enjoy with fair wages.

Many now exchange goods for services or gold and hundreds of self-sufficient communities have sprung up. They generate their own energy, grow their own food and build their own homes.

The world has become more connected. Travel is pollution free and cheaper. Humanity has evolved its consciousness and makes decisions understanding that all life is interconnected and, as part of nature, we co-create with all its elements. Culture has become values-based, heart-centered and collaborative.

The theme of self-sufficient communities continues with the vision from Martin Blake and his co-author Sarah-Jane Sherwood. Martin lives in Singapore these days but was well known in the UK for driving the world–leading sustainability strategy at the Royal Mail.

He now works as a sustainability strategist advising corporations, governments, industry associations and NGOs.

Martin's vision also sees a crash and one that might have significant impacts on the islands discussed by Dessima above. His rebuilt world however holds less poverty and more education, equality and happiness. Self-sufficient communities are widespread and our culture has evolved to be *'values-based, heart-centered and collaborative.'*

Martin's evolution of culture will be a big change but he is not the only one to dream of that world. Silence your pragmatist again while we focus on the collaborative element of this future culture.

A common example of where collaboration creates the best outcome is in the Prisoners' Dilemma of game theory. The exercise is often used in negotiation training and was originally written in this form by Albert Tucker in 1992. It shows how apparently 'rational' individuals do not cooperate even if it is in their best interests to do so. The problem has two prisoners in jail being offered a bargain to betray their fellow criminal. If they both stay silent they both serve a minimum sentence. If only one betrays the other, the betrayer walks free and the betrayed serves the longest sentence. Finally, if they both betray each other, they both serve medium terms. The best outcome is to stay silent and the usual outcome is that they both betray each other and serve the medium term sentences. This plays out in negotiations, in arms races and in war situations. Cooperation will deliver the best result as long as you trust that the other party will play along with your strategy.

A related outcome can be the Nash equilibrium where multiple parties will not change their position until another party changes. They all know that the outcome will be improved if they all change together, but no-one is prepared to go first because if they are wrong they will suffer.

Maybe a reluctance to substantially change our culture for the better is a form of Nash equilibrium. Many people know that a changed way of working within our communities would be of benefit but no-one wants to go first for fear of losing out. If this is so, then clearly we will need to evolve further in our thinking to be able to redesign the world. Whether the redesigning happens before or after a crash, it will be necessary and our current way of thinking is not sufficient to be able to deliver it.

There are countless studies into the benefits of collaboration in every possible setting. McKinsey & Company has detailed specific cost savings generated through collaboration frameworks. Anuradha Gokhale at Western Illinois University showed that collaborating in learning environments creates an environment that improves critical thinking outcomes. Research firm, Aberdeen, found in a 2013 report that the use of social collaboration programs in businesses delivers financial and multiple other benefits. So what stops every problem or challenge being solved through engaged collaboration?

In 1973, Horst Rittel and Melvin Webber from UC Berkeley introduced the concept of 'Wicked Problems' contrasting 'wicked' problems with relatively 'tame', soluble problems in mathematics, chess and puzzle solving. The term 'wicked' implies resistance to resolution, rather than evil. The way of managing the resolution of Wicked Problems is detailed in Jeff Conklin's 2005 book, *Dialogue Mapping*.

In essence, a Wicked Problem is one that does not have a simple cause and effect and therefore does not have a simple 'best' solution. The problems are novel and complex, not fully definable and not fully understood at the outset. Furthermore, there is no 'right' answer and every solution changes the nature of the problem, often in unexpected ways. The problem solving process is therefore iterative and tends to go off at tangents at times. Critically, solving complex Wicked Problems requires collaboration to more fully understand the nature of the problem and how it might react to various interventions.

Both managing chronic illness and parenting children are Wicked Problems for which there is no 'right' answer, only ones that seem to work for a while. With both, it seems that just as you find a solution that works, the problem starts to change and that solution is no longer effective.

Using standard project management techniques to solve a complex problem will fail. We can see this all the time in companies, governments, families and with any problem that involves a degree of social complexity or community interaction.

Conklin explains why collaborative efforts are often thwarted:

> *Collective intelligence is a natural property of socially shared cognition,*
> *a natural enabler of collaboration. But there are also natural forces that*
> *challenge collective intelligence, forces that doom projects and make*
> *collaboration difficult or impossible. These are forces of fragmentation.*

He considers that 'fragmentation' is a result of the wickedness of the problem and the degree of social complexity involved in its resolution. So not only is the problem difficult to get hold of and solve but the social dynamics between the people needed for the solution will have a major impact on the outcome. He concludes that the '*antidote to fragmentation is shared understanding and shared commitment*,' and goes on to describe a way of doing this within companies.

Laurence Peter, the Canadian educator famed for the Peter Principle that states '*every employee tends to rise to his level of incompetence*', is quoted at the beginning of Conklin's book:

> *'Some problems are so complex that you have to be highly intelligent*
> *and well informed just to be undecided about them.'*

Redesigning the way the world works is certainly a complex and Wicked Problem. The more I understand about the challenges the less I can see a clear solution. There are many social complexities in how lives, communities and wealth will change. It cannot be solved by forming a task force, but rather requires long-term collaborative and creative thinking to find ways that engage and attract a large proportion of the world's population. Even then the solutions that will work will change and emerge and we will need to continually redesign to fit with the ecological needs of the planet and the cultural evolution of its human population.

This cultural evolution will deliver better ways of treating both each other and our host planet. Collaboration and co-creation will be a key feature of this. As Paul Dickinson said in Chapter 18, we will find the '*extraordinary truth that we must work together or perish.*'

* * *

Another Adelaide contributor is Sam Wells who, as I mentioned in the introduction, was one of the inspirations for both this book and for *Opportunities Beyond Carbon*. Sam is a Rhodes Scholar and spends much of his time lecturing on organisational psychology, systems and sustainability on the MBA program at the University of Adelaide.

Sam's chapter in Opportunities Beyond Carbon was sub-titled '*Time to stop the hand-wringing and start envisioning what we really want*'. It works as a great introduction to all the visions assembled here. Of all the chapters from that book, Sam's received the most comment. A bit like Sam's lectures, which is where we first met, people either loved it or hated it. Predictably the engineers and accountants found it too 'fluffy' and idealistic and those who were more in touch with their emotional side found it inspirational.

As an example, when she heard about this book, one of my (many) sisters specifically asked if there would be something more from Sam as that was the best bit in the last book.

Interestingly for me, there were two very different reactions to Sam's chapter from two of Kate's previous pain specialists, with one saying the book was good "*except for that chapter by Wells*" and the other seeing Sam's chapter as the foundation for everything else. The latter also managed to make a major step forward in the treatment of Kate's chronic illness through being able to think about the problem in an entirely different way to all the many others we had consulted.

Maybe, for jobs that involve Wicked Problems, instead of undertaking standard psychometric testing such as Myers-Briggs as part of a recruitment process, the reaction to Sam's writing could be measured. If it inspires you, then you've got the job!

Sam's vision sees the cultural evolution of humans making a step change. Cultures are of course constantly changing. When I lived in Dublin in the early nineties, the culture was such that it was impossible to imagine a landslide referendum outcome in favour of gay marriage. Major tenets of culture can change within decades or even years when the time is right.

There is also good evidence that the rate of cultural change is accelerating. Technological evolution is certainly accelerating: the speed of adoption of the first telephone compared to the uptake of smart phones is a stunning example. As we adopt different technologies our culture changes. The use of smart phones, for example, has entirely changed the norms of human communication.

Studies into step changes in cultural evolution have been conducted. Peter Richerson and Robert Boyd wrote in the 2008 book, *Explaining Culture Scientifically*, that the '*cultural evolutionary process [is] rather more rapid than ordinary genetic evolution*'. The ability to change culture rapidly stems from it being decision-driven. If the environment changes and requires a different way of thinking and behaving, the culture adapts.

This is really good news!

Richerson and Boyd trace the emergence of cultural change back to the adaptation required during the '*onset of high-frequency climate change in the Pleistocene*'. The rapid climate change experienced then was still very slow compared to our current situation. They also say that '*The psychology of humans appears to be designed to acquire and manage a cultural repertoire.*' So the psychological inadequacies we discussed in Chapter 3 may in fact be trumped by the overriding need to adapt culture to ensure survival. We may well need a crisis to force this to happen but maybe this is why so many people feel so confident that, when it becomes critical to adapt, we will just adapt - of course.

What also seems clear is that, for all the reasons we discussed before, this change will only happen when enough people feel significantly threatened by the prospect of not changing. That the increasingly known risks of inaction feel greater than the unknown risks of action. This however may not bode well for some of Dessima's low-lying islands.

Sam's world holds communities in harmony with their environment, industries as servants to '*enhance nature and humanity*' and an understanding of what it is to have '*enough*'. Communities are largely self-sufficient and grow much of their own food, presumably through some of the urban farming initiatives addressed by

George Ujvary in Chapter 14.

In his autobiographical book, *All Men are Brothers*, Mahatma Gandhi wrote, '*Interdependence is and ought to be as much the ideal of man as self-sufficiency. Man is a social being.*' For this reason the cultural norms of the day are very powerful drivers of behaviour.

To jump into the envisioned world of Sam or others, we must first change the social pressures and norms to enable a different world to emerge. This will require making connections at an emotional level and influencing core assumptions and values that lie below the culture. If the inspiring stories of the future world are told well, it will pull the community along. People might see a different world, feel what it might be like to live there, have a gut-feeling that their lives there would have more meaning, more time and more happiness.

If we do this well, then maybe we will find ourselves in a world of '*elegant self-sufficiency.*'

Nourished

Dr Sam Wells
Business School, University of Adelaide
Rhodes Scholar
Adelaide, Australia

Now we live with a strong sense of our place in Nature and of our connection to all living things, in a world that nourishes and is nourished by us. We make decisions every day about how to act in that world – we don't always agree, initially, but we are united by a shared, heart-felt vision of how we really want to experience the world, and we find ways to reflect that vision in practice.

Our shared vision honours both the profound connectedness and the essential messiness of life on earth, with all its uncertainty and the unfathomable play and interplay of self-organising forces. We are learning how to act in ways that are in harmony with and harness the power of those natural forces.

We live close to the sources of our food, energy and livelihoods. We grow healthful, non-toxic food in ways and in places that nourish the land that produces it. Non-polluting technologies generate power and long-term employment – communities are not plundered by commerce, but sustained by enterprise that builds economic, social, environmental and cultural 'common wealth'.

We finally understand what it is to have 'enough', and have travelled the path from unrestrained consumption to elegant self-sufficiency.

Section 6

SETTING OFF FROM HERE

Chapter 21

THE JOURNEY TO LETTERFRACK

"'Tis the divil's own country, sorr, to find your way in. But a gintleman with a face like your honour's can't miss the road; though, if it was meself that was going to Letterfrack, faith, I wouldn't start from here."

The Hibbert Journal: A Quarterly Review of Religion, Theology, and Philosophy

Chapter 21

THE JOURNEY TO LETTERFRACK

Just a matter of time
Frans Nauta
Entrepreneurship Lead,
Climate KIC (Knowledge & Innovation Community),
Utrecht, Netherlands

Through the last century, organisations such as the Climate-KIC Accelerator where I worked back in the early decades had the privilege of working with hundreds of clean tech start-ups every year. At least once a month I would get this wonderful sensation that they were touching the future – and it turned out I was right.

Here is a founder pitching his (and increasingly her) idea back in 2015, and the process inside my head typically went like this: 'Oh wow, this is cool'. Next something like: 'Yes, of course, this is inevitably going to happen.' Next: 'Why didn't I think of this earlier?'. The breadth and depth of the ideas of the founders never ceased to amaze me. Almost all of the environmental problems that were in the newspapers of the day were already solved. It was just a matter of time. All through the century, start-ups disrupted the clean tech space. Completely.

The question was not 'if', there were two more interesting questions: 'When (if we could speed it up?)' and 'Who (would benefit)'. Germany showed us what the 'speed it up' model looked like. With smart market incentives it singlehandedly created a booming market for wind and solar energy. The scale of the German effort forced down the prices dramatically, making green energy competitive. The faster EV adoption, cheaper storage solutions and affordable clean water technologies were all then driven by governments creating market incentives.

And who would benefit? Denmark was smart enough to anticipate the renaissance of wind energy and made a bold bet. It invested heavily at the end of the twentieth century. It reaped the benefits through the first half of the twenty-first century: billions of Euros in exports, high paying jobs and a future proof energy system. On every continent there were start-up founders dreaming of bringing their clean tech solutions to market. The winners were the countries that created a healthy start-ups ecosystem: easy access to university IP, venture capital for early stage ventures and government and corporations willing to be launching customers.

The countries that moved fast and created a support infrastructure for start-ups were the economic winners. Denmark and Germany were peanuts compared with the opportunities that lay ahead. I could tell you which countries these were but that would spoil your fun in creating these outcomes. It is a fascinating century in the lead up to 2100.

In the previous sections, we have dreamed of a beautiful future, experienced some of the journey to get there, seen what it might be like each day and revelled in the benefits that will come. We have understood why human psychology is hindering preventative action but were relieved to find out that this can be changed either through rewiring brains or, more simply, by changing our culture and its consequent behaviours. So all there is left to do is to get on with it! I think I just heard a collective sigh of relief from the few pragmatists that managed to keep reading this far!

But where do we start and what is the best path forward?

The first known version of the old Irish joke about 'If you want to get there, I wouldn't start from here' was published in 1924 about the journey to Letterfrack, a small town not that far from where my father grew up on the west coast of Ireland.

A genial Irishman, cutting peat in the wilds of Connemara, was once asked by a pedestrian Englishman to direct him on his way to Letterfrack. With the wonted enthusiasm of his race the Irishman flung himself into the problem and, taking the wayfarer to the top of a hill commanding a wide prospect of bogs, lakes, and mountains, proceeded to give him, with more eloquence than precision, a copious account of the route to be taken. He then concluded as follows: "'Tis the divil's own country, sorr, to find your way in. But a gintleman with a face like your honour's can't miss the road; though, if it was meself that was going to Letterfrack, faith, I wouldn't start from here."

Whilst it would easier to start our journey from somewhere else, our current situation is where we must begin.

From wherever you start, the most important thing is to actually start. That at least will stop you looking behind and will move you away from the current paradigm. Even if the direction of travel is uncertain, just like any Wicked Problem, the path forward will become clearer once you start testing the system and seeing how it reacts. The worst possible thing to do is nothing. Waiting for definitive instructions or for the perfect plan will just mean that we are choosing to damage the world more than we need to.

Frans Nauta tells his vision of the journey that will take place, how adoption was accelerated and which countries benefitted. The excitement he describes when he meets a new company with an amazing technology that has the potential to change the world is one that I recognise well. I have the good fortune to work with, and hopefully help, some world-leading Australian technologies doing very similar things to Frans' role in Europe. Whilst governments may be more supportive in Europe than Australia, for now, the challenge often remains the same: how do you take a good technology with strong potential and enable it to be deployed widely and live up to that potential?

Frans is a self-proclaimed 'innovation addict' who is now running Europe's largest accelerator and business ideas competition for clean tech start-ups at Climate-KIC. Frans has held many roles all of which have been connected with getting things started and changing the way people think. Amongst other things, he has been involved in establishing both Amsterdam's environmental monitoring system and its natural gas powered canal boats. I travelled on one of these boats in 2002 when I was rolling out a natural gas powered bus fleet in Australia. Frans also initiated the Dutch National Innovation Platform headed by the Prime Minister and built a research group to study public sector innovation.

Frans co-authored a 2012 book, *Agents of Change: Strategy and Tactics for Social Innovation*, which discusses case studies of innovation that have led to significant social change. There is a focus on how ordinary people accomplished extraordinary results and managed to change the way people think along the way. So Frans is certainly a useful contributor to have in this book.

In his vision, he details the early advantages won by Germany, in using policy to scale up technology deployment, and Denmark by building the industries of the future. In a simple recipe for governments around the world, Frans suggests that, '*The winners were the countries that created a healthy start-ups ecosystem: easy access to university IP, venture capital for early stage ventures and government and corporations willing to be launching customers.*' He teases us by not telling us which countries became the 'winners' and consequently were the powerhouses of the twenty-second century.

The journey towards our future world is neither obvious nor certain. The success of humans to achieve this outcome will depend on their ability to find and recognise new ways of living and then enabling these to be deployed globally. We will return to the theme of encouraging entrepreneurship and innovation policy in the next chapter, but, to me, enabling new ways of living is clearly a critical component of redesigning the world.

★ ★ ★

The Age of Madness

John Gibbons,
Journalist
CEO, Medmedia Group
Founder, www.thinkorswim.ie
Dublin, Ireland

First, the good news. Against the odds, we made it to 2100. Only fifty years ago it looked like it was game over for homo sapiens. It sounds crazy now, but back in my grandparents' time they really did carry on for a while like there was no tomorrow: tearing down rainforests, flattening mountains, poisoning the seas, waging war on nature – all in pursuit of this strange idea they called 'growth'.

There aren't that many books now, but our teachers describe the Age of Madness, as it's called, when the scientific community repeatedly warned that Earth systems were in extreme danger. But nobody listened, and few chose to act.

How could this have happened? Everyone, it seems, was competing with everyone else for money, resources, status. No one seemed to notice that this spree couldn't last forever. Even the announcement back in 2015 that half of all the world's wild animals had been wiped out failed to ring the alarm bells. And as for all the warnings about climate change, they always seemed to be about someone else, or some time in the future...

Well, that future is now. This generation has learned the hard lesson of hubris – and humility. There's barely fifty million of us now globally. Life is tough, but we're managing. This time, we're keeping it simple. They say the Earth is healing, maybe they're right. Maybe we can at last live in a world where, in the words of the poet Seamus Heaney, "hope and history rhyme".

Through the early decades of the twentieth century, the world was making decisions that have both pulled many of us out of poverty and led to our currently challenges. The 'Gusher Age' in Texas during the 1920s transformed that State from being predominantly rural to having major cities and serious wealth. The era spawned some of the world's biggest and most influential oil companies such as Texaco, Esso, Gulf Oil and Exxon. The correlated growth of the motor car was also underway with Henry Ford producing his fifteenth million Model T Ford in 1927.

The rapid deployment of the car had a slow start. From one of its earliest incarnations by Karl Benz in 1886 through to the first Model T Ford in 1908, it was seen as an expensive luxury. It was only with the business model innovation introduced by Ford on a proven technology that the global scale up started.

This might give us some clues on the way forward in terms of how to change behaviours.

Tony Seba, a lecturer in entrepreneurship at Stanford University, highlighted the rapid uptake of the motor car in a talk he gave in September 2014 when he showed a picture of New York's Fifth Avenue in 1900 with many horse-drawn carriages and a single car. He then showed a picture of the same street in 1913 with all cars and no horses.

Seba is the author of *Clean Disruption of Energy and Transportation* which forecasts a rapid uptake of both solar energy generation and electric vehicles such that both will be the cheapest options by 2020 and will comprise 100% of the new build market by 2030. He also forecasts the end of car ownership and the emergence of autonomous 'car-as-a service' which will mean an 80% reduction in both car sales and car parking in every city within ten years.

Of course, neither solar nor electric vehicles are new technologies. The technologies are improving, but it is the business and financing models that are evolving most rapidly and it will be this that drives their deployment.

The first iteration of a solar panel was shown by Augustin Mouchot at the Universal Exhibition in Paris in 1878. The first successful electric car in the US was made by William Morrison in Des Moines, Iowa in 1890. By 1900, a third of all vehicles were electric and their numbers grew strongly through the first decade of the century. The combination of Texan 'gushers' and the Model T halted their growth for the rest of that century.

John Gibbons is an Irish journalist and environmental activist and he does not see things going so well. His vision could easily sit with our pessimists in Chapter 5, but he is included here for a very specific reason.

John has run a successful medical communications business for over twenty years and is a regular commentator in the Irish media on environmental issues, including a weekly environment column in The Irish Times between 2008 and 2010. John is a virulent critic of the media's lack of responsibility in the reporting of climate change and this is why he is included in our chapter about setting off from here.

John's vision includes more bad news than good news and he recalls the '*Age of Madness*' where people decided not to act and not to listen to the scientists. Even the news, published in 2014 by WWF, that '*half of all the world's wild animals had been wiped out*' was not enough to gain attention. The fifty million survivors have experienced '*hubris and humility*' and in their redesigned world, they are '*keeping it simple*'.

On his website, John sets out this position: '*Like it or not, we live in the Era of Consequences. Neither ignorance nor cynicism is a defence. For those armed with the facts, doing nothing is no longer an option.*' This is our starting point.

If you have read this far then, for you, '*nothing is no longer an option*'.

He views the media as a critical tool in enabling the community to gain a greater understanding of the problem and the ways we can resolve it. The media tells us that climate change does not sell and is not of interest to their audience. This challenge however may be due to a lack of imagination on the part of the media and those advocating action and is not a valid reason to omit meaningful coverage of a critical issue.

In a 2015 blog post, John praises the UK Guardian newspaper, under outgoing editor, Alan Rusbridger, in seeking '*to break this communications impasse*'.

He quotes Rusbridger who explains the reason for the stand that has been taken.

'Changes to the Earth's climate rarely make it to the top of the news list. The changes may be happening too fast for human comfort, but they happen too slowly for the newsmakers – and, to be fair, for most readers. These events that have yet to materialise may dwarf anything journalists have had to cover over the past troubled century. There may be untold catastrophes, famines, floods, droughts, wars, migrations and sufferings just around the corner. But that is futurology, not news, so it is not going to force itself on any front page any time soon.'

The Guardian's '*Keep it in the ground*' campaign seeks to shame institutions and organizations, from the Bill & Melinda Gates Foundation to the Wellcome Trust, to dump their investments in fossil fuel companies. This is based on research suggesting that to keep global warming below two degrees, '*at least 80% of the world's proven fossil fuel reserves can never be burned.*' The campaign is closely aligned with Bill McKibbon's 350.org.

In hindsight, maybe society and its governments may have made some different choices if it had understood the full impacts of decisions made and industries encouraged. But that was then and this is now. We are starting our journey in the Age of Madness.

My fourteen year old son, Cormac, recently returned home from a five week school camp where he lived with five other boys and, between them, they had to do all their own shopping, cooking, cleaning and washing. This parents' delight is a program to help young teenagers become less reliant on others and to test and build their own strengths.

Cormac, being a strong willed, opinionated and fairly disorganised young man absolutely loved the trip. He came back with two major learnings which will stand him in good stead for the rest of his life. Firstly, to help him become more organised he adopted a 'panic early' strategy. If you find that in fact you did not need to panic, then there is nothing lost in getting on with things. Secondly, he learnt that he had to pick the arguments it was worth having. Getting cross over the way one of his housemates peels potatoes or digs a hole is not an issue of importance and is not something worth taking a stand on.

These two lessons provide the perfect starting point for setting off from here. Work out the important arguments to have and then panic early. With this in mind, everyone is in a position to start telling the story, changing the way they behave and influencing others. To do this well will need good communications tools, and luckily the visionaries in this book have provided you with everything you need to get started.

* * *

We'll survive and, despite John Gibbon's vision, I think that we will survive well. There will however be much collateral damage as we are already starting to see. The longer we wait to start our journey the more damage we will have.

So we just need to get going - to 'panic early'. It is not always comfortable to set off on the journey without knowing exactly where you are going or how you are going to get there. With the right mindset however, it can be exciting: there are so many paths to choose. As long as you know that selecting one path does not lock you in to that direction for ever, it can be fun to try different things. To see how to create the best life or the best community or the best world.

This is something we are all familiar with. We all set out on our lives mostly with not much idea of where we are going. When people have clear plans, the only certainty is that their lives will take unexpected paths. After a while we work out what is important and head that way, but things are still never certain or always easy.

So our journey to 2100 is just living the life of the century. If we have a rough idea of where we are going - hence our visions - we'll figure out a way of getting there as we go. The biggest risk is not starting the journey and waiting for the perfect plan. As with any entrepreneurial adventure, getting going with the best available current information is the only way to increase the chance of success.

Managing long term illness is very similar. You certainly know the desired and acceptable goals in terms of health and quality of life, but there is never a clear plan of how to get there. You have to get the advice of experts, assess what is known at the time and make what feel like the best decisions at that moment. They are not always right, but they are made with the end goal in mind. When you get pushed backwards a few steps, you just have to take a deep breath and stand up again and make the next decision. It is not easy, especially when the backwards steps sometime seem to be winning, but is the only choice to move towards the best outcome.

For our sick world, we are taking many backwards steps and we have no choice but to stand up again and make the next decision. The additional challenge with climate change is that the decision making is much, much more complex. We need to swing the views of people all over the world to be supportive of action so that our politicians have no option but to push ahead. Communities and companies can and are taking action regardless of government, but for the really big changes, government will need to be a willing partner.

So we come back to the art of communication - again. The protest movements such as 350.org have learnt much from action taken by the US civil rights movement in the 1960s and in South Africa in the 1980s and 1990s. As discussed, this is absolutely necessary and increases the pressure to avoid bad things. Simultaneously communicating in a way that attracts the community to a better future is a complementary strategy that will appeal to a wider audience.

There is much to be learnt from how the arts world communicates. Why is it that people are more interested in a pop song or a painting than in the fate of their future world? Art connects emotionally and at a very different level to everything else in our communication drenched world. It provides a lightness, it can unleash emotions, it can help people feel that they are not alone in their thoughts.

The environment movement has used this tactic on the negative side by showing pollution or animals suffering but have never managed to do it in an uplifting way. In a way that helps people feel understood and connected. In a way that gets people excited about what might happen next. There are no overnight queues waiting to buy the new improved version of the environment story.

How do we make the story of the environment as attractive as a just released iPhone?

David Fogarty is a Singapore-based journalist who works for The Straits Times and previously worked as the Asia Climate Change Correspondent for Reuters. David's vision sets out how corporate values and culture will evolve. Remembering that what gets measured gets managed, he has Gross Environmental Performance as the key measure of company investability. Anne McIvor's stock report analyst in Chapter 16 might take this as a key theme in her reporting.

Natural resources are fully valued and highly prized in this world. According to the International Institute for Sustainable Development (IISD), the term 'natural capital' is defined as *the land, air, water, living organisms and all formations of the Earth's biosphere that provide us with ecosystem goods and services imperative for survival and well-being.* IISD argues that Natural Capital forms the basis of all human economic activity and must therefore be measured and valued.

The term 'natural capital' was first used in 1973 by E.F. Schumacher in his book *Small Is Beautiful* and was popularised through the 1999 book *Natural Capitalism* co-authored by Chapter 12's Hunter Lovins.

This provides another starting point for our journey: questioning why our natural resources are not valued and suggesting how this might be achieved. Groups like the IISD are working on developing frameworks for widespread use by governments, corporations and communities to enable this to happen.

One of the keys to setting off from here is to look forward to where we want to go and not dwell too much on the past. Just because coal and oil have been invaluable to our journey to date, does not mean we need to keep using them. Bows and arrows were invaluable to historic victories until we found a better way to kill each other.

The American motivational speaker, Zig Zigler, summed this up when saying, *'The first step to getting what you want is to have the courage to get rid of what you don't.'* So we must first work out what we do not want going forward and then we can create alternative solutions.

To take my own advice for once and go back to the power of communicating through the arts, this can be said more effectively through the Missy Higgins song, '*Secret*' when she says, '*If you spend your whole life looking behind you, you don't see what's in front*'

If we set off from here with Missy in our earphones and the visions of a better world in our sights, we are sure to be heading in the right direction.

Gross Environmental Performance
David Fogarty
Assistant Foreign Editor, The Straits Times
Singapore

In the boardrooms of 2100, environmental service officers (ESOs) sit right next to the CEO.

That's because in 2100, how a major company manages its pollution, its waste and the impact of its operations on the land are the top metrics by which any corporation is measured. Shareholders and customers frown severely on any firm that pollutes the air, dirties the water, uses non-renewable energy sources or – worst of the worst – damages wetlands, forests or other natural landscapes. Companies that take CO2 out of the atmosphere, help restore forests, wetlands and rebuild fisheries attract particularly good reviews from stock analysts.

Ecosystem services, the services that nature provides to all of us, are highly valued by everyone in 2100. Governments measure ecosystem health – from coral reefs, to forests, water catchments to air quality – and report them widely. Gross Environmental Performance is a key indicator, just like inflation. Everyone is acutely aware of their own personal impact on the planet – children are taught about how nature is connected to everything we do.

Nature is highly prized and vigorously protected. Forests are given space to regenerate, ocean fisheries are allowed to recover and wetlands are rehabilitated and recharged.

The Earth at 2100 is very different from 2040, when global economies were facing collapse. Ecosystems from the Amazon to the Siberian tundra to the Pacific Ocean had been stripped of their resources, rivers were polluted and the atmosphere brimming with polluting. We were all dying. Wars were raging.

By 2050, a new global order came in and set about rapid transformation of economies away from polluting energy and mining and wasteful lifestyles. We already had the technology and by 2050 we finally had the political will to change. And we found that by using less, we ultimately had more.

Chapter 22

WITH WISDOM,
IT'S ALL ABOUT THE EXECUTION

'The secret of change is not to focus all of your energy, not on fighting the old, but on building the new'

Dan Millman,
Way of the Peaceful Warrior: A Book that Changes Lives

Chapter 22

WITH WISDOM,
IT'S ALL ABOUT THE EXECUTION

Eight Dollars per Barrel
Claus Pram Astrup
Advisor to the CEO
The Global Environment Facility
Washington DC, United States

87 years old, he was born in '13. An unlucky number, he thought, smiling to himself. But at the eve of Y2K.1 it seemed that the world had actually been lucky.

Although too young to experience it himself, Paris 2015 had started something. A spirit of global solidarity, responsibility and ambition was kindled. A global movement, where he spent most of his working life, had inevitably gathered momentum. People had since changed their way of life. Beef became the exception not the norm. Across the globe, households rapidly switched electricity demand to wind and solar, and power producers were more than happy to oblige.

Amazing improvements in battery technology revolutionized the transport sector: In 2027, the hundredth anniversary of the last Model T Ford, production of combustion engine vehicles in the US had ceased. Governments eventually caught on, and began taxing fossil fuels aggressively. Demand for crude oil and coal eventually collapsed—the current price of $8 per barrel a clear indication of excess supply—and neither were traded internationally anymore.

The world could proudly look back at a century of vision and determination. And even if there had been painful losses along the way—the great African Rhino that he had never seen in its natural habitat came to his mind—overall, the planet Earth had proven more resilient than humanity perhaps deserved.

My father's first memory was having a gun pointed at his head by a 'black and tan' soldier. His grandmother was told that, unless she told him where the uncles were, the '*kid gets it*'. Granny said they'd have to shoot him then because she knew nothing! She had called their bluff and they left with nothing. Not surprisingly, the event made a big impression on the four year old boy.

His grandmother was apparently wise, but more importantly she judged the situation correctly and executed her strategy effectively - luckily for me!

The visions presented in this book provide guidance on where we need to get to and the challenges we may face along the way. It is certain that the journey will not be straightforward and will likely resemble Edison's discovery of 10,000 ways of how *not* to make a light bulb before we succeed. For this reason, lessons from entrepreneurs and innovation policy may inform this debate to a greater extent than further input on the science of climate or the populist concerns of politicians.

Research on what makes a successful entrepreneur suggests that constancy of purpose, flexibility in approach and the ability to fail cheaply many times provide the core to success.

In Chapter 9, we looked at what makes a successful entrepreneur and how this can be applied to building a better world. Here we considered how Joseph Schumpeter's '*creative destruction*' can strike at the '*foundations and [the] very lives*' of existing firms embedded in the old way of doing things.

Successful entrepreneurship requires the ability to recognise opportunities, try out possible solutions and to fail as quickly and as cheaply as possible. The common characteristics of serial entrepreneurs is to use an effectual approach of knowing their strengths and what they can afford to lose, focussing only what they can control, building partnerships and using bad news as clues to how the system is working. The effectual worldview means that you create the future from what you have at your disposal.

Franklin D. Roosevelt summed up the life of the entrepreneur or the pioneer succinctly, '*It is common sense to take a method and try it. If it fails, admit it frankly and try another. But above all, try something.*'

Successful entrepreneurs do not just try anything and see if it works. They will instead use their knowledge of the system and of what they can control to select very specific actions that might work and, if they do not, will at least provide insight into the workings of the system.

Having a great idea or a vision of the future will help to achieve better outcomes through the optimism bias discussed in Chapter 4. If people believe they will get to their desired future state they are more likely to persevere and overcome obstacles along the way. This journey will however be far easier if it is done in an environment that is supportive of innovation and executed using the experience of those who have previously conquered the unknowable.

The British actress, Brenda Blethan, plays the lead role in a BBC drama called *Vera*. Detective Chief Inspector Vera Stanhope solves murders in the stunning scenery of Northumberland in the North of England. Her character is obsessive, disorganised and, as it says in the promotional material, '*faces the world with caustic wit, guile and courage*'.

When faced with the knowledge of the solution in one episode, she cautions her partner to act carefully, '*With wisdom, it's all about the execution*'. This might be the most important guidance we are given on our journey to 2100. We know the problem, we even know many of the possible solutions but how we execute them is going to be critical in determining their timing and success.

Claus Pram Astrup plays a key advisory role at the Global Environment Facility in Washington DC. The GEF has 183 member countries working together to address global environmental issues. Since 1991, the GEF has provided $13.5 billion in grants and leveraged $65 billion in co-financing for 3,900 projects in more than 165 developing countries. Both developed and developing countries alike have provided these funds to support activities related to biodiversity, climate change, international waters, land degradation, and chemicals and waste in the context of development projects and programs.

Claus' vision foresees '*a century of vision and determination*' where our way of living is transformed. He sees governments playing a big part in the transformation by unleashing the ideas that were developed. He pins his hopes on the Paris conference in 2015, but that is just the first step in how governments *'eventually caught on'*.

Claus' eight dollar per barrel of oil is a measure of how much the world has changed once the last internal combustion engine was made. Showing his optimism, he sees that our planet will be *'more resilient than humanity perhaps deserved.'*

One thing that governments can do immediately is to build an innovation ecosystem that encourages and supports its citizens to build a better world. This of course also has economic benefits as it encourages new businesses to grow, creates jobs and provides increased efficiency solutions to existing industry. Where its real value lies however is in its ability to help transform its country to be a global leader in the new way of living; to become one of Frans Nauta's winners.

Innovation policy is an area fraught with political danger. It encourages and facilitates lots of ventures that fail and a few that succeed. The potential for front page news about wasted money is significant and it scares elected politicians. It is however absolutely critical for countries and communities to evolve and move towards new, better ways of living. This dichotomy is the reason for so much innovation policy being poorly designed and eventually failing. The civil servants are given the task of designing a foolproof system that will guarantee success so they design something that filters anything that involves risk - or indeed innovation. In the words of Theodore Roosevelt, we need to remind our policy makers that, *'It is hard to fail, but it is worse never to have tried to succeed.'*

As well as being a Grammy-winning song for Green Day, *'The Boulevard of Broken Dreams'* is the title of a book on how to design a successful innovation policy by Professor Josh Lerner, head of Entrepreneurial Management at the Harvard Business School.

In the book, Lerner explores policy settings that have helped and, more often, those that have failed. He also provides some guiding principles for policy makers on the elements that should be considered when trying to stimulate innovation and entrepreneurship in their local economies. These principles include:

1. building a long-term stable environment that encourages risk taking, recognises long lead times and celebrates both success and failure;
2. facilitating connections with researchers, customers and investors both locally and globally; and
3. providing education to all parties and not being overly pre-scriptive in the design of the support programs.

The last point about making sure that programs are designed with flexibility is a particular challenge for governments who like to have everything strictly defined and controlled. However, programs that encourage innovation must be innovative in them-selves otherwise they will not be able to adapt to the ever changing environment.

Any city, region or national government can wisely execute in-novation policies using this framework. This will enable a multitude of ideas to be explored and trialled and the best ones to help change the world.

I have used this framework to work with regional governments in Australia to help them to design their local innovation ecosys-tems. The region that has managed to best address all elements of the framework wins a national award as Australia's most Innovative Region. Even the best regions struggle with many aspects of the framework and are continually seeking to better support their local innovators.

A framework to enable innovation to flourish in every city and region is going to be a critical part of redesigning the world. Im-portantly, the cities and regions that execute this strategy the best will become the leaders in our twenty-second century world.

The Energy-Data Nexus

Rob Day
Managing Director
Black Coral Capital
Boston, United States

In the years up to 2100, out of both necessity and opportunity, energy around the world increasingly shifted to electricity and that to clean sources of power. These forms of electricity capacity typically have very low operating costs (e.g. sunlight is free), but do require upfront capital cost.

Our appetite for data is now voracious, constrained only by available bandwidth and energy to power the equipment. Data availability has become ubiquitous and people around the world increasingly rely upon data- and thus, energy- intensive content for productivity, as a substitute for expensive physical transportation (virtual gatherings, and distributed software-driven manufacturing), and simply for entertainment.

However, power supply is not yet ubiquitous. Yes, the marginal cost of energy is close to zero, meaning consumers think nothing of demanding it in large quantities, instantaneously. And yet the physical realities of power transportation or new power generation installation mean that it is still not uniformly available in all geographies. There are pockets of massive power supply, inconsistently connected with shifting areas of demand.

Thus, a major area of investor interest over much of twenty-first century was the arbitrage of data demand and energy availability. Ways to physically provision power where and when needed, rapidly. Market schemes to trade off curtailment by one customer to accommodate a spike in demand by another. This Energy-Data Nexus is now readily apparent and continues to be a major market opportunity.

A critical component in any innovation system is that of investors backing the emerging trends. Those that are good at this manage to invest in a company cheaply when the company is still small and exit with very healthy profits once the company has grown. Of course this can be a high risk exercise and many early-stage companies with the great potential fail. In my work with some of Australia's best technologies through the Australian Technologies Competition, it is clear that the skills required to turn a good technology into a great company are far more than just technological. We start our mentoring program each year by telling the Finalists that their technology is only twenty per cent of building a successful business. This usually leads to a very quiet room full of attentive inventors!

Venture Capital is one of the major providers on this risk capital and one of the pioneers of venture investing into clean technologies is Rob Day from Black Coral Capital. Rob has been investing in cleantech and been one of the drivers of the whole US cleantech sector since 2004.

Black Coral Capital states that its target investments are '*teams who are reinventing how people buy, sell and use "resource innovations" – the next wave of cost-advantaged, sustainable solutions for the world's ever-growing demand for energy, water, food and other key resources.*' This is just investing in the future by finding and supporting the companies that are going help make the world operate more sustainably - and make good profits in doing so.

Rob's vision of the greatest investment opportunities over next century involves the connection between energy and data. He sees the greatest opportunities coming from those companies that enable data and energy to be provided instantaneously wherever and whenever it is required.

To find, encourage and better understand these opportunities Rob has been involved in many parts of the innovation ecosystem in the North East of the United States. He has chaired the regional cleantech competition, been on numerous advisory boards and provides regular media commentary. As discussed in Chapter 19, this role of 'connector' is critical in the success of any community and Rob has been a consummate cleantech connector for over a decade.

Dra

Global Complexities

Simon Divecha
Associate, MetaIntegral Academy
Founder, Greenmode
Adelaide, Australia

As I'm waking to awareness on the morning of 1 January 2100, I can't help but look back through our lives over the last century. Innovation, of course, continued to explode driving standout change as we strove to answer our sustainability imperatives. This was a scramble, a race against climate and other environmental stresses - by 2020 we had already built up a substantial ecological debt. Greenhouse gas levels alone required a sustained, multi-decade, drawdown effort.

The truly standout shifts were, however, a dance between radical technological change and upgrading our society's global and local operating systems. The two flowed together, one enabling the other. Far more sophisticated ways of working together, managing local and global complexities and updating our empathetic and intuitive self-awareness emerged.

It was not so much what we were doing to address climate change rather what climate change, and a cavalcade of other social dilemmas arising with new technologies, did to us so we could enable positive futures.

There were many dark times but, by the new century, we had realised an interconnected and caring, flourishing and exciting, collaborative and competitive, environmentally sound new world. Today, in 2100, there are inherent tensions and paradoxes between our diversity of priorities. Our transformational shifts found balance points between such polarities. Additionally, we also often see the positive aspects of our inevitable different positions in a complex world. We recognised this complexity to shift ourselves, the society around us and to become what we needed to be for viable, sustaining futures.

Simon Divecha is another Adelaide resident with a global view. He has worked on many leading projects over his twenty years working in the cross-over between sustainability and innovation. He has led teams that drove Adelaide's Solar City project, developed a $75m sustainable housing development and established a carbon management course at the University of Adelaide.

Simon's vision builds on the innovation theme above. He sees the combination of both technical and social innovation as the enabler of building our '*positive futures*'. The innovation that enabled people to work together locally and globally on different solutions led not only to solving the solutions but also to redesigning our concept of the world allowing '*our empathetic and intuitive self-awareness*' to emerge. Importantly, as with any innovation system, the outcome is not actually designed and cannot be controlled but with the right guidance, the outcome that emerges can exceed any expectations.

In addition to enabling innovation, leadership plays a critical role in how we evolve. Leadership comes from many quarters. Our political leaders get the most air-time but are not necessarily the most influential. There are leaders at every level from corporations, charities, activists, communities, churches, schools or in any group. A leader that commands respect in any forum will influence the thinking and behaviour of their followers. Leaders do not have to have an official title, it can just be someone that influences, binds and inspires a group of people. There does not even have to be a formal group to lead, as we have seen with movements inspired through social media. We all have moments of being the leader of a group, even with a small group for a short time. In those moments, good leaders will inspire people towards their long term goals.

Many of the authors in this book are significant leaders of large groups of people and with global influence. As an example, just twenty of them have a combined following of 300,000 people on Twitter. That is a lot of people globally that are interested in building a better future.

In my teaching of MBA and corporate leadership courses, I have found that those in the class have very similar ideas of what they admire in and want from a leader. They want a leader that is firm, fair, consistent, inspiring and brings to the group a higher purpose or goal that binds people together. It does not really matter whether they are extroverts or introverts, overly caring or slightly distant as long as they have those key aspects. The consistency desired is not only in their treatment of people and issues but in everything they do. If they say one thing but do another, whether at work or not, then a leader will lose respect and the loss of respect will mean they will no longer be a leader. They may still be in a position of authority but they will not be a true leader.

In my corporate life, I worked with those in positions of authority and most of them, to me, were not even close to being true leaders. In my post-corporate life, I have had the good fortune to meet and work with many people that do indeed stand the test of being a good leader and consequently inspire respect and a following.

It can be hard and risky for political leaders in Western democracies to take a firm stand on issues, particularly where there will be influential losers as a result. It is not however unheard of. Those politicians who do take a stand on a matter of principle earn long term respect. Of course they might not get re-elected but, looking on the upside, they are likely to be far more employable if they are seen as a strong leader!

Authentic Leadership is becoming a more common topic in management education and studies. Whilst presented as the latest great discovery and the current trend in how to be a leader, to me, it just feels as though it is describing what a good leader has always been. Leaders that make a difference do not need to be taught on an MBA or elsewhere that you earn respect from having integrity, honesty, empathy, openness and a long term plan with meaning.

That is not to say that the concept of Authentic Leadership does not have merit. Its greatest strength is highlighted by Bill George in his 2003 book entitled, Authentic Leadership. '*No one can be authentic by trying to imitate someone else.*' He goes on to explain that, '*you can learn from others' experiences, but there is no way you can be successful when you are trying to be like them. People trust you when you are genuine and authentic, not a replica of someone else.*'

George was the former CEO of Medtronic and argues that authentic leaders of mission-driven companies will create far greater shareholder value than financially oriented companies.

The concept fits well with John Harradine's vision in Chapter 10 that says that change all starts from '*deciding what we stand for*' and resolutely sticking to your aims. An authentic leader will do just that.

To drive the changes that are needed to build the better worlds as presented in our visions will require many authentic leaders leading many groups to behave differently. Each group and each leader will require something unique to be able to engage and make a difference.

Suhit Anantula sees a new kind of leader emerging to drive this change in his vision. Suhit works at the intersection of entrepreneurship, design and social sciences with a focus on social change. He heads Business Innovation at The Australian Centre for Social Innovation that we discussed in Chapter 9 and led the development of the Family by Family and Weavers programs there.

Suhit sees his wonderful future world as having many benefits with all of its inhabitants having an excellent quality of life. To get there he sees three critical developments: technology to delivery abundant energy globally, social innovation to drive '*social prosperity*' and humble, collaborative leaders who are responsive to change.

Great leaders inspire change and anyone can be a great leader. You can tell the stories of your vision of a better world to anyone that will listen and that will inspire change.

One of my favourite books as a young child, along with Rudyard Kipling's Just So Stories, was *Struwwelpeter* by Dr Heinrich Hoffman, which was originally published in German in 1845. It is a collection of ten wonderfully illustrated stories of all the bad things that can happen if children do not do as they are told. For instance, the story of Little Suck-a-Thumb starts with:

One day, Mamma said: "Conrad dear
I must go out and leave you here.
But mind now. Conrad, what I say,

Don't suck your thumb while I'm away.
The great tall tailor always comes
To little boys that suck their thumbs,
And ere they dream what he's about,
He takes his great sharp scissors out
And cuts their thumbs clean off, - and then,
You know, they never grow again."

Like all of the stories, this ends badly with spurts of blood from thumbless hands.

The challenge for our leaders today and in future years is to convince the rest of our race that change will not only avoid the bad outcomes but will build a world worth living in and lives worth living. You can choose to be one of these leaders in your community. If these leaders fail and we continue to suck our thumbs, then we too will find out what will '*never grow again*'.

Humble Leaders

Suhit Anantula
Strategy Designer, Business Models Inc
Director of Business Innovation,
The Australian Centre for Social Innovation
Adelaide, Australia

The baby born in the new millennium in Australia is 100 years old today. As she celebrates her hundredth birthday with her friends and family she celebrates not only her life but the world in 2100 where most of the countries of the world are better than the Australia of the year 2000. Nine billion people in the world have a way of life with economic, social and well-being benefits that were unimaginable when she was born.

As she recounts, her 30 year old grandson asks, "How did this happen?".

She explains the three things that led the world to this prosperity:

1. *Cheap, clean and common energy became available all over the world as humanity harnessed the power of the Sun. Necessity is the mother of invention and China, India and many African and South American countries worked together to create a breakthrough in technology. This was then supercharged by ingenious entrepreneurs with innovative business models to provide energy to every corner of the world.*

2. *Entrepreneurship in the corporate, social & public sector converted economic prosperity into social prosperity. Individuals from the public, social and corporate sectors worked together collaboratively to create outcomes that were socially, environmentally and economically beneficial.*

3. *The digital revolution created a new kind of leader. People who were humble, responsive to change and worked in collaboration with others.*

Most importantly, she says, the doom and gloom predictions of the early part of the century never came true because of the ingenuity of mankind.

Chapter 23

COMMON SENSE

Perhaps the sentiments contained in the following pages, are not YET sufficiently fashionable to procure them general favour; a long habit of not thinking a thing WRONG, gives it a superficial appearance of being RIGHT, and raises at first a formidable outcry in defense of custom. But the tumult soon subsides. Time makes more converts than reason.

Thomas Paine, Common Sense, 1776

Common sense is genius dressed in its working clothes.

Ralph Waldo Emerson

Chapter 23

COMMON SENSE

'Those who don't know history are destined to repeat it'
Edmund Burke

Professor Chris West
CEO, Royal Zoological Society of Scotland
Edinburgh, Scotland

In city-colonies alongside energy and food centres and ecology reserves, we have immersion pods so children can experience what the world was like after humans 'swarmed' and nearly sabotaged the planet. They can see and feel compressed into minutes the time of reckless chopping, digging, burning, befouling, breeding and fighting that happened and hear the falsehoods of leaders blinded by greed and bingeing selfishly as others starved and died. They called it 'progress'.

Most children cry on experiencing the harpooning of a whale or felling of an ancient tree. They ask us older ones, why did you let it happen? It's a fair question, hard to answer. Our world is hot, crowded and damaged but we finally realised that life was more precious than money. We discovered ourselves. We take the children and share with them the 'rewild areas' to feel the shade of trees and listen to real birdsong. They learn about ecology, not economics, so they understand that we depend on nature as it depends on us. Us older ones celebrate survival and the youngsters hope and renewal.

This isn't really about politics, economics or religion. It is a combination of common sense and deep feelings and taking responsibility, each of us as a human and as a part of nature.

'I offer nothing more than simple facts, plain arguments, and common sense.'

These are the words of Thomas Paine in his 1776 book *Common Sense*. Paine was an English-American political writer, theorist and activist who had a great influence on the thoughts and ideas which led to the American Revolution and the Declaration of Independence.

Common sense is defined in the Collins English Dictionary as *'plain ordinary good judgment'*. Building a better world that lives within its natural capital means and allows all its human inhabitants to live lives worth living seems like common sense to me. It may take some time but it can be achieved. Framing our actions and decisions on a journey towards this goal seems eminently 'commonsensical'.

There will of course be arguments about the details and, more importantly for the hundreds of millions of vulnerable people, the timing.

This final chapter will attempt to pull together all the many seeds we have sown through the book. Firstly, a summary of our challenges and why humans are struggling to act with common sense. Then a look at the solutions that have been discussed and suggestions on how this can get us moving in the right direction. Finally, it is over to you and what you can do help deliver those solutions.

★ ★ ★

Rational arguments for rapid action abound. We do not need any more of those. The rational arguments along with pessimists' catastrophes are essential, but insufficient to inspire more than a small minority. What is needed is a different way of communicating that inspires and attracts the widest possible array of people to travel on this journey.

As we have seen, the human brain has evolved to cope well with imminent threats. It is not designed to effectively assess long term risk. Furthermore the cultural norms of rich countries have evolved to provide incentives that ignore long term consequences.

There is much to be scared about in those long term consequences. The longer we dither, the more pain will be inflicted, the
more species wiped out, the larger the hordes of climate refugees
and the more climate war devastation. We stand a very real chance
of being remembered as the time thieves or the Neroan generation
that fiddled whilst the world burnt.

As the predicted collapse of mid-century is raging, what will
you do when your grandchildren ask you why you were so weak?
Why didn't you stand up? Why did you wait so long? You can
mumble you didn't have the power; you had no control; it was the
fault of others. They won't believe you.

You have the choice of what world you want to build. Whoever
you are and whatever you do, you have influence. Through your
networks you can start to work on attracting people towards a
better future. Humanity will survive – it is just a question of how
much we choose to lose along the way.

Chris West runs the Edinburgh Zoo and might well be known as
the panda-man. Having reinvigorated Adelaide Zoo with pandas in
2009 he has overseen the same experience in Edinburgh. However,
he is much more than that and is at the forefront of redefining
the role of zoos in community education and engagement about
environmental issues. His move to Edinburgh was Adelaide's loss.

Chris' vision sees the children of 2100 being shocked at the
carelessness and callousness of their forebears. The children cry at
watching this and ask 'why did you let it happen?' This future is created
through 'common sense and deep feelings and taking responsibility'.

The human decision-making process combines an assessment
of facts with the 'gut-feeling' that weighs up the many subconscious inputs on the veracity, relevance and priority of the options
available. The emotional part of the decision-making process is the
most important factor. Arguing on facts alone is therefore a futile
pursuit.

Making a decision is a trade-off and can involve sacrifice.
Aran Ralston's decision to amputate his own arm on day five was
eminently sensible, if not easy. When there are no more options left,

the sacrifices get more and more serious.

Decisions on health are similarly complex. The decisions of Kate's managers to leave her sick in Ghana for weeks in 1994 was driven by a culture that tough hard-nosed lawyers do not need to be cared for - they must either sink or swim. These same managers all ran for cover when Kate's case came to court: nothing then mattered more than protecting their own little careers. Kate was the collateral damage in a system that did not consider employee welfare a priority. Workplace practices improved quickly after the action we took against Freshfields, as it was then known, and young lawyers today are treated better. Kate's twenty years of suffering was perhaps the sacrifice - the amputation - required to change the thinking in the Magic Circle.

Wicked Problems, as discussed earlier, are complex and non-linear. They have no clear solution and are not fully understood. Building a better world, managing chronic illness and overcoming climate change are all good examples of Wicked Problems. The solving of such problems requires a different way of behaving. It needs collaboration, trial-and-error, integrative thinking and dancing with the system. These are things that the large bureaucracies of governments and corporations struggle to deliver.

An important driver of decisions is fear and this is why the pessimists are an incredibly important part of the solution. Pessimists provide the answer to 'or what?' Fear often drives action and can start the journey.

We need this fear response given what the future might hold, but at this stage there seems to be only a mild anxiety at best. Anxiety allows the human brain to switch off from the problem and get on with 'business as usual'. Fear has no 'off' switch until the threat is removed. The fear mongers will not succeed on their own but they are absolutely necessary to garner global support.

Similarly, negative psychology is very good at initiating action but it is positive psychology that seems to provide permanent changes to brain patterns. Both inputs are often needed to provide the emotional and rational reasons that humans need before making decisions.

This is where environmental communications to date have failed. They have mostly been about the negative aspects of our changing climate and with no long term goals using positive psychology to make permanent changes in thinking. For this we need visions.

For Purpose

Simon Webb
Senior Vice President
Ogilvy Public Relations
Beijing, China

Looking back on it, the inflection point for building community consensus to address climate change came when global leaders and activists started to frame their communications to communities around the world less in terms of the dire risks to humanity – severe though they turned out to be – and more in terms of the opportunities they presented.

Inspired perhaps by the early manned missions to Mars in the 20s and the Second Space Race they brought about, campaigns shifted focus to the opportunities for entire communities to rally together around a common cause. A spirit of shared endeavour was created – by drawing on stories of national achievement in the past, inspiration was found to make the sacrifices required in the present to ensure the wellbeing and even survival of future generations. The inertia shown by the first generations presented with the prospect of climate change was overrun by subsequent generations who were able to find purpose by facing this common cause.

This defining shift in community attitudes also brought about this century's defining pivot in the economy. Rising up between the failed poles of the 'not-for-profits' on the one hand which had shown themselves unable to resolve problems efficiently or at scale and the private corporations on the other, whose assiduous profit-maximising had seen them show at times a psychopathic disregard for the harm their operations engendered, the 'for-purposes' flourished.

Defined by their combination of productivity-seeking and dedication to achieving social outcomes, the 'for-purposes' now predominate all sectors in the economy having gained momentum in the late 10s and early 20s. This was after the Great Restructuring which saw the entire global financial sector reorganised into 'for purposes' after a catastrophic string of wealth-destroying financial collapses in the US, China and Europe.

As we have seen, when communities have a common purpose then they can pull together and achieve great outcomes. This is the same whether the communities are within a company, suburb, school or sporting club. A common goal draws people together to work as a team.

Simon Webb's vision above is for the emergence of a new type of organisation by 2100 that are able to be both 'for profit' and 'for good'. He calls these new organisations 'For-Purposes'. This would bridge the gap between the good intentions of charities and the efficiency delivered by corporations. In Simon's world, this outcome emerged once people stopped talking about dire risks and started considering how positive messages can deliver better outcomes.

Simon is another Beijing resident and is in the business of communication. He leads the OgilvyEarth practice in China and, amongst other things, has helped governments build support for pricing carbon and in changing consumer behaviour in relation to energy efficiency. His view that change can best be delivered through positive messaging therefore comes from practical experience in Australia and across Asia.

However, talking about hopes for a future world is problematic. Envisioning is largely a taboo activity in Western culture. It is seen as dreaming, being ungrounded, rocking the boat. Certainly not something that will help this quarter's profits. Even the work of companies like OgilvyEarth that help to create positive messages generally focus on near term projects and goals.

The human race is really just in its 'immature teenage boy'

stage of development. The rich countries have become lazy and egocentric. This spoilt teenager might turn into the confused and dishevelled lord of the manor, house and grounds in a state of decay, asking why he no longer has respect. With luck, we might instead mature into 'a fine young man' that acts more responsibly and with care and respect.

This will require significant change and with change comes grief for a lost past. The grief cycle will be strong and we will see much denial, resistance and recriminations as a result. It is easy for us who seek change to feel anger at those resisting it but we must understand that they are just acting in the way that evolution has programmed them. Those advocating change are the difficult ones. The blame can only be laid at the feet of the story tellers for not yet doing a good enough job in attracting the majority.

So the challenge we face is a complex problem with very serious long term risks that the human mind is not easily able to solve. Our cultural mores currently stop us from thinking or acting in a way that will produce solutions. Many of the wealthy feel as though they have much to lose from any change. Furthermore, our main global measure, Gross Domestic Product, serves to further exacerbate the problem through encouraging economic growth with no reference to either ecological constraints, or indeed to whether societies are more functional.

No wonder there are so many pessimists!

No person should go through the agony that Kate has suffered without a sensible concerted coordinated effort to make life better.

From a very personal point of view, the fact that we are choosing to inflict suffering on countless others by deciding not to take action that we can easily afford is reprehensible. The agony we will inflict through starvation, wars and extreme weather events will be no less than Kate has suffered, although hopefully not as long in duration.

So our task is to change the way environmental communications are undertaken in order to inspire and attract a wider part of the community. It is only through the power of attraction that the extra-ordinary is achievable. As we have seen, an envisioned future can be a wonderful place. Why would you accept anything less?

New World Order by Emily May Chandra-Hickson
Ken Hickson
Chairman, Sustain Ability Showcase Asia – SASA
Author, The ABC of Carbon
Singapore

*The most remarkable change we accept as we sit outside on
a pleasantly warm mid-winter's day alongside Lake Geneva,
Switzerland - the outside temperature is 18C and the sun is
shining – is the effective "privatisation" of the United Nations and
all its agencies, merged in with private sector and non-government
organisations.*

*Now we have thirty independently managed global business units
– corporations if you like - each one headquartered in a different
centre somewhere in the world.*

*We're part-way through the monthly Governors meeting of SWIPE
(Sustainable World for Innovation & Productivity Enterprise), the
organisation I was elected Chairman of at our annual meeting in
2099.*

*SWIPE evolved out of the International Labour Organisation (ILO)
and the World Trade Organisation (WTO), which was abolished
in 2025 after years of failing to bring about any substantive
multi-lateral trade agreements, along with members of the World
Business Council for Sustainable Development (WBCSD) and the
World Economic Forum (WEF).*

*We have representatives on the council from fifteen governments,
as well as from major industry bodies and unions, regional groups
like the Asian Productivity Council, the Zero Waste Alliance and the
former UN Sustainable Consumption and Production group.*

*SWIPE was formed in 2035 and, along with most of the other
twenty-nine international groups, has been remarkably successful in
managing global business.*

Admittedly, the world had to endure the Ten Year War in the Middle East – from 2015 to 2025 – which showed up the failings of the United Nations Security Council, as well as the former Arab League.

The peace was finally brokered by Pakistan, Turkey and Egypt, plus European and American teams and led to the establishment of three major institutions:

1. *The Arab Union of States, incorporating thirty members from Mediterranean, Africa, Middle East and South Asia.*
2. *CROW – Council of Religious Organisations Worldwide (including Muslim, Buddhist, Hindu, Christian, Jewish and other organisations), altogether twenty-five members, with a Court for Mediation, Resolution and Co-operation.*
3. *Secure World for Energy, Environment & Peace - SWEEP – to replace the UN Security Council, based in New York, and incorporating thirty member states.*

We continue to experience extreme weather events and 'natural' disasters, but we are better prepared, having adapted well to a changing climate. We are also much better at managing things since the establishment CODEM, the Crisis Organisation & Disaster Efficiency & Management and IMT3, the International Mobilisation Taskforce of Troops & Transport.

No, the world has not managed to keep the average temperature increase to two degrees Celsius above the pre-industrial levels. For the first fifty years of the twenty-first century the rising continued, with every year being hotter than the one before. By 2050, the global average temperature hit 2.50°C above the long-term average for the twentieth century, but it had at least started to level off.

Major achievements? International agreements to shut down all coal mining and coal fired power stations by 2030 and the insistence in 2016 that major oil companies (including the Middle East oil producers) invest 80% of their profits in renewable energy.

All thirty global corporations are running smoothly, as they're decentralised, lean, productive and effective. Communication, co-ordination, collaboration and co-operation are "four top C keys" to successful global business.

There's much more I could tell you about, but remarkably things are working, like a well-oiled machine, running on "clean energy" of course.

As I look at the snow-capped peaks of the Swiss Alps, I can't help thinking: Yes, we're on top of the world. Finally.

Written by Emily May Chandra-Hickson, the 64 year old mythical great granddaughter of Ken Hickson. She was appointed head of the SWIPE (Sustainable World for Innovation & Productivity Enterprise). Her mother was from Anglo-Indian Chandra family and her father was Australian born and bred. Ms Hickson served as Australia's Ambassador to the European Union for five years until 2095 and worked in corporate law for thirty years throughout Asia Pacific.

> *'When my country, into which I had just set my foot, was set on fire about my ears, it was time to stir. It was time for every man to stir.'*

Thomas Paine, Crisis Number 7, 1778

We have no choice but start from our current position and it is indeed time for every man and woman to stir.

To overcome our challenges we need to inspire action through changing the way people's minds are wired and changing the cultural norms of acceptable behaviour. Whilst not straight forward, the good news is that both of these are possible so there is plenty to hope for.

Neuroplasticity is in its early stages of understanding but appears to offer an alternative to what have previously been seen as hard-wired circuits of the brain. At an individual level, it may enable amazing changes to occur, from eradicating remembered pain to reversing the decline of a Parkinson's sufferer. If we can teach ourselves and others to view long-term threats as we do immediate ones, to short-circuit the grief precipitated by change, huge progress towards a positive future will be made. The scale up of the theory to changing community attitudes is something that does not appear to have been yet tested but it certainly offers hope.

Even better, the evolution of culture is highly malleable. Under the right circumstances, cultural change can happen very quickly. It is done through conscious decision making of how to redefine the rules of society to better cope with new conditions. This is why so many people are so confident that when the level of destruction has reached the stage of 'immediate threat', change will occur.

By that time however we risk the loss of low-lying islands and of having pushed the world to its limits. Most humans will survive but not those who happen to be poor or live in vulnerable regions. They will become just the collateral damage of the resistance to change. Those fighting for climate justice are not prepared to allow this to happen. The question for us is how do we accelerate the pace of cultural change to reduce the looming catastrophes.

The change agents working on this challenge cannot force people to accept the change. Rather they can attract people to their ideas and be Dunphy's *'midwives'* for the birth of a new order. The process of change is necessarily lumpy with periods of rapid change followed by periods of apparent stagnation. These pauses, whilst frustrating, are essential to the process in bringing everyone up to speed and ensuring buy-in across the community.

Resistance to change is natural but can be fierce. It is often based on the 'psychological capital' of those that have invested their time and effort into the waning paradigm. The greater the impact of the change, the greater the initial resistance. Our authors that have seen a crash or collapse of world order, see a very rapid emergence of the replacement philosophy and culture based on alternative principles.

In his 2100, Ken Hickson sees that the structures of global governance will be very different. This process of change will threaten the psychological capital of some of his fellow authors and will no doubt meet with plenty of resistance.

Ken is a journalist by training, working in newspapers, magazines, radio & television in New Zealand, before he succumbed to the wider world of communications, including public relations for airlines and a host of businesses throughout the Asia Pacific. Ken authored the *ABC of Carbon* in 2009 and has lived in Singapore for many years.

Ken is a story teller at heart and originally sent me a lot longer version of this vision. It sets out an evolution of the world's governments that reflects the cultural evolution described by others. To be a world that has greater equity and justice for all its inhabitants needs a greater level of collaboration across its manmade boundaries. This can only be done if the entire world's ecosystem is considered as a whole with the only boundary being the natural one of the atmosphere.

It is not possible to 'solve' Wicked Problems. Instead the best acceptable outcome can be discovered as the problem is explored. This needs a willingness to be flexible in the journey without ever losing sight of the end goal. Innovation ecosystems and entrepreneurial attitudes will be essential to enable this flexibility.

Furthermore, Wicked Problems need authentic leaders who can attract followers committed to stay the course. They also need an integrative negotiating style to seek solutions through collaboration and making the 'pie bigger' rather than just fighting for the biggest slice. Essential is the creation of credible alternative paradigms that highlight current flaws and offer a better fit for what we humans really want. The visions here provide this possibility.

Story telling has the power to change culture through recasting values and assumptions. As we have seen, a changing culture will drive changing behaviours. It all starts with the story telling.

Change will come and it is the strength of the story telling that will determine the timing of this change and thus the extent of the suffering and devastation caused in the meantime. Everyone of us can contribute to this process of change. In Chapter 4, I challenged you to write your own vision for the future. Without looking at what you wrote before, write another one. Have you been influenced by the visions of others? Can you envision your ideal future?

Having a vision of the future that aims high, a dream if you will, has no downside. You will not regret having dreamt of something better. Your only regrets will be not to have done so and to have failed to act towards creating that better world for yourself, your family and beyond. Through the process of optimism bias, the very act of having a vision of a better world is highly likely to make the world better.

As a race we mostly understand the problem and we have the wherewithal to deliver adequate solutions. The missing piece is just in the communication process that will inspire concerted global action. Like a Parkinson's sufferer who is unable to walk across a line drawn on the pavement, the world is lacking the motivation to do what it must. Communication that tells a positive message and engages at an emotional level is the missing piece. Visions of the better world are the missing catalyst that can inspire movement and help us step over the line towards this future.

As John Gibbons says, 'Nothing is no longer an option'.

Seeds of Destruction

Mark Halle
Executive Director
International Institute for Sustainable Development
Geneva, Switzerland

No sane person ever opposed sustainable development as the long-term goal for humanity. After all, the alternative is unsustainable development – a form of progress that plants the seeds of its own destruction. But if there genuinely was a consensus on this goal, why was it so difficult to reach?

The answer was unfortunately quite simple – historically our societies continued to reward unsustainable behaviour, setting up a conflict between what was right long-term, and what was beneficial short-term. We could never have approached sustainable development by swimming upstream against strong currents.

Now, in 2100 this reality has been turned on its head. Sustainable development is well advanced because behaviour that sets us on a path to sustainability is now aligned with the behaviour that offers the greatest social and economic rewards. We have set up robust and fully-accountable procedures to screen all policies, laws, regulations and standards to eliminate or invalidate those that undermine sustainable development. We have in place a policy and legislative framework that enables, encourages and rewards progress towards ongoing sustainability.

In the past, imagining such a change would have seemed almost utopian. But we all knew that major shifts could happen fast if well prepared. Anyway, we had no choice.

'Common sense and a sense of humour are the same thing, moving at different speeds. A sense of humour is just common sense, dancing.'

Clive James

I have often been criticised for making light of serious situations with humour. Whilst the criticism is often justified, to me the humour – even if it is a 'dad joke' – makes the issue more potent, more memorable and connects at a different level. Common sense dancing feels like just what we need in the debate on building a better world. If it is all too serious, then no one will want to know.

Wicked Problems can be too complicated, frightening and apparently defeating to face without humour. No doubt 'gallows humour' originates from the same need to both alleviate negative emotions and communicate emotions, ideas and thoughts that are beyond direct words. When coping with Kate's illness, humour has got us through some of the darkest of times. When all has seemed beyond hope, we have danced our way to common sense and a vision of a better life.

Pessimism can be a reality check and has its place in creating change but optimism, often communicated through humour, is even more powerful.

Mark Halle has been involved in international environmental negotiations since the 1980s and now runs the European office of the International Institute for Sustainable Development. He has seen hope being dashed time and again and wrote a withering assessment of the failures at the Rio+20 conference in 2012. Despite all that he retains a very strong and hopeful vision of his future.

Mark's vision sees that all activity is undertaken within the context of sustainable development – rather than the alternative of *'unsustainable development'*. The key for him is being prepared so that when the *'major shifts'* happen, we are able to take the opportunity.

In the words of Benjamin Disraeli, *'One secret of success in life is for a man to be ready for his opportunity when it comes'*. Mark has been working on his plan for decades so is ready. We now just need to create the right opportunity.

In any good self-help book, this last part of the last chapter gives you all the answers and sets out a clear and guaranteed path forward.

The twist I mentioned in Chapter 13 should by now be self-evident. There are no answers in this book. The only way to have the future that you really want is to create it.

The future I see is beautiful and, on both a personal and global level, I intend to create it!

Everett Rogers wrote about the diffusion of innovation and suggested that before the mainstream started taking up an idea there needed to be at least sixteen per cent of the population already on board. Until these innovators and early adopters take a risk on new technology or a new idea the rest will not move. The authors and readers of this book are all in this early group.

If rather than eighty visions, we had eighty million visions then that would still be only one per cent of the global population. If we focus on regions instead, maybe we can build up slowly. To get to the sixteen per cent, we need eighty-five million visions in North America, eighty-one million in Europe and a mere four million in Australia. Is that possible - a feasible dream? As a stubborn optimist, I can only say 'Yes!'

When I just checked on the current global population at www.populationinstitute.org it stood at 7,347,461,850 but is increasing quickly. The longer we wait the more visions we will need.

We have eighty visions but we need so many more. You can start by writing number eighty-one and then there is one less to write. To count, visions must be shared, so unless you show someone what you really want from the future, it will remain locked away as good as never having been written.

Talk about your ideas, hopes and fears with friends, family and colleagues. You are the story tellers and our world, our species - and many others - need you. The only way to have the future that you want is to be part of its creation.

Or of course, you can chose not to be involved but then, like elections, you forfeit your right to complain about how others create your future for you.

After you have written and shared your vision, there are a few other things that you might want to do.

Panic Early – Firstly, panic early and do *something*. There is no point waiting for the answer because it is not coming. By doing something you will work out eventually what is useful.

Natural Capital – In everything you do, value the natural capital that you use and the impact of your activities on it. If you can do this within an organisation, even better but do it nevertheless. When you've done it, share your findings and help others to understand the concept.

Innovation – Innovation policy, ecosystems and entrepreneurship will be what enable the world to make the change. Wherever you see an effort to encourage innovation, support it and work to incorporate it into your world. The current cultural norms will not allow the changes that are required so we must innovate to change these norms.

Media – With a few honourable exceptions, the media is missing from this debate. They are a critical component to engaging the whole community in building a better world. Wherever you can, engage with the media, tell them about good news stories, about amazing forecast futures and that you want to see success stories. Complain when they do not show something that warrants attention. Once they know that there is interest, they will engage.

Technology – The quickest uptake of technology is by combining proven technology with new business models. Of course, there are many good technologies that are not fully proven that also need to be nurtured. Help this to accelerate by being an early adopter, celebrating technology success and encouraging others to do the same.

Be heard – To be heard, all your communications must be delivered primarily at an emotional level. Decide what you want your audience to feel, and deliver your topic with that in mind. Have the rational arguments as supporting material but remember that all decisions are influenced most heavily by 'gut-feeling'.

Stubborn optimist – Above all, be a stubborn optimist.

When you get knocked down, just get up one more time and try again. It will be worth it.

Lastly, do not be put off by those claiming to be pragmatists. Pragmatists do not exist – they are just emotional beings that are better at hiding it than most! So whenever you find someone being overly pragmatic, just smile sweetly and remember this.

This is certainly not a clear and guaranteed path forward but it will at least stop you from being idle.

My vision has us emerging from the chrysalis of the industrial revolution so that we can now start to really reap the benefits of all the progress to date. Like living with chronic illness, you have to make your own life. You can choose to decide how unfair life is or you get up one more time than you feel able to and create the future.

As I write this final chapter, fittingly on World Environment Day, we have the hope of creating a future for ourselves and generations to come that we can enjoy, look forward to and of which we can be proud.

There will undoubtedly be setbacks and many passionate debates but with the strength of resolve that comes with compelling visions, the human race will continue to evolve and will, by 2100, successfully build a more functional planet.

I started my journey with a vision of disaster borne partly out of Amin Malouf's *The First Century After Beatrice*. So it seems fitting to repeat and end with the final words from that book.

Then, in the space of one walk, I build a different world. A world in which freedom and prosperity have gradually spread like the waves on the surface of the waters. A world in which the only challenge left to medicine, after it has overcome all diseases and wiped out epidemics, is to postpone ageing and death indefinitely. A world from which ignorance and violence have been banished. A world rid of the last patches of darkness. Yes, mankind reconciled, generous and victorious, with eyes fixed on the stars, on eternity.

To that species, I would have been proud to belong.

EPILOGUE

"Criticism may not be agreeable, but it is necessary. It fulfils the same function as pain in the human body; it calls attention to the development of an unhealthy state of things. If it is heeded in time, danger may be averted; if it is suppressed, a fatal distemper may develop."

Winston Churchill 20th Century British Prime Minister
New Statesman interview, 7 January 1939

EPILOGUE

Criticism is an essential part of improvement and an essential part of avoiding a 'fatal distemper'. The criticism in this book levelled at the way the world currently works is an attempt to help the world select its improved future as early as possible. Those pretending to be pragmatists can easily dismiss all of this and continue on their path of ignorance or of incremental change. As has happened numerous times through history, the world will change and this change will be driven by human leadership.

By influencing or being this leadership, you will help to design our future world.

As this book goes to print, the global anticipation about the importance of the Paris Conference of Parties in December 2015 is growing. Countries are announcing their emissions targets for 2025 or 2030. Even laggards such as Australia are choosing to play the game and make announcements. National leaders feel obliged to be part of the movement regardless of their personal beliefs.

There has been much coverage of Catholic and Muslim religious leaders coming out with strong statements about respecting our environment and ensuring that the poor are not further disadvantaged through a lack of action.

At a United Nations Summit held in New York on 25 September 2015, world leaders adopted the 2030 Agenda for Sustainable Development, which includes a set of seventeen Sustainable Development Goals (SDGs) to end poverty, fight inequality and injustice, and tackle climate change by 2030. This was hailed as a major step forward to building a better world.

There is much optimism that some sort of binding global agreement will be reached in Paris.

The communication of the outcomes in Paris will be fascinating to watch. Those tied to the current world view will exclaim that there was no real agreements reached and the pessimists will shout that what was agreed was nowhere strong enough to prevent disaster. The reality will be that it will be another important step towards a solution that will work - eventually!

What will almost certainly be lacking from the coverage will be many voices talking about creating a better world using messaging that is really heard throughout the community. The weaknesses in environmental communications will take some time to change.

The other story of this book is my wife Kate's health. This provides both the context for the difficulty in solving complex problems and the awful reality of coping with severe chronic pain.

Over the course 2015 as this book has come together, Kate's health has declined. She now rarely has a day that is not 'bad'. A day on which she can go further than bed or the sofa is seen as an achievement. The level of pain is worse than it has ever been. This level of suffering is exhausting and wears away at human resilience.

She has had very low moments where all she can say is that she is *'scared of the pain and that it will just get worse'*. At these moments, suicide sometimes seems the only option for relief.

There are moments of happiness - and humour - but mostly it is just the slog of getting through each day without doing any of the things that she would like to do.

Stubbornness is however in abundance in our family so we are still exploring new options and new treatments. We wait for the medical profession to better understand the mechanism of pain and to then offer solutions that make more of life bearable. We hope that we can last until that day comes.

We already have viable solutions for climate change, so to me solving that seems like a much more manageable problem! Through our current failure to communicate effectively, we are condemning millions of people to pain and suffering. That is not my vision.

The publishing of this book is only the first step in the VISIONS 2100 project. By encouraging people everywhere to write and share their visions of a better world, this project will make a difference to our collective future. The extent of its influence is not within my control - that system is far too complex! It is what you are happy to accept as your future that will really determine our collective fate.

My VISION for 2100 is overleaf. Please share yours at **www. Visions2100.com**.

John O'Brien
Adelaide
September 2015

Post script: Australia's 'mere blip' discussed in Chapter 16 was deposed on 14 September 2015!'

Free at Last!
John O'Brien
Managing Director
Australian CleanTech
Adelaide, Australia

It is hard to believe that less than 100 years ago, organisations used to speak proudly of 'human capital' being its 'best asset' as if employees were property. Life is 2100 is far removed from this short-sighted approach.

Our natural and social capital are now also treated with more respect. The circular economy is in full swing. Everything is fully recyclable or able to be repurposed. Most things are shared.

The world is changed in other ways beyond recognition. The climate migrations and water wars changed what was valued and how the world was run. Lives are cherished with most people now focussed on building a better world and not running a 'rat-race'. Our leaders succeed because of their authenticity. Complex societal problems are assigned to the Innovation and Creativity Programs at the many Complexity Institutes. Education is entirely based around systems thinking, common wealth and emotional comprehension. Medics better understand human physiology and can finally control chronic pain effectively.

Of course we still have problems. Human greed is still there and people abuse the system. Criminal convictions for Avarice are however starting to decline as the new global culture gets bedded down. Equity and justice remain primary concerns for our global authorities.

Humans have emerged from the chrysalis of the industrial revolution and are at last starting to reap the real benefits of progress. Our culture of sharing dreams and creating one's own future has finally given people the freedom of being human - of being 'Free at last!'

ACKNOWLEDGEMENTS

The support of so many people has made this project a reality. The eighty visionaries took time out of their very busy schedules to paint their pictures of the future. Some of these people are right in the eye of the storm that will become the Paris climate conference and it was an honour to receive both their support and their contributions. Some are better known than others but it was a privilege to receive such open and heartfelt thoughts of what they each want or fear from our future.

The challenge of communicating widely and effectively is one that is acknowledged in many quarters. The support of many of those at the forefront of global climate communications is a demonstration that this is seen as a critical issue.

The contributors to this book, with many of their peers, are the ones taking risks and helping us towards a better world. Luckily, they too are stubborn optimists and we all owe a great deal of gratitude to them all for their dedication to creating a better world. I have a dream of assembling all of them in a single room to share each other's company and build on the ideas shared here to bring this future world into existence. That would be quite a party.

A number of the authors suggested and introduced people they thought would be interested in participating in this project and I owe extra thanks to them. Tessa Tennant made some wonderful introductions after a random chat in a taxi in Beijing, Kristin Alford connected me with some of Australia's leading thinkers and Ken Hickson provided the introduction to the Nobel Laureate amongst others. My sister Maureen and cousin Luan also made some valuable introductions to contributors. Another sister, Brenda, made some more great suggestions but sadly the Dalai Lama did not get back to me!

The inspiration to start on this project came from the combination Sam Wells and John Wright in their respective chapters in *Opportunities Beyond Carbon*. Painting a vision of the future to change paradigms is a powerful starting point to start a journey so thanks to them both.

To make some sense of my tendency to wander off at tangents when writing, I coerced three people to review and edit with the request that they 'be brutal'. The text here is a far improved version from the one they originally received so my thanks to my sister, Aileen, to Sam Wells (again!) and to my wife, Kate. The remaining flaws in the book, and there are many, are merely an indication that they were too kind to be really brutal!

As the book has evolved, I spent much time talking with publishers around the world. Like so much of my working life, its current form is not one that neatly fits into a category. Whilst this first edition (an optimists' statement if ever there was one!) is coming to print through my own resources, I did receive many good wishes, encouragement and introductions through this process. Matt Lloyd from Cambridge University Press and Peter Ginna previously of Bloomsbury Press were particularly helpful in making introductions.

I hope you have found my winding thought process of interest, but there are more important voices than mine. The contributing authors give you a wealth of insight so hold on to these visions and thank each of them for me if you happen to bump into them. However, the most important voice is your own, so if you do write and share your own vision for a better world, acknowledge your own part in making it come true.

The influence of my wonderfully complex childhood family, full of strong spirits, wild adventures and a feeling that respect must first be earned, provided me with the foundations on which to build this book. I wish could spend more time being inspired by them.

My sons, Jack and Cormac, are turning into wonderful young men and do a fantastic job of reminding me of my limitations in all things – particularly humour and height! They are, mostly, a pleasure to live with and I am counting on them to report back on which of these future worlds is in place in 2100.

Finally, I also owe a huge debt of gratitude for the support and encouragement received from my wife, Kate. Her life is not easy and that I do not have a sensible, stable job makes it no easier. That she also let me talk about her health and our lives shows a level bravery only surpassed by her strength of character in coping with her debilitating pain.

FURTHER READING

Introduction

O'Brien, J., (2009) *Opportunities Beyond Carbon*, Melbourne University Press

Carson, R., (1962) *Silent Spring*, Houghton Mifflin

Dallaire, R., (2012), *Shake Hands with the Devil: the Failure of Humanity in Rwanda*, AWB

Kuhn, T., (1962), *The Structure of Scientific Revolutions*, University of Chicago Press

Maalouf, A., (1994), *The First Century After Beatrice*, Abacus

Meadows, D., (2001), *Dancing with Systems*. Whole Earth, Winter, (pp. 58-63).

Chapter 1

Avery, G.C., Bergsteiner, H., (2011), *Sustainable Leadership: Honeybee and Locust Approaches*, Routledge

Collins, J., Porras, J., (1996), *Building Your Company's Vision*, Harvard Business Review, Sept-Oct

Short, D., (2005), *Hope & Resiliency: Understanding the Psychotherapeutic Strategies of Milton H. Erickson*, Crown House Publishing

Wood, J.M., Chapman, S., Fromholtz, M., Morrison, V., Wallace, J., et al (2004) *Organisational Behaviour: A Global Perspective*, Third Edition, Wiley

Chapter 2

Carson, R., (1962) *Silent Spring*, Houghton Mifflin

Intergovernmental Panel on Climate Change (IPCC), (2012), *Summary for Policymakers. Managing the Risks of Extreme Events and Disasters to Advance Climate Change Adaptation*

Sachs. J.D., (2015), *The Age of Sustainable Development*, Columbia University Press

Watts, J., (2010), *When a Billion Chinese Jump: How China Will Save Mankind - or Destroy it*, faber & faber

Chapter 3

Gifford, R. (2011). The dragons of inaction: Psychological barriers that limit climate change mitigation and adaptation. *American Psychologist*, 66, 290–302.

Gilbert, D., (2007), *Stumbling on Happiness*, Vintage

Gilding, P., (2012), *The Great Disruption: Why the Climate Crisis Will Bring On the End of Shopping and the Birth of a New World*, Bloomsbury Press

Greenfield, S., (2015) *Mind Change: How Digital Technologies Are Leaving Their Mark on Our Brains*, Random House

Lertzman, R., (2015), *Environmental Melancholia: Psychoanalytic dimensions of engagement*, Routledge

Maslin, M.A., Brierley, C.M., Milner, A.M., Shultz, S., Trauth, M.H., Wilson, K.E. (2014), *East African climate pulses and early human evolution*, Quaternary Science Reviews

Przybylski, Kou Murayama, A.K., DeHaan, C.R., Gladwell, V., (2013), *Motivational, Emotional, and Behavioral Correlates of Fear of Missing Out*, Computers in Human Behavior Journal 29

Thaler, R.H., Sunstein, C.R., (2009), *Nudge: Improving Decisions About Health, Wealth, and Happiness*, Pemguin Books

Zichermann, G. & Linder, J., (2013), *The Gamification Revolution: How Leaders Leverage Game Mechanics to Crush the Competition*, McGraw-Hill Education

Chapter 4

Carver, C. S., Scheier, M. F., Segerstrom, S. C., (2010), *Optimism*, Clinical Psychology Review, 30, 879–889.

Reynolds, J., Baird, C. (2010), *Is There a Downside to Shooting for the Stars?*, *Unrealized Educational Expectations and Symptoms of Depression*, American Sociological Review February 2010, vol. 75, no. 1 151–172

Ware, B., (2012), *The Top Five Regrets of the Dying: A Life Transformed by the Dearly Departing*, Hay House

Chapter 5

Gower, P., (2004), *Psychology of Fear*, Nova Science Publishers

McKibben, B., (2006), *The End of Nature*, Random House

Chapter 6

Dunphy,D., Griffiths,G., Benn,S., (2003), *Organizational Change for Corporate Sustainability*, Routledge

Freeman,J., (2011),'*Psychology for the sake of the environment*', in Mendonca, A., Cunha, A, & Chakrabarti, R. (Eds.) *Natural Resources, Sustainability and Humanity: A Comprehensive View*

Funnell,A., (2012), *The Future and Related Nonsense*, ABC Books

Mbongeni A., Mdletye, M., Coetzee, J., Ukpere, W., (2014), *The Reality of Resistance to Change Behaviour at the Department of Correctional Services of South Africa*, Mediterranean Journal of Social Sciences, MCSER Publishing, Rome-Italy,Vol 5 No 3.

Murtagh, N., Gatersleben, B., Uzzell, D., (2012) *Self-identity threat and resistance to change: Evidence from regular travel behaviour.* Journal of Environmental Psychology

Renesch,J., (2011), *The Great Growing Up: Being Responsible for Humanity's Future*, Hohm Press

Chapter 7

de Grey, A., (2008), *Ending Aging: The Rejuvenation Breakthroughs That Could Reverse Human Aging in Our Lifetime*, St. Martin's Griffin

Landry, C., (2008), *The Creative City: A Toolkit for Urban Innovators*, Routledge

Chapter 8

Klein, N., (2015), *This Changes Everything: Capitalism vs the Climate*, Simon & Schuster

Reddy, R., (2004), *Do Men and Women Negotiate Differently - and Why Does it Matter?* Princeton

Chapter 9

Damasio,A., (1994), *Descartes' Error: Emotion, Reason, and the Human Brain*, Penguin Group

Meadows, D. (2001), *Dancing with Systems*. Whole Earth, Winter, (pp. 58-63)

Sarasvathy, S., (2009), *Effectuation: Elements of Entrepreneurial Expertise*, Edward Elgar Publishing

Schumpeter, J.A., (1942), *Capitalism, Socialism and Democracy*, Harper Perennial

Chapter 10

Gilding, P., (2012), *The Great Disruption: Why the Climate Crisis Will Bring On the End of Shopping and the Birth of a New World*, Bloomsbury Press

Kuhn, T., (1962), *The Structure of Scientific Revolutions*, University of Chicago Press

Nair,C., (2011), *Consumptionomics: Asia's Role in Reshaping Capitalism and Saving the Planet*, Wiley

Chapter 11

Avery, G.C., Bergsteiner, H., (2011), *Sustainable Leadership: Honeybee and Locust Approaches*, Routledge

Dunphy,D., (2003), *Organisational Change for Corporate Sustainability: A guide for leaders and change agents of the future*, Routledge

Green Growth Knowledge Platform (2015), *Third Annual Conference Report: Fiscal Policies and the Green Economy Transition: Generating Knowledge – Creating Impact*

Hart, S., (2005), *Capitalism at the Crossroads*, Wharton School Publishing

Meadows, D.H., Meadows, D.L., Randers, J., Behrens, W.W., (1972), *The Limits to Growth*, Universe Books

Chapter 12

Doherty, P., (2005), *The Beginner's Guide to Winning the Nobel Prize*, The Miegunyah Press

Chapter 13

Bumpus, A., Tansey,J., Henríquez, L.P., Okereke,C., (2015), *Climate Change, Carbon Governance and Business Transformation*, Routledge

Gould.,S.J., (1989), *Wonderful Life, The Burgess Shale and the Nature of History*, W.W. Norton & Company

Maslin, M.A., Brierley, C.M., Milner, A.M., Shultz, S., Trauth, M.H., Wilson, K.E. (2014), *East African climate pulses and early human evolution*, Quaternary Science Reviews

May,Vol. 8, No. 5, Pages 781-797

Wood, P.B., (2008), *Role of central dopamine in pain and analgesia*, Expert Review of Neurotherapeutics,

Zimmer, C., (2014), *The New Science of Evolutionary Forecasting*, Quant Magazine, July

Chapter 14

Copenhagen Cleantech Cluster (2012), *Global Cleantech Report 2012*
Rode, P., Stern, N., Zenghelis, D., (2012) *Global Problems: City Solutions*, LSE Cities

Chapter 15

Lincoln, S., (2006), *Challenged Earth: An Overview of Humanity's Steward-ship of Earth*, Imperial College Press
Updike, J., (1996), *The Witches of Eastwick* , Ballentine

Chapter 16

Kurzweil, R., (2006), *The Singularity is Near*, Penguin Books
United Nations Industrial Development Organization, (2007), *Energy, industry modernization and poverty reduction: a review and analysis of current policy thinking*
Vinge, V., (1986), *Marooned in Realtime*, St Martin's Press

Chapter 17

Drucker, P., (1954), *The Practice of Management*, HarperCollins
Mackay, H., (2013), *The Good Life: What makes a life worth living?*, McMillan

Chapter 18

Amabile, T., Hadley, C.N., Krame, S.J., (2002) *Creativity Under the Gun*, Harvard Business Review, August
Dickinson, P., Leonard, R., Svensen, N., Morris, S., (2000), *Beautiful Cor-porations: Corporate Style in Action*, The Financial Times
Newman, P., Beatley, T., Boyer, H., (2009) *Resilient Cities: Responding to Peak Oil and Climate Change*, Island Press
Newman, P., Kenworthy, J., (1999), *Sustainability and Cities: Overcoming Automobile Dependence*, Island Press

Chapter 19

Diamond, J., (2005), *Collapse: How Societies Choose to Fail or Survive*, Allen Lane Penguin Books
Rans, S.A., (2005), *Hidden Treasures: Building Community Connections by Engaging the Gifts of* *, A Community Building Workbook from the Asset Based Community Development Institute, School of Education and Social Policy, Northwestern University

Chapter 20

Conklin, J., (2005), *Dialogue Mapping: Building Shared Understanding of Wicked Problems*, John Wiley & Sons

Cross, R.L., Martin, R.D., Weiss, L.M., (2006), *Mapping the value of employee collaboration*, McKinsey Quarterly

Gandhi, M., (1958), *All Men are Brothers*, Columbia University Press

Gokhale, A.A., (1995), *Collaborative Learning Enhances Critical Thinking*, Journal of Technology Education, Volume 7, Number 1, Fall 1995

Rittel, H.W.J., Webber, M.W., (1973), Dilemmas in a General Theory of Planning

Richerson, P.J., Boyd, R., (2008), *Cultural Evolution: Accomplishments and Future Prospects. Explaining culture scientifically*: 75-99

Chapter 21

Cels, S., De Jong, J., Nauta, F. (2012), *Agents of Change: Strategy and Tactics for Social Innovation*, Brookings Institution Press

Hawken, P., Lovins, A., Lovins, L.H., (1999), *Natural Capitalism: Creating the Next Industrial Revolution*, Back Bay Books

Schumacher, E. F., (1973), *Small Is Beautiful: Economics as if People Mattered*, Harper Perennial

Seba, T., (2014), *Clean Disruption of Energy and Transportation: How Silicon Valley Will Make Oil, Nuclear, Natural Gas, Coal, Electric Utilities and Conventional Cars Obsolete by 2030*

The Hibbert Journal: A Quarterly Review of Religion, Theology, and Philosophy, Volume 22, 1924

Tyrrell, P., (2006), *Founded on Fear: Letterfrack Industrial School, War and Exile*, edited by Diarmuid Whelan, Irish Academic Press

Chapter 22

Champy, J., (2009), *Authentic Leadership*, Leader to Leader Institute, Volume 2009, Issue 54, pp 39–44, Autumn (Fall) 2009

George, B., (2003), *Authentic Leadership: Rediscovering the Secrets to Creating Lasting Value*, Jossey-Bass

Hoffman, H., (1848), *English Struwwelpeter*, George Routledge & Sons

Lerner, J., (2012), *Boulevard of Broken Dreams: Why Public Efforts to Boost Entrepreneurship and Venture Capital Have Failed--and What to Do About It*, Princeton University Press

Chapter 23

Hickson, K., (2009) *The ABC of Carbon: Issues and Opportunities in the Global Climate Change Environment*, ABC Carbon

Rogers, E., (1962), *Diffusion of Innovations*, Free Press

INDEX

Lightning Source UK Ltd.
Milton Keynes UK
UKOW02f1358271115

263587UK00001B/36/P